Communism
and the
Conscience
of the West

Communism
and the
Conscience
of the
West

ARCHBISHOP
FULTON J. SHEEN

TAN Books
Gastonia, North Carolina

Communism and the Conscience of the West published by
TAN Books 2022

Cover & interior design by www.davidferrisdesign.com

Cover image: A portrait of the famous Catholic Archbishop Fulton J. Sheen (1895 - 1979), New York, 1964. (Photo by Bachrach /
Getty Images).

ISBN: 978-1-5051-2325-8
Kindle ISBN: 978-1-5051-2326-5
ePUB ISBN: 978-1-5051-2372-2

Published in the United States by
TAN Books
PO Box 269
Gastonia, NC 28053

www.TANBooks.com

Dedicated to

MARY GRACIOUS MOTHER-HEART

of the

WORLD'S SAVIOUR

in

PRAYERFUL HOPE

of

THE CONVERSION OF RUSSIA

CONTENTS

Publisher's Note .... *IX*

Preface .... *XIII*

1: The Decline of Historical Liberalism and
   the Rise of the Antireligious Spirit 1

2: Is Communism the Enemy of the Western World? 37

3: The Philosophy of Communism 49

4: The Basic Defects of Communism 71

5: Communism Speaks for Itself 105

6: How to Meet Communism 119

7: The Attitude Toward the Family
   in Russia and America 139

8: Passion 159

9: Russia and the Faith 177

10: Our Lady of Fatima and Russia 203

Prayer to Obtain a Favor Through the Intercession
of Venerable Fulton J. Sheen.. *225*

Endnotes.. *227*

PUBLISHER'S NOTE

ARCHBISHOP FULTON J. SHEEN (1895–1979) was one of the greatest theologians of the twentieth century. As the first Catholic televangelist on prime-time television, his program, Life is Worth Living, inspired an audience of nearly thirty million people weekly, more listeners than St. Paul ever could have reached during a lifetime of preaching. With his eloquent writing and preaching on television and radio, he movingly and masterfully portrayed life, eternity, love, sorrow, joy, freedom, suffering, marriage, and so much more. His memorable style was distinguished by his booming voice, his Irish wit and wisdom, and his warm smile.

In this carefully selected set of books, Sheen offers clear guidance on the problems affecting all people in today's world, including key ideologies that seek to destroy the Church and society, including Marxism and Freudianism, what is today called "Cultural Marxism." His spiritual and practical wisdom cover a wide variety of subjects that range from discussions of down-to-earth spiritual and moral problems to provocative conversations on the meaning of life, family, education, Christianity, world affairs, and more. Together they add up to a stirring and challenging statement of Bishop Sheen's whole philosophy of life and living. With ease, Sheen shows the relationship between human reason and religion. He shows that the world of today has reached a point of irrationalism that is in utter contempt of lasting truths. With honesty and capable scholarship, Sheen has something to say for everyone. His works are of immediate concern to all men and women seeking understanding, belief, and purpose in these troubled times.

Bishop Sheen reminds us that if we are to help cure the modern world of pessimism and despair, hatred and confusion, we must enlist as warriors of love and peace. Sheen's daily Holy Hour before the Most Blessed Sacrament was the catalyst behind his preaching and writing but also his great love for the Blessed Mother. She was the woman he loved most, "The World's First Love," in addition to his great love for St. Thérèse, patroness of the foreign missions.

Sheen wrote over seventy books, many of which are still widely read today. When the first nationwide Catholic Hour was inaugurated in 1930 on NBC, Sheen was chosen as the first preacher. He hosted this nighttime radio program for twenty years from 1930 to 1950 before moving to television where he had his own show on prime-time TV from 1952 to 1957. Sheen twice won an Emmy for Most Outstanding Television Personality and was featured on the cover of Time magazine. But more important than any earthly awards, Fulton Sheen's tireless evangelization efforts helped convert many to the Faith, especially Communist organizer Bella Dodd.

Entombed in a side altar at the Cathedral of Saint Mary of the Immaculate Conception in Peoria, Illinois, Sheen's cause for canonization was officially opened in 2002. May readers be inspired by Archbishop Fulton J. Sheen, a timeless voice described as one of the greatest Catholic philosophers of our age.

PREFACE

Every book should contain at least one idea. The one idea in this book is that the philosophy of communism and to some extent the Revolution of Communism are on the conscience of the Western world. This idea is not new. It has always been a part of the Christian tradition that the guilt of humanity at any one segment of the circle is to some extent the guilt of the circle itself. Closely allied to this is the other idea that the so-called Russian problem is not primarily economic or political but philosophical: it revolves around the nature of man. Here too the conscience of the Western world is involved, for the Western world generally has lost the concept of man as a creature made to the image and likeness of God, and reduced him either to a component part of the universe, to an economic animal or to a "physiological bag filled with psychological libido." Once man became materialized and atomized in Western thinking, it was only natural for a totalitarianism to arise to gather up the fragments into a new totality and substitute the collective man for the individual man who was isolated from all social responsibilities.

This distortion of the true nature of man was due principally to the philosophy of historical liberalism, which saw man as endowed with no higher destiny than the economic. There is no word more "dangerous" than liberalism, because to oppose it is the new "unforgivable sin." The word can be used in three senses: (a) As a philosophy which believes in the progressive achievement of civil, social, political, economic and religious liberties within the framework of a moral law. (b) As an attitude which denies all standards extrinsic to man himself, measures freedom as a physical power rather than a moral power and identifies progress by the height of the pile of discarded moral and religious traditions. (c) As an ideology generally identified with the doctrine of *laissez faire*. The first kind of liberalism is to be encouraged, prospered and achieved. The last two are false for reasons well known to those who are familiar with Laski, Hocking, Tawney, Weber and the Papal Encyclicals. It is the third kind of liberalism, called historical liberalism, with which we are very briefly concerned in this book. A little-known fact is that communism and the Catholic Church are one in their opposition to historical liberalism, but for very different reasons. The vast majority of profound thinkers who see the dangers of monopolistic capitalism as well as totalitarian capitalism are also opposed to it. Professor William Ernest Hocking among others points out three defects: "(1) It has shown itself incapable alone, of achieving social unity. (2) It has cultivated a pernicious separation of individual rights from individual duties. (3) It has lost its emotional force, because its emotional basis was in a serious degree unrealistic."*

* *Lasting Elements of Individualism*, p. 40.

But this is giving undue importance to a word and an idea which plays no major role in this book and distracts from the general idea intended to be expressed, namely that up to this time Western civilization has been the superior civilization of the world. This was due not to the fact that it was "white"—though many imperialists among others assumed that it was—but to the fact that it was Christian. As Western civilization loses its Christianity it loses its superiority. The ideology of communism rose out of the secularized remnants of a Western civilization whose soul was once Christian. Communism is therefore, as Waldemar Gurian has said, both an "effect and a judgment" on Western bourgeois civilization.

For that reason communism is not treated as an economic doctrine, which it is not primarily, but as a philosophy of life. Nor is it viewed as a challenge to monopolistic capitalism, which itself stands in such need of regeneration. Rather communism is seen as the dehumanization of man by making him a social animal for whom an economic machine is the total meaning of existence. Communism represents an *active* barbarism outside Western civilization which has made inroads because of the *passive* barbarism within, which manifested itself in the general demoralization of society. It is the passive barbarism from within which contributes to some extent to active barbarism without for, as Toynbee shows, sixteen out of the nineteen civilizations which have decayed from the beginning of history until now, decayed from within.

The basic struggle today is not between individualism and collectivism, free enterprise and socialism, democracy and dictatorship. These are only the superficial manifestations of a deeper struggle which is moral and spiritual and involves above all else whether man shall exist for the state, or the state for man, and whether freedom is of the spirit or a concession of a materialized society. It has not been given to every age in history to see the issue as clearly as it has been given to our own, for we have a double incentive to work for the peace and prosperity of the world: the first is the Gospel in its fullness, the second is the communism of Soviet Russia. The first teaches us that happiness comes from living rightly; the second, that misery comes from acting wrongly.

The author expresses his thanks to the publishers for their careful editing, to the Reverend Marcellus Scheuer, O. Carm., for reading the manuscript, and to Mr. Blair Taylor for his many helpful suggestions.

CHAPTER ONE

The Decline of Historical Liberalism and the Rise of the Antireligious Spirit

It is a characteristic of any decaying civilization that the great masses of the people are unconscious of the tragedy. Humanity in a crisis is generally insensitive to the gravity of the times in which it lives. Men do not want to believe their own times are wicked, partly because it involves too much self-accusation and principally because they have no standards outside of themselves by which to measure their times. If there is no fixed concept of justice how shall men know it is violated? Only those who live by faith really know what is happening in the world; the great masses without faith are unconscious of the destructive processes going on, because they have lost the vision of the heights from which they have fallen. The tragedy is not that the hairs of our civilization are gray; it is rather that we fail to see that they are. As Reinhold Niebuhr put it: "It is a strange irony of history that a commercial and industrial civilization which might have had special reasons for being apprehensive about its vitality and longevity, should have been particularly optimistic." The basic reason for this false optimism he attributes to the fact that our civilization is mechanical rather than organic. Nothing is more calculated to deceive men in regard to the nature of life than a civilization whose cement of social cohesion consists of the means of production and consumption.[1]

The very day Sodom was destroyed, Scripture describes the sun as bright; people saw Noah preparing for the flood one hundred and twenty years before it came, but men would not believe. In the midst of seeming prosperity, the decree to the angels goes forth but the masses go on in their sordid routines. As Our Lord said: "For as in the days before the flood, they were eating and drinking, marrying and giving in marriage, even till that day in which Noe entered into the ark, and they knew not till the flood came, and took them all away; so also shall the coming of the Son of man be." (Matthew 24:38, 39) Well may Our Saviour say to us what He said to the Sadducees and the Pharisees in His time: "When it is evening, you say: It will be fair weather, for the sky is red. And in the morning: Today there will be a storm, for the sky is red and lowering. You know then how to discern the face of the sky: and can you not know the signs of the times?" (Matthew 16:2, 3)[2]

Do we know the signs of these appointed times? Most people are afraid to face the unpalatable fact that not a single *positive* major objective for which this war was fought has been achieved. Few realize that barbarism is not only outside us, but beneath us; that science, by making us spectators of reality, has blinded us to the necessity of being actors, and that the atomic bomb, by putting human power in our hands, has hidden the weakness of our hearts. The signs of our times point to the truth that we have come to the end of the post-Renaissance chapter of history which made man the measure of all things. More particularly the three basic dogmas of the modern world are dissolving before our very eyes. We are witnessing first, the liquidation of the economic man, or the assumption that man who is a highly developed animal has no other function in life than to produce and acquire wealth, and then like the cattle in the pastures, be filled with years and die.

The basic assumption of bourgeois civilization was that the best interests of the world, the state and the community could be served by allowing each individual to work out his economic destiny as he saw fit. This is known as the principle of *laissez faire*. As far as possible individual life is unregulated by the state, whose function is purely negative, like that of a policeman. The less the state does, the better. It was not long until the evil of this principle manifested itself. If every individual is to be allowed to work out his economic destiny as he sees fit, it will not be long until wealth is concentrated in the hands of the few and the vast majority are reduced, as Hilaire Belloc showed, to a slave state.[3] Thus from a false economic system which insisted only on *personal* right to property and forgot the *social use*, the world reacted to a totalitarian economy which insisted on *social use* and forgot *personal* rights. As a result the *homo oeconomicus* died and the *homo politicus* was born.[4]

Secondly, the modern world is witnessing the liquidation of the idea of the natural goodness of man, who has no need of God to give him rights, no need of a Redeemer to salvage him from guilt, because progress is automatic and inevitable, thanks to education and science. This false assumption had its roots in Rousseau, who reinterpreted the Christian tradition by making man naturally good and blaming institutions and civilizations for evil. Comte, Darwin and Spencer were subsequently invoked to support the idea that man was on the road to becoming a god. But modern history has completely dissipated this false philosophy of man, as the interval between wars shows man becoming increasingly dehumanized. The interval between the Napoleonic and Franco-Prussian wars was 53 years, the interval between the Franco-Prussian War and World War I was 43 years, and the interval between World War I and World War II was 21 years—and this at a time when man has all the *material* conditions necessary for his happiness. Having lost the purpose of life which religion supplied, modern man became increasingly frustrated as his disappointed hedonism turned to pessimism. Thus man, who isolated himself from the religious community, now by reaction finds himself absorbed by the political community as despair becomes the dominant note of contemporary philosophy and literature.[5]

The third idea being liquidated today is rationalism understood in the sense that the supreme purpose of life is not the discovery of the meaning and the goal of life, but solely to devise new technical advances to make this world a city of man to displace the City of God. Rationalism properly understood is reason concerned with ends and means to an end; modern rationalism is reason concerned with means to the exclusion of ends. This was justified on the grounds that progress made ends impossible. The result was that man, instead of working toward an ideal, changed the ideal and called it progress. Paul Tillich says that "the decisive feature of the period of the victorious bourgeoisie is *the loss of control of human reason over man's historical existence*."[6]

Reaction has set in and man who surrendered his reason in the proper service of the term discovers that the state has pre-empted it as *planning* reason, so that now there is no reason but state reason which is Fascism, or class reason which is communism as there was once a race reason which was Nazism. Other manifestations of irrationalism are to be found in Freudianism which makes the subconscious the determinant principle of life, or Marxism which supplants reason with historical determinism, or astrologism which puts the blame on the stars.[7]

In more general terms, our day is witnessing the end of historical liberalism. Liberalism is a dangerous term to use simply because the modern mind never makes a distinction. If liberalism means a system which believes in progress toward freedom as the *right* to do whatever man *ought*, then liberalism is to be encouraged. If liberalism means a progressive repudiation of law and truth in the sense that freedom means the *right* to do whatever man *pleases*, then it is to be condemned. In the latter sense, the liberal is opposed to the reactionary though both have something in common; they never see permanence and change together. They take one to the exclusion of the other. The reactionary seizes upon permanency to the exclusion of change, and the liberal upon change to the exclusion of permanency. The reactionary wants things to remain as they are; the liberal wants change though he is little concerned with direction. The reactionary wants the clock but no time; the liberal wants the time but no clock. The reactionary believes in staying where he is, though he never inquires whether or not he has a right to be there; the liberal, on the contrary, never knows where he is going, he is only sure he is on his way.

The terms reactionary and liberal are so relative they mean little to thinking men who have either a knowledge of history or a remnant of reason. For example, the liberal of the last generation invoked liberalism to free economic activity from state control; the liberal of today invokes liberalism to extend state control of the economic order. The old liberal was a defender of capitalism; the new liberal is reacting against capitalism and wants some form of collectivism or state control. The old liberal wanted liberty of press, speech and conscience within the framework of democracy; the new liberal, reacting against the old liberalism, wants the liberty without the framework as its safeguard. The old liberal rebelled against taxation without responsibility; the new liberal wants the taxation as a handout without responsibility. The old liberal 50 years ago was materialistic in science. His son, who calls himself a liberal, is today's reactionary for whom science is idealistic. The French liberals who protested against the authority of king and altar in the name of liberty were reactionaries, for they did not believe in extending that liberty to the proletariat. Many liberals who wrote they believed in the equality of all men kept slaves. To change it around, every reactionary is protesting against the last liberal. Sometimes in one man the liberal and the reactionary meet, as they did in the case of Milton. Milton was a liberal who favored a free press and protested against licensing of books; and then when a handsome salary was offered him he reacted against his liberalism and became an official censor of books.

We have in the world reactions against reactions; revolts against revolts; the reactionary and the liberal are on a seesaw, and think they are going places because they are going up and down or see their momentary triumph over their opponent. The new liberals are at war against the old liberals; the new rebels in rebellion against the old rebels. The liberal of today will be the reactionary of tomorrow. This so-called liberalism is only a reaction against the latest liberalism.

When we say liberalism is dying, we mean neither liberalism in the sense of a progressive acquisition of rational freedom, nor a progressive deterioration of rational standards, but historical liberalism with its roots in the seventeenth century or even earlier, which in the economic order became capitalism, in the political order nationalism, in the social order secularism, and which by reaction today has become totalitarianism.

Classic treatises on the history and development of historical liberalism are known to all scholars. Harold J. Laski, for example, in his work *The Rise of European Liberalism*, referring to its relation to an earlier philosophy of history writes: "It was in the interest of profit-making that Liberalism had broken the discipline of the medieval *Respublica Christiana*. . . . As an organized society, the liberal man at bottom had no defined objective save the making of wealth, no measurable criterion of function and status save ability to acquire it. . . ."[8] The more remote background of historical liberalism is to be found in the classic treatise of R. H. Tawney, *Religion and the Rise of Capitalism*, in which he closely links up Puritanism with the rise of capitalism.[9] "A creed which transformed the acquisition of wealth from a drudgery or a temptation into a moral duty was the milk of babies. . . . The good Christian was not wholly dissimilar from the economic man."

From a divergent point of view, but still correlating the break-up of religious unity to the rise of economic man is the equally important treatise of Max Weber, *The Protestant Ethic and the Spirit of Capitalism*. His thesis is that it was the change of moral standards which converted a natural frailty into a virtue.[10]

In any case it is becoming increasingly clear that historical liberalism is like a sundial, which is unable to mark time in the dark. Liberalism can function only in a society whose basis is moral, where the flotsam and jetsam of Christianity are still drifting about the world. From another point of view, historical liberalism is a parasite on a Christian civilization, and once that body upon which it clings ceases to be the leaven of society, then historical liberalism itself must perish. The individual liberties which historical liberalism emphasizes are secure only when the community is religious and can give an ethical foundation to these liberties. It may very well be that historical liberalism is only a transitional era in history between a civilization which was Christian and one which will be definitely anti-Christian.[11]

The second great truth which the signs of the times portend is that we are definitely at the end of a nonreligious era of civilization, which regarded religion as an addendum to life, a pious extra, a morale builder for the individual but of no social relevance, an ambulance that took care of the wrecks of the social order until science reached a point where there would be no more wrecks, and which called on God only as a defender of national ideals, or as a silent partner whose name was used by the firm to give respectability but who had nothing to say about how the business should be run.

The new era into which we are entering is what might be called the religious phase of human history. By *religious* we do not mean that men will turn to God, but rather that the indifference to the absolute which characterized the liberal phase of civilization will be succeeded by a passion for an absolute. From now on the struggle will be not for the colonies and national rights, but for the souls of men. There will be no more half-drawn swords, no divided loyalties, no broad strokes of sophomoric tolerance; there will not even be any more great heresies, for heresies are

based on a partial acceptance of truth. The battle lines are
already being clearly drawn and the basic issues are no longer in doubt. From now on men will divide themselves into
two religions—understood again as surrender to an absolute. The conflict of the future is between the absolute who
is the God-man, and the absolute which is the man-God;
the God Who became man, and the man who makes himself God; brothers in Christ and comrades in Antichrist.

The Antichrist will not be so called; otherwise he would
have no followers. He will not wear red tights, nor vomit
sulphur, nor carry a trident nor wave an arrowed tail as Me-
phistopheles in *Faust*. This masquerade has helped the Devil
convince men that he does not exist. When no man recognizes, the more power he exercises. God has defined Himself
as "I am Who am," and the Devil as "I am who am not."

Nowhere in Sacred Scripture do we find warrant for
the popular myth of the Devil as a buffoon who is dressed
like the first "red." Rather is he described as an angel fallen
from heaven, and as "the Prince of this world," whose business it is to tell us that there is no other world. His logic is
simple: if there is no heaven there is no hell; if there is no
hell, then there is no sin; if there is no sin, then there is no
judge, and if there is no judgment then evil is good and
good is evil.[12] But above all these descriptions, Our Lord
tells us that he will be so much like Himself that he would
deceive even the elect—and certainly no devil ever seen in
picture books could deceive even the elect. How will he
come in this new age to win followers to his religion?

The pre-Communist Russian belief is that he will come
disguised as the Great Humanitarian; he will talk peace,
prosperity and plenty not as means to lead us to God, but
as ends in themselves. He will write books on the new idea
of God, to suit the way people live; induce faith in astrology

COMMUNISM AND THE CONSCIENCE OF THE WEST

so as to make not the will but the stars responsible for sins; he will explain guilt away psychologically as inhibited eroticism, make men shrink in shame if their fellow men say they are not broad-minded and liberal; he will be so broad-minded as to identify tolerance with indifference to right and wrong, truth and error; he will spread the lie that men will never be better until they make society better and thus have selfishness to provide fuel for the next revolution; he will foster science, but only to have armament makers use one marvel of science to destroy another; he will foster more divorces under the disguise that another partner is "vital"; he will increase love for love and decrease love for person; he will invoke religion to destroy religion; he will even speak of Christ and say that He was the greatest *man* who ever lived; his mission, he will say, will be to liberate men from the servitudes of superstition and Fascism, which he will never define; he will organize children's games, tell people whom they should and should not marry and un-marry, who should bear children and who should not; he will benevolently draw chocolate bars from his pockets for the little ones, and bottles of milk for the Hottentots.

He will tempt the Christian with the same three temptations with which he tempted Christ. The temptation to turn stones into bread as an earthly Messias will become the temptation to sell freedom for security, making bread a political weapon which only those who think his way may eat. The temptation to work a miracle by recklessly throwing himself from a steeple will become a plea to desert the lofty pinnacles of truth where faith and reason reign, for those lower depths where the masses live on slogans and propaganda. He wants no proclamation of immutable principles from the lofty heights of a steeple, but mass organization through propaganda where only a common man directs the idiosyncrasies of common men. Opinions not truths, commentators not teachers, Gallup polls not principles, nature not grace—to these golden calves will men toss themselves from their Christ. The third temptation in which Satan asked Christ to adore him and all the kingdoms of the world would be His, will become the temptation to have a new religion without a Cross, a liturgy without a world to come, a religion to destroy a religion, or a politics which is a religion—one that renders unto Caesar even the things that are God's.

In the midst of all his seeming love for humanity and his glib talk of freedom and equality, he will have one great secret which he will tell to no one: he will not believe in God. Because his religion will be brotherhood without the fatherhood of God, he will deceive even the elect. He will set up a counterchurch which will be the ape of the Church, because he, the Devil, is the ape of God. It will have all the notes and characteristics of the Church, but in reverse and emptied of its divine content. It will be a mystical body of the Antichrist that will in all externals resemble the mystical body of Christ. In desperate need for God, whom he nevertheless refuses to adore, modern man in his loneliness and frustration will hunger more and more for membership in a community that will give him enlargement of purpose, but at the cost of losing himself in some vague collectivity. Then will be verified a paradox—the very objections with which men in the last century rejected the Church will be the reasons why they will now accept the counterchurch.

The last century rejected the Church because it was infallible; it refused to believe that the Vicar of Christ would be immune from error when he spoke on matters of faith and morals as chief shepherd of Christendom. But the twentieth century will join the counterchurch because it claims to be infallible when its visible head speaks ex cathedra from Moscow on the subject of economics and politics, and as chief shepherd of world communism.

The Church was critically spurned in the last few centuries because it claimed that it was Catholic and universal, uniting all men on the basis of one Lord, one faith and one Baptism. No man, the nineteenth century claimed, could be a good American, a good Frenchman or a good German if he accepted shepherding, albeit spiritual, from a spiritual head. But in the new era, what the modern lost soul will like particularly about the counterchurch is that it is catholic or international. It breaks down all national boundaries, laughs down patriotism, dispenses men from piety to country which the Christ enjoined, makes men proud that they are not Americans, French or British, but members of a revolutionary class under the rule of its vicar who rules from the Kremlin.

The nineteenth century rejected the Church on the ground that it was intolerant, excommunicating heretics who did not accept the apostolic traditions, teaching as it did that Christ founded only one Church, that Truth is one, that its dogmas were like living things, and that like a babe, one had to accept the whole child or nothing. But in this evil hour, the sons and grandsons of those who so objected are embracing the counterchurch simply because it is intolerant, because it purges its heretics, liquidates its Trotskyites and excommunicates all those who do not accept the party line: that there may be not one fold and one shepherd, but one anthill and one anteater.

The liberal world rejected the Church because it was too dogmatic with its exact definitions of Hypostatic Union and Immaculate Conception, too hierarchical with its bishops who derived their authority from the Apostles, and claimed to be guardians of the faith and morals of the people. But lo and behold, millions today are embracing the counterchurch for these reasons; they love its infallibly defined dogmas of dialectical materialism, economic determinism and its labor theory of value; they like its hierarchy of approved party leaders who as bishops of the new counterchurch derive their authority from the apostles, Marx and Lenin, and who in their role of secret police keep the errant in the party line, even to the consummation of the world.

The modern mind resents any reference to the Devil. The fact is, however, that, though contemporary atheism has not convinced us there is no God, it has convinced us that there is a devil. When man forgets he has a soul he also forgets that there is a competition for it between the forces of good and evil. Those who penetrate the surface of things more deeply than others have seen that if there is no devil, then all the evil in the world must be attributed to human nature, and no member of the human race wants to believe his species is that diabolical.

Paul Tillich, for example, seriously considers the demonic as a factor in history and as a correlative to the state of grace. "In both phenomena it is the creative original forces which, bursting the form, break into the consciousness. In both instances the spirit is raised out of its autonomous isolation; in both instances subjugated to a new power, which is not a natural power but grows out of the deeper stratum of the abyss which also underlies nature. The paradox of the possessed state is as strong as the paradox of the state of grace; the one is as little to be explained as the other by casual thinking, by categories of rational observation of nature. The difference is only that in the state of grace the

same forces are united with the highest form which con-
tradict the highest form in the possessed state. Therefore
grace has a fulfilling and form-creating effect on the bearer
of the form, while demonry has the consequence of destroying the personality through robbing it of being and
emptying it of meaning. Divine ecstasy brings about an el-
evation of the being, of creative and formative power; the
demonic ecstasy brings about weakening of being, disintegration and decay. Demonic inspiration does indeed reveal
more than rational sobriety; it reveals the divine, but as a
reality which it fears, which it cannot love, with which it
cannot unite."[13]

Berdyaev has also admitted the demonic element in
history.[14] He starts with the proposition that man, having
no source of life within himself, must seek it either in what
is higher or lower than himself, and ends by confronting
man with the alternative of God or Satan. "Being is only
free when it is united in that love through which it is allied to God. It is only in and through God that everything
is linked up and brought into unity. Apart from God everything is alien and remote and is held together simply
by force. Satan by dint of his superior spiritual powers has
succeeded in leading men astray by suggesting to them that
they will become as gods. But by the pursuit of evil and
by the substitution of himself for God, man, so far from
becoming the God-like being of his dreams, becomes the
slave of his lower nature, and, at the same time, by losing
his higher nature becomes subject to natural necessity and
ceases to be spiritually determined from within. He is deprived of his freedom. Thus evil involves that displacement
of the true centre of being and that complete revolution
of the hierarchy of the universe which involves not only
the spirit's being possessed in its pride by the material

principle, but the actual substitution of the material for the spiritual. The hard and resistant appearance of the material world is simply the result of its having lost its true centre in the spiritual world."[15]

The best presentation of this subject for those inclined to deny either evil or the demonic is the brilliant work of Denis de Rougemont, *The Devil's Share*, which he introduces with the suggestion that the knowledge of true danger may cure us of false fears. Meeting immediately the difficulty that Satan, though a myth, has personality, he answers: "The Devil *is* a myth, hence he exists and continues to be active. A myth is a story which describes and illustrates in dramatic form certain deep structures of reality."[16]

"This Devil has not sprung from a series of more or less authentic or ancient texts. For he is a permanent agent of human reality as we live it when we really live, in our state of free creatures, that is to say, constantly placed before choices, in contradiction and perplexity, paradox, tragedy. All this assumes and poses the existence of a good and of something other than the good. Otherwise where would choice, tragedy, liberty lie? When this non good, this evil assumes a meaning, we name it Devil, and I accept this name."[17]

C. S. Lewis in a fanciful series of letters exchanged between Wormwood, a devil on earth, and Screwtape, a devil in hell, teaches sound spiritual lessons in reverse. Particularly interesting is the advice given to the young devil who is trying by argument to win a soul away from God ("The Enemy") to materialism.[18] "I note what you say about guiding your patient's reading and taking care that he sees a good deal of his materialist friend. But are you not being a trifle naïve? It sounds as if you supposed that argument was the way to keep him out of the Enemy's clutches. That might have been so if he had lived a few centuries earlier.

At that time the humans still knew pretty well when a thing was proved and when it was not; and if it was proved they really believed it. They still connected thinking with doing and were prepared to alter their way of life as the result of a chain of reasoning. But what with the weekly press and other such weapons we have largely altered that. Your man has accustomed himself, ever since he was a boy, to have a dozen incompatible philosophies dancing about together inside his head. He doesn't think of doctrines as primarily 'true' or 'false,' but as 'academic' or 'conventional' or 'ruthless.' Jargon, not argument is your best ally in keeping him from the Church. Don't waste time trying to make him think that materialism is true! Make him think it is strong, or stark, or courageous—that it is the philosophy of the future. That's the sort of thing he cares about."*

Joseph Roth in one of the strongest books on the subject, *The Anti-Christ*, despite its extremist tendencies, does much to arouse men's consciousness to the reality of the Devil. "For we have been struck with blindness, with the blindness of which it is written that it will come upon us before the end of time. We have long failed to recognize the nature and appearance of the things with which we have contact. Like those who are physically blind we have merely names for all the things of this world which we can no longer perceive. It is as though we were building a horizontal Tower of Babel which the blind, who are unable to recognize proportion, believe to be vertical and to be growing ever higher; and they think that everything is in order for they understand one another perfectly . . . whereas their comprehension of the proportion, form, and colour

---

* From C. S. Lewis, *Screwtape Letters*. Copyright 1943 by The Macmillan Company. By permission of The Macmillan Company, publishers.

of things is only that of men without sight. Terms which were originally applied correctly, and which fitted the phenomena of this world, are applied by them in a false and inverted sense. That which is raised they call flat, and that which is flat they call raised, since a blind man cannot distinguish between what is lofty and what is level. At the time of Babel it was only the tongues and ears of men that were confused. A few of the builders could still comprehend one another by the language of the eyes, which are called the mirror of the soul. Now, however, the eyes of men are blinded (and tongues are only servants, while eyes are masters, in the hierarchy of the human senses). How can we still hope that Antichrist has not yet come? This faith and this hope are further evidence of our blindness. For just as a man without sight can be persuaded that night is day and day is night, so can we, who have lost our eyes, be made to believe that Antichrist is not here, that we are not smouldering in the glow of his eyes, that we are not standing in the shadow of his wings."[19]

Transcendent to all these writers are the Russians of the nineteenth century who in a prophetic way saw the twentieth century as one in which the Devil would exercise great sway over men and Antichrist would appear as the Great Humanitarian. Fyodor Dostoevsky saw man as capable of reaching heights undreamed of by reason, and yet degrading himself to an abyss of evil which would terrify even its own victims. Man, to him, summarized all the tensions of the world. As the prophet of totalitarianism he saw the twentieth-century world organizing in a collective fashion to rebel against playing the game according to God's rule, and setting man up as the master. In 1877 he wrote: "It seems to me that this century will end for old Europe with something colossal. I mean with something, if not exactly like the events of the French Revolution of the 18th century, yet nevertheless so colossal, so irresistible and so terrifying that it will change the face of the earth at any rate in Western Europe."[20] In the fifth section of his great work *Brothers Karamazov* the Grand Inquisitor, who is Antichrist, appears full of pity for man, a humanitarian with a seeming passionate interest in mankind, but really their enemy because he is the destroyer of their freedom. He appears even like Christ to deceive the elect. "He came softly, unobserved, and yet, strange to say, every one recognized Him. The people are irresistibly drawn to Him, they surround Him, they flock about Him, follow Him. He moves silently in their midst with a gentle smile of infinite compassion. The sun of love burns in His heart, light and power shine from His eyes, and their radiance, shed on the people, stirs their hearts with responsive love. He holds out His hands to them, blesses them, and a healing virtue comes from contact with Him, even with His garments. An old man in the crowd, blind from childhood cries out, 'O Lord, heal me and I shall see Thee!' and, as it were, scales fall from his eyes and the blind man sees Him. The crowd weeps and kisses the earth under His feet. Children throw flowers before Him, sing, and cry hosannah. 'It is He—it is He!'"

The Antichrist speaks to Christ, who never answers, bidding Him give up freedom for security. "Judge Thyself who was right—Thou or he who questioned Thee then? Remember the first question; its meaning, in other words was this: 'Thou wouldst go into the world, and art going with empty hands, with some promise of freedom which men in their simplicity and their natural unruliness cannot even understand, which they fear and dread—for nothing has ever been more insupportable for a man and a human society than freedom. But seest Thou these stones in this parched and barren wilderness? Turn them into bread, and mankind will run after Thee like a flock of sheep, grateful and obedient, though forever trembling lest Thou withdraw Thy hand and deny them Thy bread.' But Thou wouldst not deprive man of freedom and didst reject the offer, thinking, what is that freedom worth, if obedience is bought with bread? Thou didst reply that man lives not by bread alone. But dost Thou know that for the sake of that earthly bread the spirit of the earth will rise up against Thee and will strive with Thee and overcome Thee, and all will follow him, crying 'Who can compare with this beast? He has given us fire from heaven!' Thou didst promise them the bread of Heaven, but, I repeat again, can it compare with earthly bread in the eyes of the weak, ever sinful and ignoble race of man? And if for the sake of the bread of Heaven thousands and tens of thousands shall follow Thee, what is to become of the millions and tens of thousands of millions of creatures who will not have the strength to forego the earthly bread for the sake of the heavenly? Or dost Thou care only for the tens of thousands of the great and strong, while the millions, numerous as the sands of the sea, who are weak but love Thee, must exist only for the sake of the great and strong? No, we care for the weak too. They are sinful and rebellious, but in the end they too will become obedient. They will marvel at us and look on us as gods, because we are ready to endure the freedom which they have found so dreadful and to rule over them—so awful it will seem to them to be free. But we shall tell them that we are Thy servants and rule them in Thy name. We shall deceive them again, for we will not let Thee come to us again. That deception will be our suffering, for we shall be forced to lie."[21]

Equally powerful is the prophetic outlook of Vladimir Soloviev who at just about the beginning of this century wrote *Three Conversations.*[22] He pictures a young man at thirty-three becoming discouraged in his uncontrollable self-love to a point of suicide. Driven mad by the thought that Christ was greater than he, he throws himself into an abyss: "He heard a strange metallic voice, seemingly without soul or feeling, yet very clear. 'My beloved son, to thee goes my great favor. Why didst not thou seek me? Why didst thou worship the other, the foolish one and his Father? I am the God and Father. The other, the wretch that was crucified is a stranger to me and to thee. Thou art the chosen one, the only son, my equal.

"'I love thee and ask nothing of thee. Thou art full of great beauty, thou art great and powerful. Do thy duty *in thine own name not mine.* I am not jealous of thee, I love thee. The one whom thou worshiped before as God demanded obedience, boundless obedience till the very death on a cross. He did not help him on his cross. I am not asking thee anything and yet I shall help thee. Because of thee, because of thy wonderful self, because of my great unselfish love for thee I shall help thee. Partake of my spirit. My spirit delivered thee in beauty and now my spirit delivers thee *in power.*'"

He writes a book under the inspiration of Satan entitled *The Open Road to Peace and Prosperity for the World*, which has fantastic sales all over the world. Many Christians accept it, though Christ's name is not mentioned, justifying themselves: "In the past all sacred matters have been so misused by unauthorized zealots, that a truly deep religious writer has to watch his step. As long as the contents are fully of the Christian spirit of love and charity, what else would one ask?" Finally the superman is made President of the United States of Europe, and all the world accepts his dominion and authority. Exiling the Holy Father from Rome to pronounce himself the "World Emperor of Rome," he issues the manifesto: "People of the world! I promised you peace and now I have given it to you. But the world is only wonderful to live in as long as there is prosperity for all. Peace without prosperity is peace without joy. Come to me all who are hungry and cold and I shall feed you and I shall warm you."

At the beginning of the fourth year of his reign the World Emperor calls a World Council of Churches in Jerusalem, and 3,000 representatives of Catholicism, Protestantism and Orthodoxy attend as well as half a million pilgrims. Among the members of the council there are three that warrant special attention. The first is Pope Peter. The Pope has no faith in the Emperor of the World. The real though unofficial leader of the Orthodox Christians is Father John, well known among the Russians. The head of the Evangelical members of the Council is a scientific German theologian, Professor Ernest Pauly. The opening of the council is very impressive. The two thirds of the great temple which are dedicated to the unity of all cults, are filled with benches for the members, while the remaining third is taken up by a platform at the center, on which there is an imperial throne. The various members of the Council have their services in their own churches and the opening of the Council is devoid of any religious ceremonies. When the Emperor together with the great magician appears, the orchestra starts to play the hymn of the United Nations which by that time has become the Imperial International hymn.

At the close of the hymn, the Emperor rises from his throne and with a magnificent gesture thanks the musicians and addresses the Council: "Christians, Christians, of all denominations, my loyal subjects and brethren. From the very beginning of my reign I have never had occasion to be displeased, you have always fulfilled your obligations. You have been faithful. This is not enough for me. My sincere love for you, brothers, is craving for reciprocation. I am anxious to bring about a state of affairs whereby there would not be a sense of duty but a feeling of deep love with which you would recognize me your leader in every enterprise you undertake for the benefit of humanity. Besides, I do wish to consummate a deed of special charity. Christians, is there any way that I could make you happier? Is there anything that I can give you? My Christians, let me know the thing that is dearest to you so that I may exert my efforts in that direction."

When he stops a great roar fills the temple. The members of the Council are whispering to one another. Pope Peter carries on a grave discourse with those surrounding him. So does Professor Pauly. Father John bends over a group of Eastern Bishops and Catholic monks and endeavors to impress them with his thoughts. After several minutes of silence the Emperor addresses the Council again, now with a slight note of annoyance: "Beloved Christians, I understand how very difficult it is to come to any direct answer. I am going to help you. Since time immemorial you have been divided into so many parties and groups that you really have no common goal. You have not even reconciled yourselves on many things. I shall endeavor to unite all of the parties and groups and I shall bend to fulfill the real craving of each group. Beloved Christians, I know that a great many of you deem spiritual authority as the most precious heritage of Christianity. Beloved brother Catholics, I fully understand your point of view and I dearly want to rest my royal scepter upon your spiritual head. So you will think these are not empty words I am declaring now that in accordance with my royal will the supreme Archbishop of the Catholic Church, the Pope of Rome, is being reinstated from now on upon his throne in Rome, given with all the rights and privileges that were ever bestowed upon him from time immemorial and beginning with the reign of Constantine the Great, and all I ask for you, my Catholics, is that you consider me at the bottom of your heart to be your only protector and benefactor. Whoever will recognize me as such let him come to me."

At this moment the Emperor points a finger at the empty benches on the platform. Amidst joyous cries, "*Gratias agimus! Domine! Salvum fac magnum imperatorem,*" nearly all the Princes of the Catholic Church, the Cardinals, the Bishops and most of the faithful laymen and nearly one half of all the monks mount the platform and after bowing in the direction of the Emperor seat themselves. Down below, straight and silent as a statue of marble, sits Pope Peter II. The Emperor throws a glance of amazement at the Holy Father, then turns to the others, raising his voice. "Beloved brethren, today I will sign an edict. In this edict I am bestowing upon the world a museum of Christian archeology and a sum of money for promoting the study of the ancient Christian folklore, legends and other antiquities. This museum will be situated in our imperial city of Constantinople."

A great portion of the Hierarchy of the East and North, half of the former old Believers and more than half of the Orthodox priests and monks and laymen, crying joyfully, walk up on the platform and seat themselves. Father John does not move. He sighs loudly and when the crowd with him becomes very thin he leaves his bench and walks up toward Pope Peter and his circle. The other Orthodox who did not join those on the platform follow John. The

Emperor speaks again, "It is known to me, Christian brethren, that there are many among you who deem that there is nothing more sacred to Christians than freedom to study the Bible. I can assure you that in a few days I am receiving a request to become an honorary Doctor of Theology at the University of Tübegean."

More than one half of the scholarly theologians move to the platform although some are a little uneasy and some look at Professor Pauly, who has not moved, but figuratively has grown to his seat. He bends his head very low. All of a sudden one of them jumps down from the platform and runs to Professor Pauly and his dwindling group. Professor Pauly lifts his head, rises and walks between the empty benches toward Father John and Pope Peter. Down below remain three little clusters of men squirming around Father John, Pope Peter and Professor Pauly.

With a sad voice the Emperor addresses these groups. "You are strange people. What else can I do for you? What else are you demanding? I do not know. Tell me this, Christians who are now deserted by the majority of your brothers and leaders of your own people, condemned by the voice of your people, what is it that you hold most sacred in Christianity?"

Hearing this, Father John rises like a tall white candle and answers humbly, "Great Emperor, there is only one thing that is dearest to us in Christianity, and that is Christ Himself. It is He, and everything comes from Him and we know that within Him lives the spirit of physical Divinity. We are ready to receive from you all kinds of blessings just so long as we recognize in your generous hand the Holy Hand of Christ the Son of God, and when you ask us what there is that you can do for us our answer is, simply confess before us here the Christian Creed. Say 'I believe in our

Lord Jesus Christ the Son of God. . . .' Confess in His name and we will receive you with love. We will receive you as a forerunner of His, a forerunner of His second glorious coming to this earth."

Father John keeps looking at the Emperor, who is silent. Then he suddenly turns toward his flock and cries: "Children, the Antichrist!" At that very moment a great bolt of lightning enters the temple and strikes the old man. There is a terrific roar of thunder. Everything becomes quiet for a moment and when the deafened and blinded Christians come back to their senses, Father John lies stretched out dead on the floor. Suddenly one ringing word sounds through the temple and the word is "*Contradicitur!*" Pope Peter II rises and with his face flushed with anger he lifts his staff in the direction of the Emperor. "Our only ruler is Jesus Christ, the Son of the Living God! You heard what you are! Out of here! Cain, the killer of a brother! Out, you vessel of the devil! Forever and ever I oust you, a dirty dog, from the fold of the Church and I am giving you back to your father, the devil." Louder than the last anathema comes the roar of thunder. And the last Pope falls lifeless.

In the temple there remain two lifeless bodies and a close circle of Christians half dead from fright. The only one who does not lose his head is Professor Pauly. He takes a piece of paper left by one of the royal secretaries and begins to write. When he finishes he stands up and reads aloud: "In the name and glory of our only Redeemer, Jesus Christ, the World Council of Christian Churches has assembled in Jerusalem. After our good Brother John, the representative of Eastern Christianity condemned the great impostor as the enemy of God and accused him of being the real Antichrist, as foretold in the prophecies, Peter, the representative of Western Christianity, rightfully and eternally excommunicated the impostor from the Church of God. Today I am standing here before the bodies of two martyrs, killed for their belief in truth. Being witness for Christ, the Council orders: Stop all intercourse with the one who was excommunicated, with all of those who recognize him. All the faithful, depart into the wilderness and wait there for an early coming of the real Lord Jesus Christ."

Because the signs of our times point to a struggle between absolutes we may expect the future to be a time of trials and catastrophes for two reasons: firstly, to stop disintegration. Godlessness would go on and on if there were no catastrophes. What death is to a sinful person, that catastrophe is to an evil civilization: the interruption of its godlessness. Why did God station an angel with a flaming sword at the Garden of Paradise after the Fall, if it were not to prevent our first parents from entering the garden and eating of the tree of life, which, if they ate, would have immortalized their evil? God will not allow unrighteousness to become eternal. Revolution, disintegration, chaos must be reminders that our thinking has been wrong, our dreams have been unholy. Moral truth is vindicated by the ruin that follows when it has been repudiated. The chaos of our times is the strongest negative argument that could ever be advanced for Christianity. Catastrophe becomes a testimony to God's power in a meaningless world, for by it God brings a meaningless existence to nought. The disintegration following an abandonment of God thus becomes a triumph of meaning, a reaffirmation of purpose. Adversity is the expression of God's condemnation of evil, the registering of Divine Judgment. As hell is not sin, but the effect of sin, so these disordered times are not sin, but the wages of sin. Catastrophe reveals that evil is self-defeating; we cannot turn from God without hurting ourselves.

The second reason why a crisis must come is in order to prevent a false identification of the Church and the world. Our Lord intended that His followers should be different in spirit from those who were not His followers. "I have taken you out of the world, therefore the world hateth you." (John 15:19) Though this is the Divine intent, it is unfortunately true that the line of demarcation between the followers of Christ and those who are not is often blotted out. Instead of black and white, there is only a blur. Mediocrity and compromise characterize the lives of many Christians. Many read the same novels as modern pagans, educate their children in the same godless way, listen to the same commentators who have no other standard than judging today by yesterday and tomorrow by today, allow pagan practices such as divorce and remarriage to creep into the family. There are not wanting so-called Catholic labor leaders recommending Communists for Congress, or Catholic writers who accept presidencies in Communist-front organizations to instill totalitarian ideas in movies. There is no longer the conflict and opposition which is supposed to characterize us. We are influencing the world less than the world influences us. There is no apartness. Well indeed might St. Paul say to us what he said to the Corinthians: "What has innocence to do with lawlessness? What is there in common between light and darkness? What harmony between Christ and Belial?" St. Paul is here asserting that those who were sent out to establish a center of health had caught the disease; therefore, they lost the power to heal. Since the amalgamation of the Christian and the pagan spirit has set in, since the gold is married with an alloy, the entirety must be thrust into the furnace that the dross may be burned away. The value of the trial will be to set us apart. Evil must come to reject us, to despise us, to hate us, to persecute us, and then shall we define our loyalties, affirm our fidelities and state on whose side we stand. How shall the strong and weak trees be manifested unless the wind blows? Our quantity indeed will decrease, but our quality will increase. Then shall be verified the words of Our Master: "He that gathereth not with me scattereth." (Matt. 12:30)

These are Times of Troubles, and it is not so much a Third World War that is to be feared as the rebirth of Leviathan, the coming of the Day of the Beast, when there will be no buying or selling, unless men have been signed with the sign of the Beast who would devour the child of the Mother of Mothers. All great minds, non-Christian and Christian, see these days as perilous. Spengler believed that we are at the winter of civilization;[23] Fisher at the death rattle of European civilization;[24] Sorokin, at the end of sensate culture;[25] Berdyaev at the end of the days of reason illumined by faith;[26] Marx at the collapse of capitalism;[27] Lippman, at an hour when men feel it is no longer wise, necessary or useful to pass on to succeeding generations the good Christian heritage of the past;[28] Toynbee, at the third stage of crisis in the Greek drama. The three stages are *Hybris* or pride that came from material prosperity, showing itself in power; the second *Nemesis* or arrogance or contention against God, in which man arrogates to himself the attributes of Deity, and finally *Ate* or disaster, in which Divine Justice will humble the vain pretension of men.[29] Going back farther, Lord Gray, at the close of the First World War, said that the lights were being put out all over Europe and they would not be lighted again in our generation. Before that a great German poet and a Russian novelist warned people of the signs of the times. Writing in 1834, in *Religion and Philosophy in Germany*, Heine warned, look out for Germany when the Cross of Christ no longer casts its spell over His people.

"Christianity has—and that is its fairest merit—somewhat mitigated that brutal German lust for battle. But it could not destroy it; and once the taming talisman, the Cross, is broken, the savagery of the old battlers will flare up again, the insane rage of which Nordic bards have so much to say and sing. That talisman is brittle. The day will come when it will pitiably collapse. Then the old stone gods will rise from forgotten rubble and rub the dust of a thousand years from their eyes; and Thor will leap up and with his giant hammer start smashing Gothic cathedrals . . . and when you hear a crash as nothing ever crashed in world history, you will know that the German thunder has hit the mark. At that sound the eagles will fall dead from the sky and the lions in the farthest desert of Africa will pull in their tails and slink away into their royal caves. A play will be performed that will make the French Revolution seem like a harmless idyll in comparison. . . ."

In 1842 Heine, friend of Karl Marx, the founder of communism, saw the evil effects of his philosophy and warned: ". . . Communism is the name of the terrible antagonist which sets agrarian rule in all its consequences in opposition to the *bourgeois regime* of to-day. It will be a terrible conflict—how will it end? *That* the gods and goddesses only know who know the future. This much do we know, that Communism, though it be at present but little discussed, and now yearns away its life in forgotten garrets on wretched straw-pallets, is still the gloomy hero to whom a great if transitory part is assigned in the modern tragedy, and which only waits its cue *(Stichwort, replique)* to enter on the stage. We should never lose sight of this actor, and we will from time to time give accounts of the secret rehearsals in which he is preparing for his debut. Such indications are perhaps more important than reports of electoral intrigues, party quarrels, and cabinet intrigues.

". . . You will have seen the result of the elections in the newspapers. Here in Paris there is indeed no need of looking into them—you can see it clearly written in every face. Yesterday they all had a hot and sultry look, and people's minds betrayed an excitement such as is only to be seen in great crises. The birds prophetic of storm, well known to us of yore, whirred invisibly through the air, and the sleepiest heads were suddenly awakened from their two years of repose. I confess that I myself, feeling the wind of these terrible wings, experienced a dire beating of my heart. . . . What would be the end of this movement for which Paris has, as usual, given the signal? It would be a war, the most terrible war of destruction, which—more's the pity!—will call the noblest races of civilisation into the arena, to their joint destruction. I mean Germany and France. England, the great sea-serpent, which can always glide back into its watery nest, and Russia, which in its vast forests of firs, steppes, and ice fields has also the securest lairs—these two cannot be utterly destroyed in a common political war, even by the most decided defeats; but Germany is, in such a case, in far greater danger, and even France may suffer terribly in her political existence. But this would be, so to speak, only the first act or prologue to the grand drama. The second will be European or the world Revolution, the gigantic battle of the disinherited with the inheritors of fortune, and in that there will be no question of nationality or of religion, for there will be but one fatherland, the Earth, and but one religion, that of happiness in *this* life. Will the religious doctrines of the past in every country unite to a desperate resistance, and thus form a third act in the great play? Or will the old Absolute tradition enter again on the stage, but this time in a new costume and with new watchwords to incite and goad? How will this drama end?

I do not know, but I think that at last the head of the great water-snake will be crushed, and the skin pulled over the head of the bear of the North. And then perhaps there will be only *one* flock and *one* shepherd—a free shepherd with an iron crook—and one great herd of men all shorn and all bleating alike. Wild and gloomy times come roaring on, and the prophet who would write a new Apocalypse must imagine new beasts, and those so terrible that the old symbols of St. John as compared to them will seem like soft doves and amorets. The gods hide their faces out of pity to the sons of mankind, their nurslings for so many years, and perhaps out of fear as to their own fate. The future has an odour as of Russian leather, blood, blasphemy, and much beating with the knout. I advise our descendants to come into the world with thick skins. . . ."[30]

The Holy Father says that we are at the return of the early centuries of the Church. Many others believe we are saved from utter chaos only by habits of thinking, rules of the road and conventions which depend for their validity on beliefs which have long been abandoned. With the family disintegrating, with one divorce for every two marriages in 35 major cities of the United States, with five divorces for every six marriages in Los Angeles—there is no denying that something has snapped. Beyond all these and other tragic facts, such as the attempt to ground peace on compromises between powers, rather than on justice and pledges such as the Atlantic Charter, the startling fact stands out that our times—and our times alone—have witnessed, for the first time in human history, the persecution of the Old Testament by the Nazis and the persecution of the New Testament by the Communists. Anyone who has had anything to do with God is hated today, whether his vocation is to announce His Divine Son, Jesus Christ, as did the Jew, or to follow Him as does the Christian. Every now and then in history the Devil is given a long rope, for we must never forget that Our Lord said to Judas and his band: "This is your hour." God has His day, but evil has its hour when the shepherd will be struck and the sheep dispersed. But though we speak of the emergence of the Antichrist against Christ, think not that it is because we fear for the Church. We do not; it is for the world we fear. It is not infallibility we are worried about, but the world's lapse into fallibility; we tremble not that God may be dethroned, but that barbarism may reign; it is not the Transubstantiation that may perish, but the home; not the sacraments that may fade away, but the moral law. The Church can have no words for the weeping women different from those of Christ on the way to Cavalry: "Weep not over Me; but weep for yourselves and for your children." (Luke 23:28) The Church has survived other great crises in her 19 centuries of existence, and she will live to sing a requiem over the evils of the present. The Church may have its Good Fridays, but these are only preludes to its Easter Sundays, for the Divine Promise shall never be made void: ". . . and the gates of hell shall not prevail against it." "Behold I am with you all days, even to the consummation of the world." (Matt. 28:20) "Whosoever shall fall upon that stone, shall be bruised." (Luke 20:18) Never before in history has there been such a strong argument for the need of Christianity, for men are now discovering that their misery and their woes, their wars and their revolutions increase in direct ratio and proportion to the neglect of Christianity. Christians realize that a moment of crisis is not a time of despair, but of opportunity. The more we can anticipate the doom, the more we can avoid it. Once we recognize we are under Divine Wrath, we become eligible for Divine Mercy. It was because of famine the prodigal said: "I will arise, and will go to my father . . ." (Luke 15:18) The very disciplines of God create hope. The thief on the right came to God by a crucifixion. The Christian finds a basis for optimism in the most thoroughgoing pessimism, for his Easter is within three days of Good Friday.

As we look about the world and see the new barbarism move whole populations into slavery we may ask: "Why do so many innocent people suffer? God should have pity on them." God does. One of the surprises of heaven will be to see how many saints were made in the midst of chaos, and war and revolution. John saw a ". . . great multitude, which no man could number, of all nations and tribes, and peoples, and tongues, standing before the throne, and in sight of the Lamb, clothed with white robes, and palms in their hands: And they cried with a loud voice saying: Salvation to our God, Who sitteth upon the throne, and to the Lamb. And all the angels stood round about the throne, and the ancients, and the four living creatures: and they fell down before the throne upon their faces, and adored God." (Apoc. 7:9–11) "And one of the ancients answered and said to me: These that are clothed in white robes, who are they? and whence came they? And I said to him: My lord thou knowest. And he said to me: These are they who are come out of great tribulation, and have washed their robes, and have made them white in the blood of the Lamb." (Apoc. 7:13, 14) After Our Divine Lord had pictured the catastrophes that would fall upon a morally disordered civilization, after He foretold how the military would take it, and their holy places be abominated, He did not say, "Fear," but, "When these things begin to come to pass, look up, and lift up your heads, because your redemption is at hand." (Luke 21:28)

Jews, Protestants and Catholics alike, and all men of good will, are realizing that the world is serving their souls with an awful summons—the summons to heroic efforts at spiritualization. An alliance among Jews, Protestants and Catholics is not necessary to fight against an *external* enemy, for our "wrestling is not against flesh and blood; but against principalities and powers, against the rulers of the world of this darkness, against the spirits of wickedness in the high places." (Ephesians 6:12) We desire unity of religion but not when purchased at the cost of the unity of the truth. But we plead for a unity of religious peoples, wherein each marches separately according to the light of his conscience, but strikes together for the moral betterment of the world; a unity through prayer, not hate. If Satan has his fellow travelers, then why should not God and His Divine Son? The Roman sergeant who built a temple for the Jews was a fellow traveler with them in their belief in God. The woman at Tyre and Sidon became a fellow traveler of Christ. The forces of evil are united; the forces of good are divided. We may not be able to meet in the same pew—would to God we could—but we can meet on our *knees.*

No sordid compromises nor carrying waters on both shoulders will see us through. Those who have the faith had better keep in the state of grace, and those who have neither had better find out what they mean, for in the coming age there will be only one way to stop trembling knees, and that will be to get down on them and pray. The most important problem in the world today is the soul, for that is what the struggle is about. As St. Peter told the Romans in the days of delirium: "Seeing then that all these things are to be dissolved, what manner of people ought you to be in holy conversation and godliness?" (2 Peter 3:11)

The way out of this crisis is basically spiritual, because the trouble is not in the way we keep our books, but in the way we keep our souls. The time is nearer than we think. In 1917 Lenin, addressing a group of students in Switzerland, said: "This revolution may not come in my lifetime." Within three months he was leading it. The struggle is so basically spiritual, so much concerned with the forces of Christ and Antichrist, that there is a definite planned policy put into practice by the Communists in Korea. They go to the Christian homes converted by missionaries and ask: "Do you believe in Christ?" If the householder answers in the affirmative, the Communist says he will be back next week. If then he answers: "I believe in Stalin," he keeps his house and his land. Otherwise they are confiscated and he is liquidated. And some think the struggle is between individualism and collectivism! Because the struggle is between the Kingdom of mass atheism and the Kingdom of God, St. Michael must once more be invoked as Chesterton invoked him: "O Michael, Prince of the Morning, Who didst once conquer Lucifer who wouldst make himself God, save us from our world of little gods. When the world once cracked because of a sneer in heaven, thou didst rise up and drag down from the seven heavens the pride that would look down on the most high." So now:

> "Michael, Michael, Michael of the mastering,
> Michael of the marching on the mountains of the Lord,
> Marshal the world and purge of rot and riot,
> Rule through the world till all the world be quiet:
> Only establish when the world is broken—
> What is unbroken is the Word."

CHAPTER TWO

Is Communism the Enemy of the Western World?

Few are willing to face the realities of the time in which they live because it involves too much self-reproach. Perhaps that is also the reason why we have no satire in the modern theater. We are not humble enough to laugh at our foibles and admit our own sins. Others who are more awake to the seriousness of our times are inclined to think that the cause of all the world's woe is external to our democratic way of life, and is principally due to communism. This is only partly true, and if we subscribe to it, we blind ourselves to the fact that the very existence of all modern culture is being threatened. In order to see the matter straight, put the problem bluntly: *Is communism the enemy of our Western civilization?*

That question cannot be answered without making a distinction, namely: What is meant by Western civilization? Obviously it may mean one of two things. It may mean, first of all, Christian civilization with its emphasis on human rights as an inalienable gift of God, its stress on the value and dignity of the human person because fashioned to the Divine Image, its affirmation of liberty as a derivative of the Spirit and intelligible only within law and not outside of it, and finally the sacramental use of creation aided by redemptive grace to attain the glorious liberty of the children of God.

On the other hand, Western civilization may mean our materialistic, bourgeois, capitalistic civilization, descended in part from the French Revolution, which affirms that man is only a highly evolved economic animal, that evil is due to ignorance and can be cured by education, that the primary purpose of man is either to acquire wealth or enjoy pleasure.

To return to the question: Is communism the enemy of our Western civilization? Unquestionably it is the enemy of our Christian civilization, but Christian civilization is submerged and denied a major influence in the political, economic life of our times. But communism certainly is not the enemy of our Western bourgeois, capitalistic, materialistic civilization. The truth of the matter is: Communism is related to our materialistic Western civilization as putrefaction is to disease. Many of the ideas which our bourgeois civilization has sold at retail, communism sells at wholesale; what the Western world has subscribed to in isolated and uncorrelated tidbits, communism has integrated into a complete philosophy of life. There is no identity between the two, but there is affinity. There are basic differences which will be treated later on, but there *is* a relationship. Both believe in egotism; our Western civilization believing in individual egotism; communism believing it should be collective. Our Western bourgeois world is un-Christian; Communism is anti-Christian.

Take, for example, such a subject as economics. Communism derived its notion of economics as the primary and motivating cause of all human history from the Western world of historical liberalism which claimed that the primary purpose of man was the acquisition of profit.[1] If Marx had lived in any other century than that which made economics both the be-all and end-all here, his ideas would have fallen on barren ground. There is a further similarity between capitalism and communism in that the former concentrated wealth in the hands of a few capitalists, while communism concentrates it in the hands of a few bureaucrats. To do this both historical liberalism and communism had to divorce economics from morality. The only contribution that communism makes to capitalism is to shift booty and loot from one man's pockets to another, while leaving the lust of acquisition untouched. Every Communist is a capitalist without any cash in his pockets. He is the involuntary capitalist—but his heart is just as set on materialities as the economic baron whom he would displace. Communism, from the economic point of view, is rotted capitalism, with the difference that in one case the people live off the largess of a capitalist, and in the other off the largess of the bureaucrat. The former, however, admits the right to strike and recognizes basic civil liberties; the latter does not.

In the domain of morality, is it not an accepted principle of our Western bourgeois world that there is no absolute distinction between right and wrong rooted in the eternal order of God, but that they are relative and dependent entirely upon one's point of view? Hence when the Western world wishes to decide what is right and wrong even in certain moral matters, it takes a poll—forgetful that the majority never makes a thing right, because right is right if nobody is right, and wrong is wrong if everybody is wrong. The first pool of public opinion taken in history of Christianity was on Pilate's front porch, and it was wrong. What is the difference between the bourgeois denial of absolute standards of right and wrong and communism? The latter denies an eternal order; it too says that the collectivity is the determinant. But in typical Byzantine fashion it says that public opinion is too vague and vacuous, so it concentrates the determinant of right and wrong in the party. Whatever the party decides is right, is right, and what the party decides is wrong, is wrong. There is no conscience but state conscience, no morality but state morality. Thus did the eighteenth-century idea that man in his moral actions should be different to otherworldly considerations end in a downright materialism which persecutes all who would live by an otherworldly morality.[2]

It is an accepted principle of education in our bourgeois world that religion must not be taught in school, with the result that the only group secular education actually pleases is the atheistic. In addition to this, our bourgeois, capitalistic civilization teaches that religion is an individual affair, and hence must be denied political, economic and social relevance. The Communists accept this premise of the Western world, but go a step farther and say that if it has no social relevance, then exclude it altogether. Article 125 of the Soviet Constitution accordingly denies the right to teach religion. Thus does the individual atheism of our bourgeois civilization become the collective atheism of communism.[3]

Finally, consider what is basic to any philosophy, namely the subject of man. Is there any secular university or college in the Western world, or one that is not under definitely Christian influences, which teaches that man is a creature of God, that this life is a novitiate for the next, that Christ is Redeemer of his soul, that marriage is monogamous, that self-restraint is essential to virtue and that a man ought to save his immortal soul? Rather the general teaching is that man is nothing but an evolved animal, and that he is not responsible for his sins, either because there are no sins, or because man is not really free. Man has been determined biologically, which is the Darwinian theory, or he has been determined erotically, which is the Freudian theory, or for its intelligentsia—those who have been educated beyond their intelligence—man is determined zoologically. Communism too states that man came from the beast, hence, they add, he ought to act like one, and thus they justify their philosophy of violence. It too denies personal guilt and sin, but it says that man is determined not in the Darwinian or Freudian fashion but economically, by methods of production. It makes little difference. Once man is identified with nature, so that psychology is nothing more than behaviorism, theology nothing but comparative religion, it is not long until man begins to be treated the way nature is—as a means, an instrument, a tool, and then the Moloch of collectivism swallows up the man of democracy.[4]

One might go on making comparisons, but it is clear that there is some relation between bourgeois materialism and capitalism and communism. The very fact that in World War II we chose to fight in alliance with one form of totalitarianism against the other two forms, though all were intrinsically wicked, proves not only the basic sympathy between Western materialism and communism but also the grave mistake of trying to drive the Devil out with Beelzebub. As a final proof of the affinity it would be well to inquire: Where did the philosophy of communism start? Not in Russia, but in the Western world of the last century. It is Western in origin; its philosophy is German, its sociology French and its economics English. Communism is potpourri, a hodgepodge of all the cheap, deistic, *Aufklärung*, atheistic, agnostic thinking of the Eighteenth Century, and what Leon Daudet called the "stupid nineteenth century." Karl Marx, its founder, patched the dialectics of a Hegel to the materialism of a Feuerbach, to the sociology of a Proudhon, to the economic problems born of liberalism and out of it came the philosophy we call "the enemy" of our Western civilization. Every single idea of communism is Western bourgeois in its origin.[5]

Only the dynamism of communism is non-Western, but it has swallowed whole all the bourgeois falsities, from pragmatism, that the useful is the true, to materialism, that matter alone matters. Because it has never corrected the abuses of our Western world, but only intensified them, communism has made us realize how wrong we are. It has not eradicated a single major premise of bourgeois capitalistic civilization, but only urged collective egotism, to crush individual egotism. It has accepted our degenerate standards of the primacy of economics. Because it has only revised the capitalistic system by making it supply an increasing number of state services at the cost of freedom, it can make only one contribution to our Western world and that is to compel us to strike our breasts and cry *"mea culpa, Domine"* and resolve from this day forward to purge ourselves of the towering nonsense that a man who will not covet his neighbor's goods is no longer a progressive; that a man who says that the right to work implies the duty to work with responsibility is a "reactionary," and that loyalty to conscience, to family, to country, to truth and to God makes us "Fascists."

This is not saying that there is identity between the bourgeois, capitalistic civilization and communism, because there is not. The relationship, however, is something like uranium and the cyclotron on the one hand, and the atomic bomb on the other. Communism put the elements of destruction together and they became a new kind of thing. The very fact that we are horrified when we see the effects of our materialism worked out on a world-wide scale proves that we are not yet sold on the whole philosophy of materialism. Because there is affinity between the two,[6] since there is a God in the heavens, since there is a moral law behind and beyond all nations, there is a possibility that both communism and Western civilization will perish together, perhaps even at each other's throats, or perhaps by a disease and corruption within both. We are both moving toward catastrophe, and in this the Marxist and Christian both believe. The liberal world thought that history moved in an ascending line of progress, thanks to evolution and science, until two world wars in 21 years knocked that idea into a cocked hat. But Christianity never believed that history worked that way; neither does communism believe it. The Gospel for the last Sunday of Pentecost and the Gospel for the first Sunday of Advent are Gospels of catastrophe; they proclaim that the final era of peace will not be ushered in until the final conflict between good and evil, when God shall come to judge the living and the dead and the new city of Peace will be seen descending from the Heavens. The liberal Christians who wanted a Christianity without a cross denied this tragic element in history, but the Marxists kept it and secularized it. They too believe that the city of man will not be ushered in without a great catastrophe in which the Communist dictator, not God, will come to judge the Communists and the anti-Communists, and put all the latter to death in the bloody revolution. Then in time shall be born the kingdom of man in which love will come out of hate; fraternity out of fratricide. Though utopian and violent, Marxism reveals a better insight into the historical processes than liberalism, which saw peace coming without a struggle and which denied that even a relative Easter of economic order would come without the Good Friday of self-sacrifice and effort.

Our Western bourgeois world may yet suffer for being un-Christian; communism may suffer for being anti-Christian. As many a parent who educated his child in an extremely progressive school, where the child equated freedom with doing what he pleased, is now the parent who wants to know what to do with his recalcitrant, alcoholic, neurotic son, so the Western world that taught Russia some bad ideas may soon want to know how it can be saved from a country which learned its lesson too well. A Freudian psychoanalysis cannot help the son, so neither politics nor economics can help the Western world, for the fault is deeper; the world is under the judgment of God and needs repentance.

Though Babylon fell because it was very wicked, it was none the less God's instrument for disciplining the people of Judah. Assyria was bestial, but it was the "rod and the staff" of God's anger against the people of Israel. It may very well be, therefore, that unless there is a moral revival in our Western world, a fulfillment of the pledges of the Atlantic Charter, a rebirth of family life, communism may be the instrument for the liquidation of a bourgeois civilization that has forgotten God. *Communism is not to be feared just because it is anti-God, but because we are Godless*; not because it is strong, but because we are weak, for if we were under God, then who could conquer us?

Before World War II we sold to Japan a tremendous amount of scrap iron on the principle that if we appeased, they would be friends. We got the scrap iron back, not in the shape that we sent it, but in the form of bullets at Okinawa and Iwo Jima. In like manner, for the last century we have sent into Russia all the scrap ideas of materialism that accumulated as a by-product of our abandonment of Christian civilization. Some day we will get those ideas back, not in the shape that we sent them, but after they have been transformed in revolutionary Asiatic souls—but get them back we will. Does that mean the end of civilization? It does not. It will mean the end of bourgeois capitalistic and liberal civilization as well as communism and the beginning of a new civilization and a new order. What will happen will be very much like what happened in the fall of Rome. There was a tremendous amount of energy and goodness under its old paganism, namely, the nascent energies of Christianity, but they were not permitted to exercise influence on society. The barbarian invasion broke the crust of that paganism and allowed Christianity to become a vital influence in the souls of men. In like manner, there is a tremendous amount of goodness, moral decency and godlikeness both in Russia and in our bourgeois Western civilization. Communism has millions of adherents in our Western world, but Christian civilization with its Hebraic roots and fruits has millions of adherents not only here but in Russia. Just as there is life under the shell of an egg, but that life cannot assert itself until the shell has been broken, so too the potential lifeblood of a new and better world cannot come until the shell has been broken in Russia and our Western world. Then shall there be peace as Russia receives the gift of faith, and, please God, then our own country because of its basic idealism, will understand why its symbol is the eagle flying upward and onward unto God.

It is so easy to believe that evil is extrinsic to our Western civilization and that all we need to do is to harangue against communism, but the more sober thinkers will see that communism and its defunct relatives, Fascism and Nazism, are world diseases that broke out in the weakest organs or nations which were most susceptible to contagion. They indicate the sickness of the whole world. Only because there has been a radical schism of soul, or a triple alienation of man from his God, from self and from fellow man, could these totalitarian systems arise. What this sickness is can be variously described, but certainly egotism and envy play a preponderant role. Every revolutionist, Rauschning contends, is basically not a socialist of the red, brown or black variety, but an anarchist. Socialism as such has never been a popular movement. What communism has added to socialism is anarchy as the road to power. The socialist says: "Everything will be held in common." The Communist adds: "When everything is held in common, I will own that house."

Even before the First World War, Gustave le Bon, in his *Psychology of Socialism*, saw the disease taking possession of the body of Western civilization: "It is difficult," he wrote, "to foresee how modern society can escape the formidable tyranny which menaces it. . . . Hate and envy in the lower layers; indifference, intense egotism and exclusive cult of wealth in the ruling class; pessimism among the thinkers, such are the general modern tendencies. It is doubtful if society can resist for any length of time."

In our day Emil Brunner warns: "The totalitarian state is the inevitable result of the slow disintegration of the idea of justice in the Western World."[7] Lewis Mumford, striking the same note, warns: "Today every human being is living through an apocalypse of violence. . . . Now, for the first time in human history there is no spot on earth where the innocent may find refuge. . . . Something else has been disclosed to our unwary eyes: the rottenness of our civilization itself. . . . If our civilization should perish, this will come about in part, because it was not good enough to survive."[8]

Communism is, as Waldemar Gurian has said, both an effect and a judgment on our Western world; an effect because it was born of our unfulfilled Christian duties, our abandonment of the Father's House in favor of materialism; a judgment because it reveals how wrong has been our thinking, how evil have been our deeds. War and unrest are nothing more than symptoms of a deeper breaking up. That the generations of godless humanism should have issued in Nietzsche, Oswald Spengler and the three totalitarians is suggestive that the Incarnation is true. "The Lordship of Christ, if it does not yet appear in the coming of His Kingdom, is nevertheless visible in the fact that His defeat in this world appears inevitably to involve the defeat of man: and this defeat is the more impressive because it has come when man has accumulated all the necessary implements for a successful humanist world."[9] Christ is at our doors summoning us to repentance, but only those who have religious eyes or ears know how urgent is the task.

CHAPTER THREE

The Philosophy
of Communism

Though communism has millions of followers, hangers-on
and fellow travelers throughout the world, there are actually only a few outside the Communist leaders themselves
who know anything about its philosophy. Many think that
communism is just an economic theory in which production is for use rather than for profit; others believe it to be
a defense of the worker and the disinherited, which indeed
if it were, we would all be Communists. Others believe it
is a form of collectivism opposed to the individualism of
the Western world. Basically, communism is none of these
things. Rather it is a complete philosophy of life, what the
Germans called a *Weltanschauung*, an integral comprehension of the world, different from all other secular systems
in that it seeks not only to dominate the periphery of life
but to control man's inner life as well. Communism has a
theory and a practice; it wishes to be not only a state but
a church judging the consciences of men; it is a doctrine

of salvation and as such claims the whole man, body and soul, and in this sense is totalitarian.

It has its origin in the brain of a German, Karl Marx,[1] who on both his mother's and father's side, though his father was a lawyer, was descended from a long line of rabbis. He was born on the fifth of May in the year 1818 in the city of Treves, Germany. At the age of six, Karl Marx along with his family was baptized and became a member of one of the Christian sects, not for religious but for political and business reasons.

It is his philosophy rather than his life which interests us. The first stage in the development of his thought began when, at the age of 19, he enrolled at the University of Berlin to study law, but in his own words, "above all to wrestle with philosophy." At that particular time German universities were obliged to teach the philosophy of Hegel, who had died in 1831. Marx plunged into the almost unintelligible abstractions of Hegel, whose philosophy was known as dialectical idealism: *idealism*, because it was concerned with ideas, thoughts, spirits, mind, for the reality of the universe is not things but ideas; *dialectical*, because it described the method by which thoughts or ideas developed, namely by contradiction.

For Hegel there are no immutable truths or principles. Ideas are fluid and are arrived at by a debating or dialectical process, in which like a tennis ball they are batted back and forth over the net until a point is scored. First there is the *affirmation* of an idea, then its *negation* by another idea, and finally a *synthesis* of the two. Suppose the problem under discussion is the decoration of a room. One group says: let us do it in blue; another group argues against it in favor of green and finally out of the conflict of ideas there emerges a synthesis of opinion that it be done in red. This is indeed an oversimplified explanation of Hegel, so simple that if Hegel heard it he would turn over in his grave, but it is often the business of philosophers to complicate and obscure the simple things of life.

Marx was tremendously impressed with the dialectical side of Hegel which denied any truth is permanent, or any principle immutable. In the year 1841 Marx presented to the University of Jena a doctoral thesis, so dialectical in character that the second sentence contradicted the first and the third united the two. Then he started all over again. In the preface to this bizarre piece of writing, Marx wrote a summary of his thesis: "I hate all the gods."

A more elaborate presentation of the foundation of dialectical materialism necessitates a study of Hegel (1770–1831), who said that any element (idea, sentiment, human institution, emotion) has an essential tendency to beget the contrary, and as a result to transform itself into a new thing which *includes* and yet surpasses the first two antagonistic terms. This process with its three stages he called thesis, antithesis and synthesis, or position, opposition and composition. Every synthesis is a conquered or overcome contradiction. In the synthesis, the thesis and antithesis are said to be "*Aufgehoben*" that is, transposed, sublimated, transfigured. The dialectical law applies to any newly created synthesis, which in its turn as thesis begets a new antithesis and then becomes a new synthesis. Hegel thus makes contradiction the fundamental law of thought, "That which moves the world in general is contradiction and it is laughable to say that one cannot think contradiction."[2]

Now begins the second stage in the development of Marx's philosophy. The very year Marx received his doctorate there appeared the most popular attack on religion that had been delivered in Germany up to that time. While

other Germans like Strauss and Bauer were trying to destroy Christianity through historical criticism, Ludwig
Feuerbach in his *Essence of Christianity* tried to destroy it by
a full-fledged materialistic philosophy. Marx read the book
and his enthusiasm is recorded as "unbounded." Feuerbach
had killed the idealism of Hegel, which he never liked anyway, and he destroyed all religion by showing that it is an
illusion projected by the brain of man. This pleased Marx
tremendously. Feuerbach did this by denying thought,
ideas, mind and spirit, and by affirming that matter is the
basic reality. "Man is only what he eats."

Now that the gods were dethroned, Marx got what he
thought was a brilliant idea. Wouldn't it be wonderful to
take the dialectical method which Hegel applies to ideas,
and apply it to matter and to history? Marx then summoned
to the altar of his own construction the groom of dialectics
which came from the house of Hegel and united it in marriage to the materialism of the house of Feuerbach and out
of that union came the child dialectical materialism which
Marx adopted as the philosophy of communism. Reality
then became for Marx not spirit made manifest through
moving matter as Hegel thought, but matter paramount,
and moving spirit. All thought, all spiritual existence thus
became merely a product of dialectical matter.[3]

From now on Marx would see contradiction at the
very heart of reality. There is no need of a God to explain
matter, because matter itself is endowed with motion. It
develops by shocks, oppositions, clashes, struggles, catastrophes. The whole universe is dialectical. *Reality is
revolutionary*. Marx now took the position that knowledge
is not speculative (spiritual) but practical (materialistic).
We know the world only by living in it and undergoing
what Marx called "revolutionary practice." Materialism

of the Feuerbachian variety was corrected because it had two defects which Engels reveals through his *Anti-Dühring*. It took a too mechanistic view of the universe and it left no room for process. Marx and Engels "corrected" this mistake by applying the dialectics they took from Hegel to the materialism they took from Feuerbach and out of it came *Dialectical Materialism* or the *philosophy of communism*. From now on, not ideas would grow by contradiction but reality. Thesis, antithesis, synthesis would be descriptions not of the unfolding of spirit, but stages in revolution which would produce a Communist society.

That brings us to the next phase in the development of Marxist philosophy: the influence of French sociology. Marx had read and was tremendously impressed with a pamphlet written by Proudhon on the subject of property, in which Proudhon was trying to apply the dialectics of Hegel to economics. One night at the lodgings of the famous Russian revolutionist Bakunin, Marx met Proudhon and expounded to him the beauties of dialectics as applied to matter and also to politics with which he was concerned because of Hegel's emphasis on the state. Proudhon the Frenchman told Marx he was typically German, 'way up in the air with his abstractions and too little concerned with economics. The big problem, said Proudhon, is economic, not political, social, not Hegelian, and if he, Marx, wanted to keep his dialectics, he should apply it in some way to property. This Proudhon did by stumblingly suggesting that perhaps capital was the affirmative side of dialectics, which in turn begot its contradiction, which was labor. Somewhere there ought to be a synthesis which would involve changes of property. Where the Frenchman led, the German followed, and when Marx left the garret of Bakunin that night the complete philosophy of communism was born. Proudhon became the inspiration of the main cog in Marxist communism. Dialectical materialism applied to economics became *economic determinism* and applied to history became *historical materialism*, both of which are here discussed as a unit.

As Hegel used history as a method of investigation, so too would Marx, but in the sense that history was now to be interpreted materially rather than ideally. What interested Marx was not the origin of historical phenomena, but rather their development and change; he was seeking for the dynamic of history. His system repudiates the idea that men freely make their own history. He has recourse to the myth that history is determined by inner laws which are proper to the economic development of mankind. Even granted that men have motives, Marx considers that there is a still more basic analysis to be made, namely, what factor in history determines men's motives. As Engels interpreted Marx's thought: "We have seen that the many individual wills active in history for the most part produced results quite other than those they intended—often quite the opposite; their motives therefore in relation to the total result are likewise of only secondary significance. On the other hand, the further question arises: What driving forces in turn stand behind these motives? What are the historical causes which transformed themselves into these motives in the brains of the actors?"[4]

While Marx is willing to admit that there are certain factors such as religion and literature and great heroes who have influenced history, he nevertheless challenges the contention that these factors are basic. Starting with the assumption of Franklin that man "is a tool-producing animal," Marx says that it is at this point that man is distinguished from the animal; therefore, production must be the basic force in history.[5]

When Marx speaks of production as being basic to man he does not refer merely to the technical process of making things. He includes this but also two other factors, namely, the material upon which man works and his own psychological and physical contribution. Marx is now prepared for the fundamental principles of his economic determinism, namely that the art, literature, morality, religion, law, in any given age are the results of the economic methods of production in use at any time.[6] As Marx put it in the *Communist Manifesto*: "In every historical epoch, the prevailing mode of economic production and exchange, and the social organization necessarily following from it, form the basis upon which it is built up, and from which alone can be explained, the political and intellectual history of that epoch."[7] If there is a system in existence which recognizes personal property rights there will be a system of morality to protect those rights such as the commandment: "Thou shalt not steal." Where there are no personal property rights there need be no such moral commandment because there would be such an abundance of prosperity that no one would ever want to steal.

Until, however, communism comes to pass, so long as there are private property relations prevailing in methods of production, there will necessarily be classes. One of these classes will own and the other class will work. In Marxist language one will be the exploiting class and the other the exploited class. History is full of this struggle of class conflict. As the *Communist Manifesto* puts it: "The history of all hitherto existing society is the history of class war." Class war is the essence of all history and all ideas are merely ideological forms in which men become conscious of this conflict and fight it out. Reading his theory of the primacy of economics into history, Marx presents history in three sequences. First came the feudal society which by its very nature gave rise to inner conflicts and resulted in the rise to dominance of the bourgeois and the advent of capitalism. In the final phase the exploited or the proletariat class will, through co-operation with the inner forces of history, overthrow the capitalist regime and create a new art and culture more glorious than ever before. Then there will no longer be class conflict but a classless community in a golden age. In the language of Hegel, capitalism *(thesis)* in its monstrous development of an owning and exploiting class engenders necessarily an impoverished and oppressed class *(antithesis)*. Between these two a class conflict necessarily arises. The synthesis will come when the workers destroy all property personally owned, and as workers form an ensemble of workers possessing property collectively.

But how will society undergo this basic revolutionary transformation? By a "revolution in which the working class will use its political supremacy to wrest by degrees all capital from the bourgeoisie, to centralize all instruments of production in the hands of the state. . . . In the beginning this cannot be done except by means of despotic inroads on the rights of property."[8] "It may be taken for granted that bloody conflicts are coming. . . . The workers must aim at preventing the subsiding of the revolutionary excitement immediately after the victory. On the contrary, they must endeavor to maintain it as long as possible. Far from opposing so-called excesses, and making examples of hated individuals or public buildings to which hateful remembrances are attached, by sacrificing them to the popular rage, such examples must not only be tolerated, but their direction must ever be taken in hand. . . . The arming of the workers with rifles and ammunition must be carried out at once and steps be taken to prevent the rising of the

army which would be directed against the workers. . . . If
the small middle class propose to purchase the railways
and the factories the workers must demand that such railways and factories, being the property of the reactionaries,
shall be confiscated by the state without compensation. . . .
The workers need not be misled by democratic platitudes
about freedom. . . . Their battle cry must be 'the revolution
in permanence.'"[9]

The ethics of communism are the natural sequence
of its materialistic belief. The Communist theory of ethics
is that all moral standards grow out of certain economic
conditions. "All moral theories are the product in the last
analysis of the economic stage which society has reached at
that particular epoch."[10] Morality as consonance with the
Eternal Law of God reflected in conscience is denied, since
it is not God but economics which makes morality. There
would logically be a repudiation of both the Jewish belief in
a Divine Law as expressed in the Ten Commandments and
the Greek view of a Divine Order expressing itself in purpose and fixed behavior, once one translated Hegel's idea
of a flux in the world of ideas to flux in the world of reality
and history. Then there can no longer be any transcendent
order, but only the historic process itself which moves by
dialectical necessity to a classless society. If a man is a member of the Communist class he is predestined as was the
Calvinist of old, except that his heaven will be the classless kingdom on earth. If however a man belongs to the
"exploiting class," then he is historically doomed. There
is a certitude of election in the perverted Pauline sense to
those who are now not in Christ, but in Marx. All morality
to Communists is therefore "class morality." When classes
are done away with through revolutionary expropriation
of those who own property, there will no longer be any

need of what the Communist calls "bourgeois morality." As Lenin said: "We deny all morality taken from superhuman or non-class conceptions. We say that this is a deception, a swindle, a befogging of the minds of the workers and peasants in the interests of the landlords and the capitalists."[11]

Underneath Communist ethics is the principle "the end justifies the means." The needs of the revolution determine morality; hence whatever fosters the revolutionary overthrow of democracy and the violent dispossession of those who own property is a morally good act; whatever hinders the revolution, such as a refusal to take orders from the dictator, and the refusal to think the way you are supposed to think, is a morally bad act. As Lenin put it: "We say that our morality is wholly subordinated to the interests of the class struggle of the workers. . . . We deduce our morality from the facts and the need of the class struggle of the proletariat. That is why we say that a morality taken from outside of human society does not exist for us, it is a fraud. For us morality is subordinated to the interests of the workers' class struggle."[12]

The Communists find no ethical contradiction when, for example, they extend a friendly hand to religion one year and the next year persecute it; or when they ally themselves with democracy at one time, and the next time seek to overthrow it; or when they sign a treaty with Nazism and then fight against it. When conditions change, new techniques must be developed, but all are equally true and moral to the Communist as long as they further the revolution. But is there any limit to chicanery, duplicity and deviltry? Absolutely none! As Lenin said: "It is necessary . . . to use any ruse, cunning, unlawful method, evasion, concealment of the truth."[13] Stalin added approvingly: "Dictatorship means nothing more nor less than the power which directly rests on violence, which is not limited by any laws or restricted by any absolute rules."[14]

Because Communist ethics is based on a complete repudiation of a moral order under God, it does little good to complain against it that it leaves us no room for compassion, brotherly love and sympathy. As a matter of fact the Communist "saints" are "canonized" to just the extent that they suffer all things for the sake of their class morality. The Communist "is damned always to do what is most repugnant to him: to become a slaughterer in order to abolish slaughtering, to sacrifice lambs in order that no lambs may be slaughtered, to whip people with knouts so that they may learn not to let themselves be whipped, to strip himself of every scruple in the name of higher scrupulousness, and to challenge the hatred of mankind because of his love of it—an abstract and geometric love."*[15]

The Communist idea of religion is difficult to determine, blurred and confused as it so often is by propaganda which, for tactical purposes only, declares itself in favor of religion. The truth on this subject is that communism and atheism are intrinsically related and that one cannot be a good Communist without being an atheist and every atheist is a potential Communist. Since the thought of Marx on the subject of religion was inspired principally by Feuerbach, it is necessary to examine the three works which had the most influence on Marx, *The Essence of Christianity* (1841), *Preliminary Thesis for the Reform of Philosophy* (1842) and *Fundamental Principles of the Philosophy of the Future* (1843).[16]

---

* From Arthur Koestler, *Darkness at Noon.* Copyright 1941 by The Macmillan Company. By permission of The Macmillan Company, publishers.

As regards the origin of belief, Feuerbach contended it was psychological. A man who does not have a consciousness of his own supreme nature attributes the qualities which he lacks, such as goodness, disinterested love, to a being outside himself, and thus the idea of God is born. Every act of love of God is begotten of a want of self-love; the exaltation of the Divine is built on the ruins of the self-debasement.[17] It is much better to love oneself rather than God,[18] and to declare oneself divine rather than to empty oneself of divinity. Each man must make the choice between himself and God. "I deny God," means for me, "I deny the denial of myself," writes Feuerbach, as anthropology takes the place of theology. The idea of God according to Feuerbach is theoretically stupid and practically harmful since it is nothing else than a projection of imaginary ideals of a human nature not yet conscious of its divinity. Religion appears then as an *alienation* of human nature by which man is rendered a *stranger* to himself. By ceding to another that which is rightly one's own, there results a fission or dispossession which distorts the true nature of man.

It follows that human nature must be restored to itself. This is done first by identifying self with the attributes formerly attributed to Divinity. "Religion progresses as it suppresses relationship with God, and develops into a religion under a new form, a superior form, the cult of man."[19] Secondly, human nature passes from a negative to a positive state by the deliberate edification of man, which is called "absolute humanism." From now on it is a question of destroying the ancient separation of heaven and earth, so that humanity can concentrate on its own soul, on all the forces of its heart and on the present. This concentration alone will produce a new life and new great characters and great actions. In place of immortal individuals, the new religion "demands men completely healthy of body and 'spirit.'"[20] This religion he calls 'Anthropotheism' or religion conscious of itself.[21] "The Christian religion is the name of man united with the name of God in the same name: the God-man; the name of man here being understood as an attribute of the Supreme Being. The new philosophy conforming to the truth makes the attribute the subject and the subject the attribute."[22] "The task of philosophy is not to know the infinite as finite, but the finite as the infinite, or better still to place not the finite into the infinite, but the infinite into the finite."[23]

Engels in his *Ludwig Feuerbach* tells with what enthusiasm he and Marx became Feuerbachians, which is indeed confirmed by Marx himself. "You, theologians and speculative philosophers, let me give you some advice. . . . There is no other way to arrive at truth and liberty than by that which passes by Feuerbach. This torrent of fire is the purgatory of the present."[24] Like Feuerbach, Marx insisted that to choose God was to sacrifice man. Using the language of Feuerbach he wrote: "Religion is the affirmation not of self-consciousness, but the consciousness alienated from self."[25] In his *Critique of the Philosophy of Law of Hegel* Marx was true to his master in contending that "the criticism of religion is the first condition of all criticism. . . . Once the holy image which represents the aberration of man from himself has been unmasked the task of philosophy is to demask the aberration." "The great merit of Feuerbach is to have furnished the proof that philosophy is nothing but religion put into thought and developed by thought."[26] "Feuerbach represents materialistic humanism in the order of thought, as communism represents it in the order of social action."[27] Marx was an atheist before he was Communist, historically and logically. The intrinsic relation between the two he noted as follows: "Communism begins where atheism begins."[28]

In Theses 6 and 7 on Feuerbach[29] Marx corrects his master for ignoring the economic factor in belief. Marx too believed that religion is a compensation not for a want of divine consciousness in man himself, but for the privations of life. To express this idea he borrowed the phrase of Charles Kingsley and called religion "the opium of the people." Marx believed that when the proletariat takes over the forces of production, then there will disappear all need for religion which kept man in subjection. In another work he interprets Christianity as individual spirituality and as such makes it the parent of all forms of individualism such as liberalism and capitalism.[30]

Under Feuerbachian inspiration Marx argues that man has been alienated from himself in two ways: by religion and private property. Religion alienates a man from himself by subordinating him to God; private property alienates a man from himself by subordinating him to an employer. It follows that if a man is ever to be restored to himself, both religion and private property must be destroyed. From this argument of Marx it is clear that any system which would socialize production but not persecute religion is only half Communistic and leaves man half enslaved. Engels energetically affirmed this intrinsic relation between atheism and communism by saying that the "internal putrefaction of all institutions has its foundation in religion."[31] Marx in the same vein states that "the suppression of the alienation which reigns in the domain of production under the form of private property, *entails necessarily* the suppression of all those alienations which constitute or vitiate the diverse institutions and diverse human activities. The religious alienation as such operates in the domain of conscience in the *foro interno* of man, but economic alienation is that of life itself—its suppression embraces both sides."[32]

Marx is concerned not merely with the suppression of religion, but with the installation of what Feuerbach called the "new humanism." Atheism for Marx is therefore not something *negative*, for he makes the distinction between "negative" atheism or the suppression of God, and "positive" atheism which is humanism.[33] The purpose of persecution of religion is to restore man to himself. Thus from an entirely different point of view, the intrinsic relation of atheism and communism is once more forced upon us. "The criticism of religion has for its purpose . . . to *make man move about himself as his own sun.* . . . Religion is only the illusory sun which moves around man, so long as he does not move around himself."[34]

"The criticism of religion ends in the doctrine that man is the Supreme Being for man."[35] Marx furthermore distinguishes between theoretical and practical humanism in order to bring out the unbreakable bond between anti-God and anticapitalism philosophies, or between atheism and communism. *Theoretical humanism* is the giving to man by the suppression of religion consciousness that he is an absolute being and possesses the power to become the most perfect being possible. *Practical humanism* is the consequent realization of man's true nature as a social being in a socialist society devoid of private property. "Just as atheism which suppresses God is the beginning of the theoretical humanism, so Communism as the suppression of private property . . . is the beginning of practical humanism."[36] This indissoluble bond between the two Marx reaffirms by a tribute to Feuerbach. "As Feuerbach represents in theory, so socialism, both French and English, represents in practice how materialism coincides with humanism."[37]

A little noted aspect of Marxism is that its hatred of capitalism is based not on human dignity as the "pinks" would have it, but upon the *absolute divinity of man.* "Being radical means to take things by their root. The root for man is man himself. . . . The criticism of religion ends in the doctrine that *man is the supreme being for man* and in the *categorical imperative* of over-throwing all social relations in which man is degraded, subjected, abandoned, and despised."[38] Here Marx deduces negatively the destruction of capitalism, and positively communism, from atheistic humanism. In this passage at least Marxism is Communist because atheistic.

If it be objected from time to time that communism is not antireligious, it must be retorted that any concessions made to religion are for ulterior motives related to world revolution. As Lenin wrote: "Our program rests in its entirety on a *scientific* philosophy and notably on a materialistic philosophy. . . . Our propaganda therefore necessarily embraces atheism."[39] "One ought not to confine the struggle against religion to an abstract ideological presentation; one ought to tie up the struggle to a concrete practical class movement which is capable of eliminating the social roots of religion. . . . It would be a great error to think that the apparent 'moderation' of Marxism to religion is to be explained by 'tactical' considerations, such as the desire *de ne pas effaroucher.* On the contrary, the political line of Marxism is tied up indissolubly with its philosophical basis."[40] But though communism denies God, it affirms another god—the Communist collectivity before which men must prostrate themselves, to whose new shrines, the factories, they must make their pilgrimages; to whose will, expressed by the dictator, they must make complete abandonment of self; before whose secret police, as the new priesthood with unholy orders, they must take their brew of propaganda, and though they have not an empty tomb to give them hope, they still have the cadaver of Lenin, periodically injected with embalming fluids, to give the appearance of life where there is only death and decay.

To the credit of Marx it must be said that he foresaw the inherent weakness of historical liberalism as few saw it while it was in its heyday. It may be said that only three others saw it as clearly, and they saw it from totally different angles: Pius IX, Dostoevsky and Nietzsche. But though he was able to announce the crisis of capitalist society, he was unable to offer a solution, because he started with the basic assumption of capitalism itself, namely, the primacy of the economic. Communism to this extent is monopolistic capitalism with a fester.

The philosophy of dialectical materialism is nothing but a crazy quilt made up of patches of Hegel and Feuerbach sewed together to cover up the nakedness of its own ideas. One might just as well try to make a living organism out of the head of an ox, the body of a canary and the tail of an ichthyosaurus, as to take the split ends of Hegelian and Feuerbachian hairs and make them a living philosophy. What Marx failed to see was that Hegel in his philosophy was trying to secularize and prostitute and humanize the theological doctrine of Father, Son and Holy Ghost in thesis, antithesis and synthesis, as Marx himself later on would take another Christian doctrine, the Kingdom of God, and secularize it into a classless society where all men would be brothers without a Father. The dictionary has a stronger name for that kind of society.

The errors, such as his confusion of contradiction and opposites, are so obvious to a thinking mind that there is no need of refutation. Dialectical materialism was only a nineteenth-century form of animism. As the primitive peoples assumed that spirits inhabited the stones and flowers and thunder and the clouds, so Marx believed that thought and mind and reason inhabited matter, and that eventually he could pull them out as a magician pulls rabbits out of a hat. Once he assumes that matter is revolutionary, he goes to history to try to make it prove that his theory was right that all history is economically determined. But this was too unsound. First of all, if history is dialectical, why is it that history stops being dialectical when communism comes? Why should not communism beget its opposite, such as Trotskyism, and why should not both turn into something else, for instance, Fascism? Marx constantly confuses *cause* and *condition*. A window is a condition of light, not its cause. Economic methods of production do *condition* law, literature, art, philosophy, etc., but they do not *cause* or *create* them. Like most impractical men—and Marx was impractical, because he was supported most of his life by a rich friend—Marx isolates one factor from life, namely, the economic, and allows it to go to his head like wine on an empty stomach. If the economic method of production were "the real ultimate driving force of history" then why should it be necessary for man to add his revolutionary fervor? Why not just sit back and read the *Daily Worker* until it happens? But if man can add something to history or hasten the revolution with his emotions, then may not these emotions against capitalists be dismissed as by-products of economics?[41]

Did not Lenin and Stalin have something to do with furthering the revolution? But if their consciousness has been economically determined, then why praise them for doing the inevitable? If change in production creates new ideologies what causes changes in production? Shall invention be ignored and is invention the triumph of mind over matter? Either men are *determined* by economics or they are *conditioned*. If they are only *conditioned*, then one must turn in his Marxian badge; if they are *determined* then they are not free, and if they are not free then why prattle about freedom? Marxists try to escape the dilemma by saying that "freedom is necessity"—which makes just as much sense as to say that blindness is eyesight.

Furthermore, to say, as communism does, that a moral code is necessary only to justify a capitalist method of production is nonsense, because the Christian moral code existed centuries before a capitalistic method of production came into being and therefore was not necessary to sustain it. Nor can it be alleged, as communism does, that the Christian moral code was always based on the defense of property, because the more one practices the Christian code the less one becomes attached to property. That is why there is the vow of poverty in strict religious communities, that, like their Master Who had not whereon to lay His Head, those who take the vow may be poor in spirit. If, as communism alleges, the Christian moral law is a class morality, why is it that it has produced saints in all classes from peasants to kings, and why is it that the greatest number of saints have come from what the Communists would call the proletariat class? If the Christian moral were ever intended to be a defense of a ruling class, then the Saviour would never have chosen His Apostles from fishermen, nor would the Church have canonized a John Bosco or a Little Flower.

There is not a single Russian idea in the whole philosophy of communism. It is bourgeois, Western, materialistic and capitalistic in its origin. It was a creature of its age and could never have arisen in the thirteenth or even the eighteenth century, because the influence of Christianity was still too strong in the world. Only when the organism of the Western world began to weaken could the germ infect it. If the intellectual origin of communism is Western, how did it ever get into Russia? Obviously through the dissemination of ideas by those who became the apostles of Marx. The concrete event through which it became effective in its final form happened during the First World War. Germany, anxious to save herself, felt that her cause would be helped if she could woo Russia away from the Allies. One way of doing this was to start a revolution in Russia. Accordingly, the German General staff tossed 31 revolutionists into a boxcar marked "Extraterritorial," and attached it to a train leaving indirectly for Russia. In this boxcar was Vladimir Ulyanov, better known as Lenin, who, on arriving in Petrograd, mounted an armored car and began preaching the revolution. As General Ludendorff, in justifying his position, said: "In having sent Lenin to Russia, our Government took upon itself a special responsibility, for, from a military point of view, his journey was justified. Russia had to fall." There was something fitting about Germany assisting in the birth of communism in Russia. Germany had already given birth to the idea of communism, so now it would give birth to its reality. Russia paid back its debt to Germany in 1939, when the ignominious treaty between the Nazis and the Communists was signed, which allowed the Nazis for two years to overrun Europe, and which proved that there was no radical opposition between Nazism and communism. On the occasion of signing the treaty, Molotov said: "Fascism is only a matter of taste, and our friendship has been sealed in blood." Unfortunately it turned out to be the blood of Poland.

So much is communism a secularization or a dedivinization of Christianity that it can be presented as an ersatz for Christian doctrines.[42]

Trinity: Three Persons in one God: Father, Son and Holy Ghost.

Matter: Three processes in one theory: capital, labor and communism; thesis, antithesis and synthesis.

Messias: Christ the Son of the Living God, foretold by Jewish history.

Revolutionary Proletariat: Foretold by the history of economic methods of production.

Redemption from sin: Christ on the Cross nailed by the evil of men.

The Revolution: The exploiter on the cross nailed by the exploited.

Church: Mystical Body of Christ, governed by one visible head.

The Mystical Community of Collectivity: The dictatorship over the proletariat.

The Last Judgment: The separation of the good and the evil.

The violent expropriation of the property owners and the liquidation of the enemies.

Bible: Revealed Word of God.

Das Kapital: Revealed word of Marx.

Heresy: Deviation from Divinely revealed Truth.

Deviation from the apostolic teachings of Marx, Lenin, such as Trotskyites and Mensheviks.

Sacrifice: The condition of spiritual union with God.

Class Struggle and violence, the condition of a classless society.

Final Destiny: Kingdom of God in Heaven.

Destiny: Kingdom of Man on earth.

Sacraments: The Divinely ordained channels of communion with Divinity.

Decorations: The Order of Lenin, etc.

CHAPTER FOUR

The Basic Defects
of Communism

The Catholic Church is sometimes praised for its opposition to communism. This compliment is deserved, for the Church is the only solid moral force in the world that has been consistently opposed to the new barbarism. The Church foresaw the evils of totalitarianism and condemned each in turn. The Church condemned Fascism in the Encyclical *Non Abiamo Bisogno* which was written in Italian because Fascism was a national phenomenon;[1] it condemned Nazism in the German language in the Encyclical *Mit Brennender Sorge* because Nazism was a racial phenomenon. It condemned communism in the universal language of Latin in the Encyclical *Divini Redemptoris,* because communism is an international phenomenon. Communism in its turn has concentrated its attacks principally upon the Church, for the instinct of communism is infallible when it comes to knowing its enemy. It wastes no time on small fry; it has no delusions about the opposition. It knows that Christ not only claims to be Divine, but is Divine. Its persecution of the Church is indirect praise—it pays the beautiful tribute of hostility. If it ignored the Church, if it directed no arrows against our shields, then would the Church know that its faith had faltered and its fires had gone out, and its salt had lost its savor.

The Church, however, is embarrassed at being praised as anti-Communist, because such praise is for being anti-something rather than pro-something; for a way of thinking that would make the Church admired because it hates an enemy, rather than because its ideals are loved. The sentiments of friendly praise are like those of a fat woman toward her physician. She admires him because he is the enemy of her overweight, but she does not like him because he recommends a diet to cure her of obesity.

Every now and then there is a superficial coincidence of the ideals of the Church and the world, as there was on Palm Sunday when the Saviour was acclaimed as King by the masses. But the same Saviour has taught His Church that we must distrust the hosannas of the world, for within five days, the King met death on the throne of the Cross, with no other purple than that of His own blood, and no other scepter than a nail. The Church is never a true influence in society when the world regards it as a morale builder, whose business it is to rubber-stamp the policies of a party in power. For the sake of clarity a word ought to be said about why the Church is *not* opposed to communism.

It is not opposed to communism because communism is anti-capitalistic. If by capitalism is meant, not diffused ownership of property, but monopolistic capitalism in which capital bids for labor on a market, and concentrates wealth in the hands of the few, then from an *economic point of view alone*, the Church is just as much opposed to capitalism as it is to communism. Communism emphasizes social use to the exclusion of personal rights, and capitalism emphasizes personal rights to the exclusion of social use. The Church says both are wrong, for though the right to property is personal, the use is social. It therefore refuses to maintain capitalism as an alternative to the economic side of communism. Monopolistic capitalism concentrates wealth in the hands of a few capitalists, and communism in the hands of a few bureaucrats, and both end in the proletarianization of the masses. The true Christian must rid himself of the delusion that in opposing communism the Church thereby puts itself in opposition to all those who would seek thus to change the present economic system. The Christian concept denies there is an absolutely owned private property exclusive of limits set by the common good of the community and responsibility to the community. The more anonymous and impersonalistic property becomes, the less is the right to it. The Church agrees with communism in its protest against the injustice of the economic order, but it parts with it in the collectivity being made the sole employer, for this reduces the individual to the status of a serf or a slave of the state. Concentration of wealth is wrong whether it is done on the Hudson or the Volga.

The Church is not opposed to communism because the Church is a defender of the *status quo*. In every movement one must distinguish between *protests* and *reforms*. One can protest against a headache without advocating decapitation. The protests of communism are often right; but the reforms are wrong. The Church agrees with some of the protests of communism. In fact, there is a far better critique of the existing economic order based on the primacy of profit in two Encyclicals of Leo XIII and Pius XI than there is in all the writings of Marx. But the reforms of communism are wrong, because they are inspired by the very errors they combat. Communism begins with the liberal and capitalistic error that man is economic, and, instead of correcting it, merely intensifies it until man becomes a robot in a vast economic machine. There is a closer relation between communism and monopolistic capitalism than most minds suspect. They are agreed on the materialistic basis of civilization; they disagree only on who shall control that basis, capitalists or bureaucrats. Marx himself admitted he got many of his economic ideas from liberal economists such as Ricardo and the author of an anonymous work on interest. Capitalistic economy is godless; communism makes economics God. It is Divinity itself. Capitalism denies that economics is subject to a higher moral order. Communism says that economics is morality. Communism is not a radical solution of our economic problem; however violent be its approach, it does not touch the roots of the evil. The Communist solution of the problem is like the cynical way Oscar Wilde suggested a woman can reform a man: "The only way a woman can reform a man is by boring him so completely that he loses all possible interest in life."

Those who look to the Church in this hour of peril to pluck out of the fire the chestnuts of liberalism, secularism, materialism, and monopolistic capitalism are doomed to disappointment. That plea sounds to the Church like the plea of the thief on the left side of the Saviour, who asked Our Lord to save him from the cross—not for virtue—but that he might go on with his ordinary life, which was the business of stealing. It is so easy for those who have made their money under a given system to think that that system must be right and good. Conservatism is for that reason often nothing else than a pseudo philosophy for the prosperous. The Church, however, knows that the disorganization of the world is largely due to the fact that it is not organized by any conscious acceptance of purpose other than the immediate interest of a capitalistic class on one hand, or a Communist class on the other hand. That is why the economic policy of the Church is consistently in opposition to both capitalism and communism.

The Church is not opposed to communism because it believes that Russia is the enemy of the world. The Church makes a distinction between an ideology and a people. The ideology is wicked; the people are good. Actually only about three per cent of the population of Russia belong to the Communist Party—and there is no other party to which the people may belong. In other words, there are about 194,000,000 people in Russia who are not members of the only party permitted to exist. The distinction between American Communists and the Soviet Government is spurious, just as the distinction between American Bundists and Hitler was spurious, but the distinction between the Soviet Government with its police tyranny and the Russian people is solid, and it is on this basis that we argue. Some years ago, Yargoslavsky, the head of the godless movement, admitted that half of the population of Russia was still religious. His number is probably far below the fact, because the higher he made the number of believers, the greater was his admission of inefficiency in atheistic propaganda. There is no way of measuring it, but it may be that there is a more genuinely religious fervor, a greater spirit of sacrifice, and a more truly Christian spirit in the broad masses of the Russian people than there is in the United States. When finally the yoke of slavery, terrorism and secret police has been lifted from the Russian people, there will be less need of educating them in the Way of the Cross than there will be of educating us; their pent-up spiritual aspirations will unfold in that hour in the flowing of a Christianity that will be a model and an inspiration to the world.

As to the positive position of why the Church is opposed to communism, the best exposition is contained in the Encyclical *Divini Redemptoris*.

"In such a doctrine as is evident, there is no room for the idea of God; there is no difference between matter and spirit, between soul and body.

"There is neither survival of the soul after death nor any hope in a future life.

"Insisting on the dialectical aspect of their materialism, the Communists claim that the conflict which carries the world toward its final synthesis can be accelerated by man. Hence they endeavor to sharpen the antagonisms which arise between the various classes of society.

"Thus the class struggle with its consequent violent hate and destruction takes on the aspects of a crusade for the progress of humanity. On the other hand, all other forces whatever, as long as they resist such systematic violence, must be annihilated as hostile to the human race.

"Communism, moreover, strips man of his liberty, robs human personality of all its dignity, and removes all the moral restraints that check the eruptions of blind impulse.

"There is no recognition of any right of the individual in his relations to the collectivity; no natural right is accorded to human personality, which is a mere cog-wheel in the Communist system.

"In man's relations with other individuals besides, Communists hold the principle of absolute equality, rejecting all hierarchy and Divinely-constituted authority, including the authority of parents.

"What men call authority and subordination is derived from the community as its first and only font.

"Nor is the individual granted any property rights over material goods or the means of production, for inasmuch as these are the source of further wealth, their possession would give one man power over another. Precisely on this score, all forms of private property must be eradicated, for they are at the origin of all economic enslavement.

"Refusing to human life any sacred or spiritual character, such a doctrine logically makes of marriage and the family a purely artificial and civil institution, the outcome of a specific economic system. There exists no matrimonial bond of a juridico-moral nature that is not subject to the whim of the individual or of the collectivity.

"Naturally, therefore, the notion of an indissoluble marriage-tie is scouted. Communism is particularly characterized by the rejection of any link that binds woman to the family and the home, and her emancipation is proclaimed as a basic principle. She is withdrawn from the family and the care of her children, to be thrust instead into public life and collective production under the same conditions as man. The care of home and children then devolves upon the collectivity.

"Finally, the right of education is denied to parents, for it is conceived as the exclusive prerogative of the community, in whose name and by whose mandate alone parents may exercise this right.

"What would be the condition of a human society based on such materialistic tenets? It would be a collectivity with no other hierarchy than that of the economic system. It would have only one mission: the production of material things by means of collective labor, so that the goods of this world might be enjoyed in a paradise where

each would 'give according to his powers' and would 'receive according to his needs.'

"Communism recognizes in the collectivity the right,
or rather, unlimited discretion, to draft individuals for the
labor of the collectivity with no regard for their personal
welfare; so that even violence could be legitimately exercised to dragoon the recalcitrant against their wills.

"In the Communistic commonwealth morality and law
would be nothing but a derivation of the existing economic
order, purely earthly in origin and unstable in character. In
a word, the Communists claim to inaugurate a new era and
a new civilization which is the result of blind evolutionary
forces culminating in a humanity without God.

"When all men have finally acquired the collectivist mentality in this Utopia of a really classless society,
the political State, which is now conceived by Communists merely as the instrument by which the proletariat
is oppressed by the capitalists, will have lost all reason
for its existence and will 'wither away.' However, until
that happy consummation is realized, the State and the
powers of the State furnish communism with the most
efficacious and the most extensive means for the achievement of its goal.

"Such, is the new gospel which bolshevistic and atheistic communism offers the world as the glad tidings of
deliverance and salvation! It is a system full of errors and
sophisms.

"It is in opposition both to reason and to Divine
Revelation.

"It subverts the social order, because it means the destruction of its foundations; because it ignores the true
origin and purpose of the State; because it denies the rights,
dignity and liberty of human personality."

Some of these points bring immediately to mind a few of the many basic defects in both the philosophy and practice of communism.

Communism is an opiate for the masses in the sense that it deadens and paralyzes the *human intellect*. An opiate is a drug which deadens the higher intellectual powers of man, but allows the lower powers to function, such as the vegetative and the animal. Under the influence of a drug, a man cannot think, but he can breathe; he cannot will, but he can digest; he cannot follow a reasoning process, but his blood circulates. He is no longer a man but an animal. Communism is an opiate in the sense that it completely destroys human reason. Under its system a man cannot make his own decisions but must accept those handed down by the dictator; he has no conscience, because there is only a state conscience; he has no personal thoughts, because there is only state-controlled thought. That is why Communists so often stultify themselves; at one time hailing the Nazis as their friends, the next minute howling them down as enemies; at one moment they praise their American leader as a great thinker, and at another, when an article appears in a French magazine inspired by Moscow, 59 out of 60 members of the Executive Committee berate him as the enemy of the party line.

In saying that communism is the opium of the people because it drugs man into becoming a termite, it is not denied that Marx originally used the expression "opium of the people" in relation to religion, but that was because of two reasons: First, Marx was baptized a Christian not for religious but for political reasons. It was only natural for a man who himself used religion as an opium to think that everyone else should use it the same way. Marx knew nothing about religion except what he read from Hegel and

Feuerbach. He therefore may be excused from misunderstanding its nature on the grounds of ignorance. Secondly, in saying that religion was a kind of mystical ersatz for a rational improvement of man in the world, he was really not attacking Christianity at all, for it has never been a postulate of Christianity that souls should be extricated from an evil world, or that there was a divorce between world salvation and soul salvation. What he was actually attacking was Buddhism, which believes that the world is intrinsically wicked, and that souls should have no interest whatever in its economic and political welfare.

The term "opiate" more properly belongs to Marx's system which destroys the intellectual function of man, which function constitutes his specific difference from the animal. The absolutely rigid party discipline which Communist ideology demands can be purchased only at the expense of intellectual bankruptcy. The very inflexibility of its literature, the frequent necessity of party purges to eliminate all who challenge authority, the stultification of about-face changes in the party line, all mean the complete abdication of the individual's right to think for himself.

The former editor of the *Daily Worker*, Louis Budenz, describes this derationalization of man as "The Red Strait Jacket": "The first requisite for a Communist is to understand that he is serving Soviet Russia and no other nation or interest. Never will he be permitted to express one word of reservation or criticism of the Soviet Government, its leaders or their decisions. Whatever they say or do is always 100 percent right, and America can be right only by being in complete agreement with the Soviet Union. Never, during the 25 years of its existence, has the *Daily Worker* deviated from that rule; never has it ceased to prostrate itself before the Soviet leadership.

"The professional Communist can't be like the average American and say: 'This may be good but there are features of it that are deficient.' If it is Soviet-spawned he must say in effect: 'This is infallibly correct. There are no flaws in it whatsoever. Anyone even hinting at a flaw is to be denounced as a liar and a slanderer of the Soviet Union.' The Communist has to think through a method by which he can defend every act of the Soviet leadership and blacken the reputation of everyone daring to whisper that it may be wrong. By that device, the Communists frequently have been successful in politically blackmailing a number of 'liberals' who fear to be out of step with Soviet Russia, but whom the Communists secretly despise." *[2]

Because of the basic antirational character of its philosophy, it is only natural to find inconsistencies, such as insisting on the one hand that everyone within the ranks follow its dictation, and then on the other hand asking for fellow travelers and united fronts with those who avowedly do not accept all its theories. Within its own circle it proclaims antireligion, but outside its circle a support for professional "religionists" who speak well of the Soviet foreign policy. Harold Laski believes this is the principal reason why labor distrusts Communists. "Quite intelligibly and logically the Labour Party looks with suspicion on proffers of alliance from communists on the ground that they propose to do within its ranks what they would not permit within their own. Their policy, in brief, of an allegiance which does not admit of open-minded co-operation with alternative views, naturally promotes distrust of the very united front they hope to secure. And any action they

---

* From Louis Budenz, *This Is My Story*. Copyright 1947 by Whittlesey House, McGraw-Hill Book Company. Quoted by permission of the publisher.

take to promote a rigorous obedience in their own ranks only strengthens that mistrust by emphasising the dubious sincerity of co-operation they offer."[3]

A second difficulty with the philosophy of communism is its antidemocratic and antihuman character because it denies the value of the individual man. Communism corrects the mistake of monopolistic capitalism which made man a "hand," by making him an "ant" in a collective anthill. It is generally overlooked, but Karl Marx actually stated that the purpose of communism was to destroy the spiritual nature of man. Referring to the religious revolution of the sixteenth century Marx said: "As the Reformation of those days began in the mind of a monk, so today it must begin in the brain of a philosopher. If the Reformation was not the true solution, it was at any rate a true indication of the task. It is no longer a question of the conflict of the layman with the priest outside of himself, but with his own inner priest, his own clerical nature."[4]

According to Marx, the supernatural man, filled with the Holy Spirit, was destroyed a few centuries ago; now the natural man, endowed with an immortal soul, must be destroyed. It was because of the spiritual nature of man that Karl Marx repudiated democracy. Writing in 1843, he said that the democratic conception of man, namely, that "not one man alone, but each man has a value as a sovereign being," is the essence of democracy—which indeed it is. He rejected that kind of democracy by saying it was founded on "the illusion, the dream and the postulate of Christianity, namely, man has a sovereign soul."[5]

Here Marx teaches the fundamental differences between democracy and communism, namely, democracy insists on the value of every man, regardless of his race, his rank or his color. But Marx had no use for individuals as such, unless they belonged to his group. In the first edition of the first volume of *Das Kapital* he stated: "I speak of individuals insofar as they are personifications of economic categories and representatives of special classes of relations and interests." Man has a value only because he is a member of the revolutionary group; when he ceases to be a member, he ceases to have value. Liquidation, transfer of populations into Siberia, the denial of suffrage, concentration camps and all the other paraphernalia of communism follow in the train of this degraded concept of man. That is why communism speaks of the proletariat, but never the poor; the proletariat serves the revolution; the poor serve nobody, they stand in need of service. A Christian will help a Communist in need and there are many Christians who have; but no Communist would help a Christian in need unless he promised to aid the party. As Molotov said: "Bread is a political weapon"; which means that only those who think his way may eat.

Marx himself was a person in revolt against the world, but in a certain sense from another point of view he was not only the first Communist, but also the last, for his philosophy completely abolished personality. His early complaints against capitalism, that it crushed human personality, were right; but once he adopted the antipersonalism of Hegel, who admitted the domination of the general over the individual, and the materialism of Feuerbach, who ridiculed spirit, Marx made it impossible for the person to be in revolt against the world. Rather he made a world in revolt against a person. Marx was right in protesting against the complete isolation of the individual from society, but he developed a kind of demonic offertory in which the self-surrendering aspect of human personality to the community ends in self-destruction. This is because Marx denied the spiritual character of man. Because Christianity is built on the spiritual nature of man it can receive man into the mystical solidarity of Christ, without at the same time destroying all the values of personality. Communism asks man not to live by the grace of Christ, but by the grace of the collective society. But since the social collective is the creation of man himself, there is a vicious circle: man has no food for his spirit, he lives on himself, feeds on himself. By absorbing man into the collectivity, communism not only destroys personality which is the condition of democracy, but also creates the mass-man which is the negation of democracy, as De Tocqueville pointed out as far back as 1848.[6] For democracy, human personality is the supreme value, for communism the masses are. The person is self-governed; the masses are directed by alien forces or propaganda; the person is self-determined; the masses are dictator-determined.[7]

The Communist conception makes personality a function of the class, and the class a function of the dialectical process. Each man receives his being and status from and through the collectivity. In a democracy man has rights which are God-given; under communism the rights are state-given and therefore they can be state-taken-away. Here is the crucial point at issue in the world today. If the issue were collectivism and individualism, or capitalism and communism, then it could be ignored. But the problem today is the value of a man, or rather the survival of man.

The communion of men one with another is a consummation devoutly to be wished, but it can never be achieved on a compulsory basis, or by the exterior organization of society, which impoverishes human personality and negates the spiritual in man. The rebirth of a new order cannot start with the denial of man, but with his reaffirmation as made to the Divine Image. No better start can be made than with the Christian doctrine that a man is more precious than the universe, that the universe exists for him, that society can use some human functions, but never at the cost of absorption, and that even in his evil moments man is worth addressing in the second person singular, as Our Lord did the thief in that beautiful affirmation of democracy on the cross: "This day *thou* shalt be with Me in Paradise."

Thirdly, communism labors under the difficulty of not being sufficiently violent. Communism does, of course, teach the notion of class struggle, of the liquidation of all opposition, of violent expropriation, of the use of force to gain its ends, but it is here we contend that this is not violent enough to remake the world. Christianity believes in violence, for our Blessed Lord said: "The Kingdom of God suffereth violence, and only the violent shall bear it away." (Matthew 11:12) The great difference between Communist and Christian violence is that Communist violence is directed against the neighbor, and Christian violence is directed against oneself. The Communist sword points outward to fellow man, the Christian sword points inward to egotism, to selfishness and to acquisitiveness, to lust and the thousand and one things which would make for antisocial elements in society. History supports the Christian position for never has it been known that violence and tyranny have of themselves realized liberty, or that strife achieved fraternity.

Communism boasts that it is revolutionary, but to the Christian it is not revolutionary enough. The most revolutionary document that has ever been written was penned not by Richard Wagner, or by Karl Marx, but by Our Blessed Mother, who in the Magnificat spoke of the overthrow of political and social kingdoms: "He hath put down the mighty from their seat, and hath exalted the humble. He hath filled the hungry with good things; the rich He hath sent empty away." (Luke 1:52, 53) The revolution of communism is concerned only with externals, not with the soul of man. It shifts booty and loot from one man's pocket to another's and thinks that because one transfers property, one destroys the *desire* for personal property. There is no magic in the dissolution of private property, for pride, miserliness and acquisitiveness still exist. All that communism does in its superficial revolution is to substitute the capitalism of power for the capitalism of money. The new capitalists no longer dispense the profits, but they do distribute the right to control the profits. There is absolutely no assurance that when things are commonly produced, man will no longer desire his neighbor's bread card, or his privilege to travel from Russia to free America. Men are not brothers because they divide an apple they have stolen from the garden of the capitalist. But if men are brothers, the apple will be divided without the stealing. No greater nonsense has ever been concocted than the idea that if you take 20 eggs from one man, and 10 from another man, and liquidate both men, and make an omelet for 30 other men who had only one egg, then everyone will be a brother. The real revolution is to uproot the selfishness that manifested itself in the concentration of eggs. Then will men begin to share their eggs because they are brothers. As it has been well said: "Under Communism when nobody has anything, everybody will have everything; and when everybody has everything, nobody will have any more than anybody. But if anybody has more than anybody, somebody will liquidate him, and then everybody will be happy except the relatives of the somebody who got liquidated."[8]

Even under communism there will still be the envy toward those who are fortunate enough to be sent to America as diplomats; and fear on the diplomats' part lest on their return they will be liquidated because they liked playing golf with an American capitalist. All economic and political revolutions are destined for frustration, either because their original aims are forgotten, or because, though they can eliminate the power of money, they cannot eliminate the lust for power. Christianity agrees with Communists when they point out the need of a revolution, but Christianity places the blame not on institutions but on men; not on legislation but on legislators; not on politics but on politicians; not on property but on man. Our Lord would never have been crucified had He put the blame on things. The Physician was killed because He found the source of the disease in the person. Save man and you save the world; dehumanize man and you wreck the world. The only place that communism ever works is in a convent or a monastery, where all the religious speak of "our cell," "our books." Such a community of goods has been built up without liquidation and concentration camps, because the revolution took place first in men's souls. The early Christians shared their goods because they all possessed the Holy Spirit of Love, but the sharing of their goods would never create the Holy Spirit of Love. Communism tries to establish the impossible: a brotherhood of man without a fatherhood of God.

Communism lacks the real revolutionary spirit of violence, and it also lacks courage. In a cowardly fashion, it always makes the revolution begin with the "other fellow," forgetful that revolutions like charity begin at home. In a penetrating development of this subject J. Middleton Murry points out how easy it is for anyone to accept

historical materialism for history, or economic determi-
nation for the other fellow; and to reduce your neighbor's
behavior to its determinant "interests." But as he truly says,
the only condition on which it can be done either honestly
or to positive advantage is that, at every moment you are
ready to apply the same reduction to yourself. Mr. Murry
believes the impotence of the Marxist Socialist movement
on the continent of Europe comes chiefly from the failure
to do this. Social Democrats, from the leaders down to the
petty party officials, have remained oblivious to the fact
that while they were ostensibly serving a movement aimed
at the destruction of bourgeois society, by the same token
they were ensconcing themselves materially and morally in
bourgeois society: that inevitably, by refusing to apply the
prophylactic of consciousness of the Self to their own "behavior" they had ceased to do the work of sharpening the
point of the unconscious purpose of the working class. Instead, they were engaged in blunting it.[9]

It would do no good to have a new system of economics
unless there were new economists; no good to have a new
legal theory, unless there were new lawyers. The new man
of the Gospel must be a converted man with a change of
soul, seeking never his own. Then he can begin to change
the world. If he is not interested in changing the world
after he has been converted, it means that he was never
converted at all. St. Paul opposed the wickedness of the
Roman Empire with greater force than Marx ever wrote
against Christianity, but he never once fell into the Marxist
error of believing that the world would become better simply because Nero and a few other tyrants were overthrown.
St. Paul brought not hate, but good news; he announced
not a distant future dream, but a realized present, namely
a changed man, and proclaimed for all subsequent history

the sublime notion that communism is not revolutionary enough; it still leaves hate in the soul of man.

Fourth, communism labors under the difficulty of not being sufficiently indignant against the injustices of the economic and political order. This is so because communism denies an independent existence to ethics and morality. Communism claims that all economic exploitation is only an economic problem, and not a moral problem. It insists that injustices are due wholly to methods of production. It leaves no place whatever for the strongest protest of all, namely, that based upon a moral and ethical order. Men can be summoned to revolution, not simply because there is a difference of methods of production, but because there has been a wrong. There is, perhaps, only one word stronger in the whole economic order than the word "wrong," and that is the word "right." Once morality is made a superstructure to economics and therefore inconsequential, then exploitation, intolerance, racial injustices are no longer morally reprehensible evil attitudes of man to man. If all exploitation is simply a matter of economic processes, then why be morally indignant at all? That all evil is due to economics is as nonsensical as to say that all the unhappy marriages in the world are due to bad economics, when the facts prove that if the economic injustices were the sole cause of unhappiness, then it would be the rich who would be happy, and the poor alone who would be miserable.

The Marxists are contradicting themselves every time they make a moral protest against exploiters, profiteers, capitalists, counterrevolutionaries, Trotskyites. Whence comes this moral wrath if reality be not moral? If all social phenomena are amoral, if there is no real distinction between good and evil in the nature of things, then why is exploitation wrong, and why should not anyone commit injustices against his neighbor? If the capitalist is a product of economic methods of production, why should he be condemned as immoral, unjust, wicked? These categories do not belong to the economic order. The Christians and Jews who believe that the ethical order is independent of economics can condemn exploitation, but the materialist of Marxism cannot without repudiating his whole system.[10]

The Communist is strongest in his protest against economic disorders only, as Berdyaev says, when he borrows the morality of Christianity. He is weak when he departs from it. That is why Christianity has no use either for a man or for a system which cannot become morally indignant and righteously wrathful, even as a just God in the face of the moral indignities of man to man. "Whether we see Marxism as a revelation of truth or as a relative reflection of economic reality, either undermines the basis of Marxism itself. Marxism has smuggled into itself both absolute good and absolute truth, and from the heights of this good and this truth it passes judgment on the world."[11]

There is something infantile about communism. As a child kicks the door because he bumped against it; as the golfer breaks his clubs because he dubbed his putt; as Xerxes beat the waters of the Hellespont because they delayed him, so Marx who bumped his shins against private property immediately begins to blame property. It is so easy for all of us to fall into that error, particularly when we do not want the better.

A fifth reason why the Church is opposed to communism is because it destroys love of one's country. Communism lacks one of the fundamental virtues that even the pagans had, namely, the virtue of piety. *Pietas* was understood as reverence for one's God, family and fatherland, because they are united. Once people lose reverence for God, they begin to lose reverence for their own country.

Religion condemns any organization which, while enjoying the blessings of our country, would instill allegiance to another country.[12] But this is precisely what the Theses and Statutes of the Third International enjoin, to which the Communist Party of the United States must subscribe: "*Every party desirous of affiliating with the Third International should renounce not only avowed social patriotism, but also the falsehood and hypocrisy of social pacifism; it should systematically demonstrate to the workers that without a revolutionary overthrow of capitalism, no international arbitration, no talk of disarmament, no democratic organization of the League of Nations will be capable of saving mankind from new imperialist wars.*"

We find a confirmation of this on pages 104 and 105 of the *Manual of Organization* which was published by the Workers Library Publishers, and edited by J. Peters. It is the oath of allegiance which is taken by all Communists in the United States. It reads: "*I pledge myself to rally the masses to defend the Soviet Union, the head of victorious Socialism. I pledge myself to remain at all times a vigilant and firm defender of the Leninist line of the party, the only line that insures a triumph of Soviet power in the United States.*" Not only does communism make its members align themselves with a foreign power, but it also makes them subscribe to a revolutionary program as dictated from above. On page 105 of the manual we read: "*Our party application carries this declaration: the undersigned declares his adherence to the program and statutes of the Communist International, and the Communist party in the United States, and agrees to subject himself to the discipline of the party, and engage actively in its work.*" And finally on page 8 we read that all the members of the Communist Party must work for a revolution in the United States. "*As the leader and organizer of the proletariat, the Communist party of the United*

States leads the working class in its fight for the establishment of a dictatorship of the Soviet Socialist Republic in the United States."

The Communists have openly avowed their want of patriotism to their country before a special committee of the United States House of Representatives. In Report No. 2290, 71st Congress, W. Z. Foster of the Communist Party in answer to questions made some revealing statements.

Q. ". . . the workers in this country look upon the Soviet Union as their country, is that right?"
A. "The more advanced workers do."

Q. "Look upon the Soviet Union as their country?"
A. "Yes."

Q. "They look upon the Soviet flag as their flag?"
A. "The workers of this country . . . have only one flag and that is the red flag. . . ."

Q. ". . . are the communists in this country opposed to our Republican form of government?"
A. "The capitalist democracy—most assuredly. . . ."

Q. "And they desire to overthrow it through revolutionary methods?"
A. "I would like to read from the program of the Communist International. . . . 'The conquest of power by the proletariat does not mean peaceful capturing . . . by means of a parliamentary majority . . . the violence of the bourgeoisie can only be suppressed by the stern violence of the proletariat!"

Q. "You take your orders from the Third International, do you?"
A. ". . . The Communist International is a world

party, based upon the mass parties in the respective countries. It works out its policy by the mass principles of these parties in all its deliberations . . . when a decision is arrived at . . . the workers, with their customary sense of proletarian discipline, accept it and put it into effect."

Q. "Do the Communists in this country advocate world revolution?"
A. "Yes. . . ."

Closely allied to want of patriotism is the sixth effect of communism, namely, its perversion of the true doctrine of liberty. Every heresy in a certain sense is a twin, because in a distortion of the balanced, living unity of truth there results a splitting asunder and divorce of that which God intended should never be put asunder. Nothing more clearly reveals this truth than the history of the doctrine of freedom. According to right reason there are two freedoms: a *minor* freedom and a *major* freedom. The first is the ground of free will or liberty of choice; the second is the liberty of fulfillment or perfection. Saint Augustine says the first makes a man free in relationship to God; the second is the attainment of perfection in God. The first is the liberty of indifference or the initial freedom which a man has *from* external coercion, and which is given him as a means that he may attain the other liberty which is that of autonomy. Liberty of indifference is freedom to choose the truth; liberty of autonomy is freedom in the truth. The first belongs to earth, the second to Heaven, or its anticipation. Once a free man by the right use of means in this world really attains to God, he loses freedom of indifference. Once God is attained there is nothing left to be desired. There will be no freedom of choice in Heaven. The first kind of freedom does not give any guarantee that man will achieve his end, because as long as man exercises freedom of choice, it is within the range of possibility that he may elect that which is not for his ultimate perfection. What a man is given metaphysically in minor liberty he has to realize morally in major liberty. This constitutes the process of redemption. As Saint Augustine said: "It is a great liberty to be able not to sin; it is the greatest liberty to be unable to sin." When both these freedoms were exercised properly in the Christian civilization, then one became the means to another. Men wanted to be free in order to fulfill certain purposes; freedom *from* something was intelligible only because it meant freedom *for* something, namely perfection of personality in God.

It happens that modern civilization has separated these two liberties. Historical liberalism has chosen the first to the exclusion of the second, and totalitarianism in its three forms of Nazism, Fascism and communism, has chosen the second to the exclusion of the first. Historical liberalism defined freedom as the "right to do whatever you please," with the result that it began to judge the good society by the absence of law and restraint. In its ideal world a man would be free politically, as he escaped the power of the state; free economically, as the right to make money escaped the authority of conscience; free religiously, as he escaped religious authority, either of the Bible or the Church. Freedom of liberalism thus began to be a physical power rather than a moral power, simply because it denied the moral necessity of willing within the fixed frame of a moral order. One of the reasons why there has been so much misunderstanding of the Church's position concerning historical liberalism is that men have not seen that the divorce of freedom from law, purpose and order ends in license.[13] The effects of the false definition of freedom as the right to be immune from restraint and law has a twofold consequence: social and economic. Socially it produced a civilization made up of crosscurrents of egotism, one at variance with the order. The world began to take on the aspect of a free-for-all which was dignified by calling it the struggle for existence. No one was interested in the common good, but only in his own tiny little self, which meant that every man was his own god in a pantheon of other gods. Economically, liberty of indifference resulted in tremendous inequalities of wealth in which poverty became the lot of the many and wealth the lot of the few. As William Ernest Hocking described the effects of the false freedom: "To be free has come to mean being loosed from old regularities, trying a little breaking away and then a little more, exploring the borderland around the rules . . . thus modernity has come to take its typical excitements in the bizarre atmosphere of a social milieu made safe for semiconventional departures from convention— safe for the risks of a dulled imagination. Its highest reach is in the flouting of standards whose meaning is no longer felt because it is sufficient to know their date—they are old. When we have reached the point of measuring the stature of our freedom by the height of the pile of our discarded inhibitions, is anyone minded to die for this eviscerated ghost of that modern liberty which once was sacred because it was important?"[14]

Something had to be done to counteract individual selfishness and economic inequalities and the flouting of standards; some way had to be discovered to lift men out of their individual egotisms and make them look for the good of all, but how make man realize that he is his brother's keeper? Religion could have done it by restoring a sense of morality and justice from the *inside*, but since religion was rejected as a solution, partly because minds had lost the love of truth, there was only one way left, and that was to *force* them to live for the general welfare; that is, seize wealth and use power to equalize the inequalities. Thus were born the dictatorships of Nazism, Fascism and communism in Europe. If the sheep will not of themselves run together in the unity of the sheepfold, then dogs must be sent barking at their heels. If individuals will not be responsive to their God-given consciences prompting them to recognize their social responsibilities, then dictators will force them to do so. The unity thus achieved came not from the *inside* through religion, but from the *outside* through force. There thus became verified what Dostoevsky had said: "Complete unfreedom leads to complete tyranny." Totalitarianism then began to apply to society the freedom of autonomy which belongs only to God; it sought to secularize the perfection which only the Heavenly Absolute can give, by transferring it to an earthly absolute. Thus as Liberalism sought liberty at the expense of the common good, so communism seeks the common good at the expense of liberty. As liberalism made the individual the end that was to be served, so totalitarianism made the collectivity the end to which the individual is only a means. From the erroneous extreme of liberalism where men said that freedom was the right to do whatever you *please*, there was now a shift to the other extreme where liberty was defined as the right to do whatever you *must*. The Communist philosopher Engels defined liberty as "necessity." A stone is free when it obeys the law of gravitation and falls to the ground when released from the hand. Man is free according to the Communist view because he knows that he must act according to the laws of the dictator. When a man knows what he must do and does it, then he is free. Thus article 125 of the

Soviet Constitution grants the citizens the right of freedom of press and speech and assembly *on condition* they are used to support the Communist system. This means that unless citizens use the press and speech and assembly to further communism, they thereby forfeit the rights. Communism supplied one defect of the liberal theory of freedom, by offering a purpose which is social, but it made this purpose so absolute as to destroy completely freedom of choice. This it did by absorbing personality into the class which is the essence of communism.

Christ said that "Truth will make you free." But if truth does not exist, then nothing is left but the compulsory organization of social happiness. Many today are prepared to accept this compulsory organization of the chaos created by a false concept of liberty, because they are afraid to bear any longer the burden of responsibility of freedom.

Just as in the subject of property, so, too, in the subject of liberty, the Christian position steers a middle course between extremes. Freedom for Christianity means neither the right to do what you *please*, nor the right to what you *must*, but rather the right to do whatever you *ought*. *Ought* implies order, law and justice. Liberty by definition is an attribute which belongs only to a person. It cannot be attributed to a collectivity or totality whether it be a nation, a state, a race or a class. The basic fallacy of communism on this point is the transfer of freedom from the person to the collectivity.

The freedom of Christianity is the freedom of a person to be a person, and not a drop in the stream of terrestrial history. Every man is a person *sui juris*, an absolute in his way, relative only to God. Once the human person becomes divorced from God according to Whose image he has been made, then man himself becomes a God, and freedom becomes absolute in an autonomous individual. The taking of man out of an organic scheme of the universe in which he is both dependent on God and, therefore, independent in the sense that he is endowed with inalienable rights, leaves him swinging between conceptions of absolute impotence and absolute independence. Unlimited liberty of choice finally makes him disillusioned and he gives himself over to some collective or historical idol. Thus do false absolutes appear to take the place vacated by the disappearance of theological absolutes in which the human purposes are ordered to God as a final end. In the psychological order, the effects of the dehumanization of man are twofold: pride and sensuality. As Reinhold Niebuhr has so well expressed it: "Man falls into pride, when he seeks to raise his contingent existence to unconditional significance; he falls into sensuality, when he seeks to escape from his unlimited possibilities of freedom, from the perils and responsibilities of self-determination by immersing himself into a 'beautiful good,' by losing himself in some natural vitality."[15] In the political order these two effects are what have already been described as historical liberalism which equates freedom with license, and totalitarianism which equates freedom with necessity and tyranny.

Because communism denies freedom of choice it substitutes for God, Who alone can give freedom of perfection, the dictator and the collective state as the source of freedom, and thus necessarily destroys human freedom. In its metaphysics is implied the very necessity of a violent revolution. Simply because it takes away from man the creative power of choice for his own reformation, it must necessarily place the energy of change in the violence of the totality. Since all personal freedom implies reason, it follows that the denial of personal freedom necessarily makes a revolution irrational. Government necessarily becomes not one of persuasion, but compulsion, and compulsion is the expression of the will, not the expression of human reason. Democracy in the true sense of the word is the rule of reason; totalitarianism is the rule of the collective will which destroys personal will. Because communism relies on power, it is necessarily linked up with fear, which accounts for the cruelty of its revolutions. "A man who is possessed by fear always begins to persecute. The man who is possessed by a persecution mania is a dangerous man, persecution is always to be expected of him. There is nothing more terrible than men possessed by fear, men who see on all sides of them dangers and conspiracies and attempts upon them. It is just these men who are in the grip of an insane fear which may be animal and mystic, who set up courts of inquisition and inflict torture and use the guillotine. . . . Violence never leads to freedom. Hatred never leads to brotherhood. The general repudiation of human dignity because of a single hostile part of humanity will never lead to the universal affirmation of the human dignity."[16]

Our generation is witnessing, whether it knows it or not, the conflict of two radically false concepts of liberty: a liberty of indifference which gives the individual the right to ignore society, and the liberty of necessity which gives the state the right to ignore the individual by absorbing him into a race of class and thus destroying his freedom of choice. Liberty of indifference forgets society, liberty of necessity forgets man. Liberty of indifference wrecks society by defining freedom as individual license; liberty of necessity wrecks humanity by defining freedom as the necessity which gives the dictator the right to absorb the person. As Leo XIII as far back as 1888 warned concerning the consequences of the false concepts of liberty: "The true liberty of human society does not consist in every man doing what he pleases, for this would simply end in turmoil and confusion, and bring on the overthrow of the State . . . likewise liberty does not consist in the power of those in authority to lay unreasonable and capricious demands upon their subjects, which would be equally criminal and would lead to the ruin of the commonwealth."[17]

Liberty is something more than an economic phenomenon as the disciples of free enterprise contend; liberty is more than a political phenomenon, as a tyrannical dictatorship claims; it is even more than the separation of right from responsibility as historical liberalism contended; it is something more than the separation of responsibilities from rights as communism contends; it is something else than free thought and something more than dictated thought. Historical liberalism was not the birth of liberty, and Communist dictatorship is not its discovery. Freedom had its roots in man's spiritual nature, before there was ever a liberal, a democrat, a Fascist, a Communist or a Nazi. Freedom does not arise out of any social organization or any constitution or any party, but out of the soul of man. That is why one finds such a lack of all discussion of civil, political and economic liberty in the New Testament, because these latter forms of liberties were merely by-products of the freedom of the spirit. Our Divine Saviour, therefore, refused to accept the offer of political friends who wished to make Him king, and place Him at the head of a rebellion. In the economic order, He refused to act as a judge between two brothers who were disputing an estate, because He found covetousness in both the brothers. Only a moral regeneration could root out that vice. Though He had little to say on the manifold social issues of His time, He was tremendously interested in granting what Saint Paul called

"the glorious liberty of the sons of God." It was the souls
of men that He set Himself to liberate. Liberty to Him and
the whole tradition of the Western world does not come
essentially from improved conditions of living, either political or economic, but rather it is a spring out of which better
conditions must flow. A free spirit creates free institutions
as a slave spirit creates a tyrannical institution.[18] From the
Christian point of view both historical liberalism and totalitarianism are half right and half wrong. Half right because
they take a part of freedom; half wrong because they ignore the other part. They separate that which never should
have been separated, namely, free choice as a means to an
end which is self-perfection. God joined choice and perfection together, and to tear them apart is to do violence
to man. Man has not been sent into this world to choose
again and again and then to die without ever having made
the supreme choice. Unless the road leads somewhere
there is no reason for taking it. As courtship looks to marriage, so choice looks to goals, purposes, perfection. The
freedom man ultimately craves is neither in the indefinite
choice of indifferent goals nor in the surrender of choice to
the kingdom of earth. Man seeks to make a choice which
will dispense him from the necessity of choosing again. He
wants a freedom which will give him an escape from the
paradox of the chase and the capture. This is possible when
one has lived for and found God. Once man attains to the
rapture of God, he captures something so infinite that it
will take an eternity of chase to sound the depths of its Life
and Truth and Love, and in that union of both capture and
chase will consist the happiness of man.

The basic defect of communism is the inescapable
fact of death. Recently a work written on the subject of
Communist philosophy had a brief chapter entitled "The

Communist Attitude toward Death," and it contained nothing of the philosophy of communism, but only an excerpt from Gorky about how science was trying to master death. Practice bears this out, for all Red funerals are glorifications of the collectivity. The perfect symbol of its philosophy is the cadaver of Lenin with its periodical injections of embalming fluid to give it the semblance of permanence.[19]

Death is the great unsolved problem of communism, because despite all the dictatorial attempts to absorb men into the collectivity, the final breath individualizes and personalizes and individuates. For a time the Communist may feel he is like fruit on the tree of the classless society, in which all hang together as tree clings to skin, and skin to pulp, and pulp to seed, so he clings to the party, the party to the politburo and the politburo to the dictator. But he must remember that a day comes when the fruit falls from the tree; the pulp may become the prey of birds, but at the core of all is a seed which prepares for another life, sans party, sans politburo, sans dictator—an immortal soul. As death separated Dives of the Gospel from his five brothers, so it will separate students from their professors whose sophisms stole their faith; it will separate the hangers-on from the crowd, whose every catchword and slogan and style they reflected; it will separate fellow travelers from the Moscovite inspiration, and every party member from the central committee. During life, force and terror and fear may extinguish personality, but death will reaffirm it. Then each man will have to learn for himself that narrow is the gate and strait the way to Eternal Life, and few there are who enter therein. There will be no attorneys to plead his case; no alienists to plead that he was not in his right mind because he did wrong; no Freudians to plead that he was not responsible because he had an Oedipus complex; all the masks will be taken off; he will step out of the ranks, away from the crowd, and the only voice he will hear will be the voice of conscience, which will not testify in his behalf, but will reveal self as he really is; its X rays will penetrate beyond all moods and phantasies, gestures and schemes and illusions; no loud orchestra will play to drown his conscience; no opiates will be served to make him forget or waft him off into the delightful irresponsibility of sleep; no cocktails will be served at heavenly bars with angelic barmaids to make him deaf to the voice of conscience; no Marxist will arise to defend him and say that he was determined by economic conditions under which he lived and, therefore, was not free; no book of the month will be read to prove that since there is no sin, there can be no judgment. There will be only the open book of his conscience where all stands revealed, for then shall he begin to know what it means to be self-determined; then shall he learn what it means to be free; death makes the personality confront itself as nothing else does in life, not even danger. Marx, who said that the person has no value except as a member of a revolutionary class, will be given the great lie; a man has value because he is a person. One by one, as the scythe of death cuts down the ranks and allows the I to speak and assert itself, communism meets its greatest enemy—its final defeat from which there is no victory. Then shall stand affirmed the Christian message . . . the most precious thing in the world is a soul that one day must go to meet its God.[20]

CHAPTER FIVE

Communism Speaks for Itself

Karl Marx on the subject of Russia and the Balkans:
"The conflict between Russian despotism and Western democracy seems to be everlasting in the Balkans. Those who are working for the survival of democracy in Europe must introduce European arts, sciences, justice, liberty and the spirit of independence into the Balkans. Future peace and the progress of humanity are closely allied."[1]

Marx on the subject of Russia and annexations:
"Russia keeps claiming that it has no annexationist designs. In order to ascertain the hypocrisy of this claim, it is sufficient to review the annexations carried out by Russia since the time of Peter the Great.

"Territories extracted by Russia from Sweden are larger than the present possessions of that country.

"The conquests from Poland form an area nearly as large as Austria. Territories which Turkey had to cede to Russia in the Balkans are identical to the area of Prussia.

What they obtained in Asia from Turkey is as large as Germany. Their acquisitions from Persia are comparable to the area of Great Britain."[2]

Karl Marx on the subject of Western civilization:
"The cowardice and stupidity of the Western nations provide Russia with opportunities. Due to their ignorance, Western statesmen are losing control of the situation. Jealousies are their perdition. Whatever they do benefits Russia. . . .

"Will the Byzantinism represented by Russia yield to Western civilization, or will it one day find an opportunity to renew its pernicious influence in forms more terrible and more tyrannical than ever?"[3]

Karl Marx on the danger of Russian aggression:
"The vital interests should render Great Britain the earnest and unyielding opponent of the Russian projects of annexations and aggrandisement. England cannot afford to allow Russia to become the possessor of the Dardanelles and Bosporus. Both commercially and politically such an event should be a deep, if not deadly blow at British power. Let Russia once come into possession of Constantinople . . . in that case the Black Sea would be a Russian lake . . . Trebizond would be a Russian port, the Danube a Russian river. But having come thus far on the way to universal empire, is it probable that this gigantic and swollen power will pause in its career? And as sure as conquest follows conquest, and annexation follows annexation, so surely would the conquest of Turkey by Russia be only the prelude for the annexation of Hungary, Prussia, Galicia, and the ultimate realization of the Slavonic Empire. The arrest of the Russian scheme of annexation is of the highest moment."[4]

Lenin[5] on the subject of relation with other states:
"We are living not merely in a state, but *in a system of states*, and it is inconceivable that the Soviet Republic should continue to exist for a long period side by side with imperialist states. Ultimately, one or the other must conquer. Meanwhile, a number of terrible clashes between the Soviet Republic and the bourgeois states is inevitable. This means that if the proletariat, as the ruling class, wants to and will rule, it must prove this also by military organization."[6]

Stalin[7] on the same subject:
"The final victory of socialism is the complete guarantee against attempted intervention, and that means against restoration, for any serious attempt at restoration can take place only with serious support from outside, only with the support of international capital. Hence the support of our revolution by the workers of all countries and, still more, the victory of the workers in at least several countries, is a necessary condition for fully guaranteeing the first victorious country against attempts at intervention and restoration, a necessary condition for the final victory of socialism."[8]

"Can the victory of socialism in one country be regarded as final if this country is encircled by capitalism, and if it is not fully guaranteed against the danger of intervention and restoration? Clearly it cannot."[9]

Stalin on the meaning of self-determination
and autonomy:
"There are two kinds of autonomy: national or cultural autonomy, and regional autonomy. National autonomy is contrary to the whole development of nations. . . . National cultural autonomy is unsuitable. Firstly, it is artificial and impracticable, for it proposes artificially to draw into a single nation people whom the very march of events, of real

events, is disuniting and dispersing to every corner of the country.

"Secondly, it stimulates nationalism, because it tends to the view which advocates the 'demarcation' of people according to national *curiae*, the 'organization' of nations, the 'preservation' and cultivation of 'national peculiarities'—a thing that is entirely incompatible with Social-Democracy. . . . Thus, *national* autonomy does not solve the problem.

"What is the way out?

"The only real solution is *regional* autonomy, autonomy for such crystallized units as Poland, Lithuania, the Ukraine, the Caucasus, etc.

"The advantage of regional autonomy consists firstly in the fact that it does not deal with a fiction deprived of territory, but with a definite population inhabiting a definite territory.

"Secondly, it does not divide the people according to nation, it does not strengthen national partitions; on the contrary, it only serves to break down these partitions and unites the population in such a manner as to open the way for division of a different kind, division according to class.

"The aim must be to unite the workers of all nationalities in Russia into *united* and *integral* collective bodies in the various localities and to unite these collective bodies into a *single* party.

"Thus *the principle of international solidarity of the workers is an essential element* in the solution of the national problem."[10]

Stalin on the subordination of self-determination to dictatorship of the proletariat:
"It should be borne in mind that besides the right of nations

to self-determination there is also the right of the working class to consolidate its power, and to this latter right the right of self-determination is subordinate. There are occasions when the right of self-determination conflicts with the other, the higher right—the right of a working class that has assumed power to consolidate its power. In such cases—this must be said bluntly—the right to self-determination cannot and must not serve as an obstacle to the exercise by the working class of its right to dictatorship. The former must give way to the latter."[11]

Stalin on the subject of appeasement:
"They [England and America] let her [Germany] have Austria, despite the undertaking to defend her independence; they let her have the Sudeten region; they abandoned Czechoslovakia to her fate, thereby violating all their obligations.

"Far be it from me to moralize on the policy of nonintervention, to talk of treason, treachery and so on. It would be naïve to preach morals to people who recognize no human morality."[12]

Stalin on the purpose of Soviet diplomacy: the union of all the nations of the world into a Soviet Republic.
"The Soviet Power is so constructed that, being international by its intrinsic nature, it systematically fosters the idea of unity among the masses and impels them towards amalgamation. . . .

"I say, there, in the West, where capitalist democracy prevails and where the states rest on private property, the very basis of the state fosters national enmity, conflicts and struggle; here, in the realm of the Soviets, where the power is built not on capital, but on labor, where the power is built not on private property, but on collective property, where the power is built not on the exploitation of man by man, but on hostility to such exploitation; here, on the contrary, the very nature of the government power fosters a natural striving on the part of the toiling masses towards unity into a single socialist family. . . .

"Let us hope that by forming our confederate republic we shall be creating a reliable bulwark against international capitalism and that the new confederate state will be another decisive step towards the amalgamation of the toilers of the whole world into a single World Socialist Soviet Republic."[13]

"In the event of any success the invaders will try to destroy the Soviet system and restore the bourgeois system in the occupied regions.

"We would be in a position to say that the victory [of socialism in the Soviet Union] is complete, if our country were situated on an island and if it had not many other [capitalist] countries around it. But since we live not on an island but in 'a system of states,' a considerable number of which are hostile to the land of socialism, thus creating the danger of intervention and restoration, we say openly and honestly that the victory of socialism in our country is not yet complete.

"This problem remains to be solved. . . . It can be solved only by uniting the serious efforts of the international proletariat with the still more serious efforts of the entire Soviet people."[14]

Stalin on the meaning of democracy:
"Democracy is of two kinds. It is clear, therefore, that democracy in the draft of the new Constitution is not the 'ordinary' and 'universally recognized' democracy in general, but *socialist* democracy."[15]

"All this talk about democracy! What is democracy within the Party? Democracy for whom? If democracy is understood to mean the right of a few intellectuals, severed from the actual revolution, to twaddle without limit and to have their own press organs, we need no such democracy, for that is the democracy of a tiny minority opposing the will of the tremendous majority."[16]

". . . Lenin defined Soviet authority as a national form of proletarian dictatorship. . . . He quite particularly stressed the fact that dictatorship of the proletariat is the supreme model of democracy in a class community, as expressing, on one hand, the interests of the majority, and on the other, as opposed to capitalistic democracy which represents the interests of a minority. The party represents the highest type of proletarian class organization when compared with the other proletarian organizations, as trade unions, co-operatives, and State organizations whose activities must be unified and directed by the party. Dictatorship of the proletariat may be realized by the party, as its superior steering organ. Proletarian dictatorship can be complete only if directed by one party: the Communist Party which must not share that management with any other party. The task of proletarian dictatorship cannot be accomplished unless an iron discipline within the party is established. . . ."[17]

Stalin on the subject of the federation of non-Russian states into a Soviet Republic. June 12, 1920, Stalin was Commissar of Nationalities. He was asked by Lenin to prepare some theses for the Second Congress of the Communist International. The following plan was submitted to Lenin by Stalin:
"For nations which made up part of old Russia, our Soviet type of federation may and must be accounted expedient as

the road to internal unity. . . . The Soviet type of federation will *graft itself on to them* without any serious friction.

"The same cannot be said of nationalities *which did not make up part* of old Russia and which developed their own state. If they become *Soviet*, they will be made *by force of circumstances* to enter into one or another governmental bond with Soviet Russia, *e.g.*, a future *Soviet Germany, Hungary, Finland*. These peoples having their own state, their own army, their own finances, will hardly agree to enter into a federal bond with Soviet Russia. For these nationalities the most acceptable form of federation will be a confederation (a union of independent states)."[18]

Molotov on the subject of Fascism and alliance with Nazism:
"Fascism is a matter of taste. . . . Our friendship has been sealed in blood."[19]

"August 23, 1939, the day the Soviet-German non-aggression pact was signed, is to be regarded as a date of great historical importance. The non-aggression pact between the U.S.S.R. and Germany marks a turning point in the history of Europe, and not only of Europe. Only yesterday the German fascists were pursuing a foreign policy hostile to us. Yes, only yesterday we were enemies in the sphere of foreign relations. Today, however, the situation is changed and we are enemies no longer.

"Only the enemies of Germany and the U.S.S.R. can strive to create and foment enmity between the peoples of these countries.

"The Soviet-German pact has been the object of numerous attacks in the English, French and American press. Conspicuous in these efforts are certain 'socialist' newspapers, diligent servitors of 'their' national capitalism, servitors of gentlemen who pay them decently. It is clear that real truth cannot be expected from gentry of this calibre. . . ."[20]

Molotov on the secret clauses of the Nazi-Soviet Agreements signed by him and German Foreign Minister von Ribbentrop:

"On the occasion of the signing of the non-aggression treaty between the German Reich and the Union of Socialist Soviet Republics the undersigned representatives of the two parties discussed in a highly confidential conversation the problem of the demarcation of the spheres of influence of either party in Eastern Europe.

"This conversation has the following result:

"1. In the case of a politico-territorial change in the territories belonging to the Baltic states—Finland, Estonia, Latvia, and Lithuania—the northern frontier of Lithuania shall form also the demarcation of the spheres of interest between Germany and the U.S.S.R. Both parties recognize the interest of Lithuania in the Wilno territory.

"2. In the case of a politico-territorial change in the territories belonging to the Polish state, the spheres of interest between Germany and the U.S.S.R. shall be divided approximately following the line on the Rivers Narew, Vistula and San. The question as to whether the interests of both parties make it desirable to maintain an independent Polish state, and how the frontiers of this state should be fixed, can be clarified in a final manner only in the course of further political developments. In any case, both governments will solve this question by way of a friendly understanding.

"3. With respect to southeastern Europe, the U.S.S.R. emphasize their interest in Bessarabia. Germany declares her complete political disinterestedness in this area.

"4. This protocol shall be treated by both parties in a strictly secret manner."[21]

The Program of the Communist International[22]

What communism proposes to do when it comes to power:
"The ultimate aim of the Communist International is to replace world capitalist economy by a world system of communism.

"Between capitalist society and Communist society a period of revolutionary transformation intervenes, during which the one changes into the other. Correspondingly, there is also an intervening period of political transition, in which the essential state form is the revolutionary dictatorship of the proletariat.

"The characteristic feature of the transition period as a whole is the ruthless suppression of the resistance of the exploiters.

"The conquest of power by the proletariat does not mean peacefully 'capturing' the ready-made bourgeois state machinery by means of a parliamentary majority. . . . Hence the violence of the bourgeoisie can be suppressed only by the stern violence of the proletariat. The conquest of power by the proletariat is the violent overthrow of bourgeois power, the destruction of the capitalist state apparatus (bourgeois armies, police, bureaucratic hierarchy, the judiciary, parliaments, etc.), and substituting in its place new organs of proletarian power, to serve primarily as instruments for the suppression of the exploiters."

Tasks of the dictatorship:

"A. The confiscation and proletarian nationalization of all large private capitalist undertakings (factories, plants, mines, electric power stations) and the transference of all state and municipal enterprises to the Soviets.

"B. The confiscation and proletarian nationalization of private capitalist railway, waterway, automobile and air transport services (commercial and passenger airfleet) and the transference of all state and municipal transport services to the Soviets.

"C. The confiscation and proletarian nationalization of private capitalist communication services (telegraphs, telephones and wireless) and the transference of state and municipal communication services to the Soviets.

"A. The confiscation and proletarian nationalization of all large landed estates in town and country (private, church, monastery and other lands) and the transference of State and municipal landed property including forests, minerals, lakes, rivers, etc., to the Soviets with subsequent nationalization of the whole of the land.

"B. The confiscation of all property utilized in production belonging to large landed estates, such as buildings, machinery and other inventory, cattle, enterprises for the manufacture of agricultural products (large flour mills, cheese plants, dairy farms, fruit and vegetable drying plants, etc.).

"C. The transfer of large estates, particularly model estates and those of considerable economic importance, to the management of the organs of the proletarian dictatorship and of the Soviet farm organizations."

Dictatorship in relation to culture:
"The mass awakening of communist consciousness, the cause of socialism itself, calls for a *mass change of human nature*, which can be achieved only in the course of the practical movement, in revolution. Hence, revolution is not only necessary because there is no other way of overthrowing the *ruling* class, but also because only in the process of revolution is the *overthrowing* class able to purge itself of the dross of the old society and become capable of creating a new society.

"One of the most important tasks of the cultural revolution affecting the wide masses is the task of systematically and unswervingly combating religion—the opium of the people."

Nature of Communist tactics:
". . . The dictatorship of the proletariat presupposes the existence in every country of a compact Communist Party, hardened in the struggle, disciplined, centralized, closely linked up with the masses.

"*The Party* is the vanguard of the working class and consists of the best, most class-conscious, most active, and most courageous members of that class.

"The Communist Party must secure predominant influence in the broad mass proletarian organizations (Soviets, trade unions, factory committees, co-operative societies, sport organizations, cultural organizations, etc.). It is particularly important for the purpose of winning over the majority of the proletariat, to gain control of the *trade unions*, which are genuine mass working class organizations closely bound up with the everyday struggles of the working class.

"The Communist Party must extend its influence over the masses of the urban and rural poor, over the lower strata of the intelligentsia and over the so-called 'little man.' *i.e.*, the petty-bourgeois strata generally."

Variability of tactics:
"In determining its line of *tactics*, each Communist Party must take into account the concrete internal and external situation, the correlation of class forces, the degree of stability and strength of the bourgeoisie, the degree of preparedness of the proletariat, the position taken up by the various intermediary strata in its country, etc. The Party determines its slogans and methods of struggle in accordance with these circumstances, with the view to organizing and mobilizing the masses on the broadest possible scale and on the highest possible level of this struggle.

"When a revolutionary situation is developing, the Party advances certain transitional slogans and partial demands corresponding to the concrete situation; but these demands and slogans must be bent to the revolutionary aim of capturing power and of overthrowing bourgeois capitalist society. The Party must neither stand aloof from the daily needs and struggle of the working class nor confine its activities exclusively to them. The task of the Party is to utilize these minor everyday needs as a *starting point* from which to lead the working class to the *revolutionary struggle for power*."

United front:
"When there is no revolutionary upsurge, the Communist Parties must advance *partial* slogans and demands that correspond to the everyday needs of the toilers, linking them up with the fundamental tasks of the Communist International. The Communist Parties must not, however, at such a time, advance *transitional* slogans that are applicable only

to revolutionary situations (for example, workers' control of industry, etc.). To advance such slogans when there is no revolutionary situation means to transform them into slogans that favor merging with the system of capitalist organization. Partial demands and slogans generally form an essential part of correct tactics; but certain transitional slogans go inseparably with a revolutionary situation. Repudiation of partial demands and transitional slogans 'on principle,' however, is incompatible with the tactical principle of communism, for in effect such repudiation condemns the Party to inaction and isolates it from the masses. Throughout *the entire pre-revolutionary period* a most important basic part of the tactics of the Communist Parties is the *tactic of the united front*, as a means toward most successful struggle against capital, toward the class mobilization of the masses and the exposure and isolation of the reformist leaders."

CHAPTER SIX

How to Meet Communism

There is much misunderstanding concerning what a nation and a people should do to combat communism. Immediately there come to mind four ways in which it should not be done. Communism should not be met by vituperation, name-calling and personal hate. Hate is like a seed—it grows. By hating Communists we advance communism, for communism grows in discord just as disease thrives in dirt. As Manzoni wrote: "Few things so corrupt a people as the habit of hate."[1] Only a spurious distinction between individual and social morality has made possible the appeal to hate in the struggle of nations. Pius XII in his Christmas Message of 1940 declared that one of the first victories to be won is "victory over hate which is today dividing the nations." Communism is an ideology and as such is intrinsically wicked, but Communists are persons, made to the image and likeness of God and, therefore, should be subjects of our kindness and charity, that we may prove ourselves worthy children of the Heavenly Father. There is no erring soul that cannot attain to the treasures of Redemption. It is precisely out of love for the sinner that the sin is hated. "The very fact that we hate in our brother his fault and the absence of good is because of our love of our brother."[2] Not even the violence of communism abrogates, but rather renders more imperative, the Christian law.

Communism should not be attacked on the grounds that it is opposed to the monopolistic capitalistic system, because *from an economic point of view alone* neither system is satisfying. There is an affinity between these two in that they both start with the primacy of the economic; both make man an economic animal; both assume that man has no other goal in life than the economic which is either to make profits, as does monopolistic capitalism, or to socialize production, as does communism. Both take sovereignty away from God; the first, by making an individual absolute owner of property, the other by making the bureaucrats of collectivism the absolute owners.[3]

Neither is communism to be met altogether on the false assumption that if economic conditions were bettered we would do away with communism. Communism is not just an economic system; it is a philosophy of life. Conditions were very good in the Garden of Eden, but Lucifer started his revolt there. Bad economic situations are only a *condition*, but never a *cause* of communism. In vain will any Christian think that he has eliminated the Communist menace by equating collective bargaining with the Kingdom of God. It is the basic principle of Marxism that any attempt to reconcile capital and labor so that they both co-operate in peace and prosperity is a betrayal of communism.

Finally, we are not to think that we are called on to be God's agents to execute vindictive judgment on the

Communists, but to see the whole world as seated in sin. When a germ infects a body, it generally does not so localize itself that a surgeon can take out a quart of blood and liquidate the evil. The germs are so diffused through the body that the whole body must be saved. So, too, there is evil throughout the world; communism is one of its principal symptoms. The Christian point of view is to see ourselves as part of a guilty world. In fact, the more innocent we are, the more we are to feel that guilt, because then we better recognize our oneness with our fellow men. Our Lord was innocent, but He took on Himself the sins of the world. How can we be bearers of one another's burdens, as Scripture enjoins, unless it be by seeing that when we touch the circle of humanity at any one point, we touch humanity? Our mission is not exclusively to protest against the evils of our materialistic civilization, not merely to challenge its assumptions, or even diminish its severities—but in some way to see ourselves as citizens of a guilty world. Guilt is social as well as personal, because man is formed for fellowship. There is no thought more salutary in the present crisis than the recognition that much of it is due to our own unfulfilled Christian duties. This note of humility in the face of the world's evil was once struck beautifully on a national scale by Abraham Lincoln, in his second inaugural: "The Almighty has his own purposes. 'Woe unto the world because of offences! . . .' If we shall suppose that American Slavery is one of those offenses which, in the providence of God, must needs come, but which, having continued through His appointed time, He now wills to remove, and that He gives to both North and South, this terrible war, as the woe due to those by whom the offense came, shall we discern therein any departure from those divine attributes which the believers in a Living God always ascribe to

Him? Fondly do we hope—fervently do we pray—that this mighty scourge of war may speedily pass away. Yet, if God wills that it continue, until all the wealth piled by the bond-man's two hundred and fifty years of unrequited toil shall be sunk, and until every drop of blood drawn with the lash, shall be paid by another drawn with the sword, as was said three thousand years ago, so still it must be said 'the judgments of the Lord, are true and righteous altogether.'"

This brings us to only a few positive ways of meeting communism, not any one of which is exclusive, nor are the combined suggestions exhaustive.

Political: Communism can be met politically by choosing candidates in elections not on the basis of political parties, not on the basis of the economic class, but on the basis of their own moral worth. There are two general ways in which the American people choose candidates to represent them in government. One way is on the basis of parties. This has lost much of its meaning, for the party which started out to defend State rights is today the party which is in favor of Federal control, and the party which began with emphasis on Federal rights is today the party which stresses State rights. The more recent way is on the basis of classes. Here one chooses the group which can *promise* (not necessarily fulfill) the greatest increase of comfort and luxury to one class as against another class, or which is most willing to empty the public treasury for bounties to one group rather than another. But this, too, is losing its meaning as people are beginning to see that not the advantage of one class but the public good is paramount.

There remains the one standard that has not yet been universally used, namely, the choosing of candidates on moral grounds. A nation always gets the kind of politicians it deserves. When our moral standards are different, our legislation will be different. As long as the decent people refuse to believe that morality must manifest itself in every sphere of human activity, including the political, they will not meet the challenge of Marxism. Contemporary history proves that modern political leaders, devoid of a moral inspiration and relying solely on a mass basis, prove ineffectual in time of crisis as did the Kerensky regime and the Weimar politicians. Being the creation of a confused mass group and not primarily defenders of the right, they prove in the end to be only transitional phases in a movement toward a revolutionary regime. The apathy of an electorate to moral leadership is always reflected in the apathy of their politicians. "What men do not see is that the fracturing of the spiritual community means the loss of inclusive and unifying moral sanctions over the whole of man's activities. . . . The modern world has no cement to bind together personal morals and the morals of political and economic life."[4] If a time ever comes when the religious Jews, Protestants and Catholics have to suffer under a totalitarian state denying them the right to worship God according to the light of their conscience, it will be because for years they thought it made no difference what kind of people represented them in Congress, and because they never opposed the spiritual truth to the materialist lie. St. Paul said: "Woe is me if I preach not the Gospel," (I Corinthians, 9:16) and woe unto us, if the believing element in our country does not allow its belief in God and morality to seep down into its action in the polling booths. The first effective campaign against communism is to wage war against our temptation to abandon the spiritual in the realm of the political. Nothing can do men of good will more harm than apparent compromises with parties that subscribe to antimoral and antidemocratic and anti-God forces. We must have the courage to detach our support from men who are doing evil. We must bear them no hatred, but we must break with them.

Economic: The economic way to meet communism is to make capitalists out of workers by a wide diffusion of private property. Before suggesting how this can be done, a word about the morality of property is necessary. The moral law affirms that the right to property varies in direct ratio and proportion to its nearness to personality. For example, a man may not use the word "mine" in exactly the same way when applied to his food, clothing and shelter, as to his yacht or his Rembrandt. The nearer things are to personality, which is the source of responsibility, the stronger the right to ownership; the farther away they are from personality, the weaker is the claim. It used to be when property was real rather than financial, as it is today, that the right to property was inseparable from responsibility. A man owned a horse; he could show a title to it; he could say, "It is mine." But the responsibility for the horse was also his. If the horse trampled the neighbor's garden he had to remunerate the neighbor. But because he owned, controlled, cared for, and managed the horse, he was also entitled to 100 percent of the profits from the horse.

With the development of finance those two things which were meant to be joined, namely ownership and responsibility, have tended to become separated. Today, too often, those who own do not labor or manage, and those who labor or manage do not own.[5] Under these conditions, stockholders become distinct from the management and labor. When the owners or stockholders surrender responsibility to management, they give up one of the essential notes of property, and hence one of the titles to profits. But the owners or stockholders claim all the profits though they have surrendered 50 percent of the title, namely responsibility. The stockholders are only the passive creators of wealth; the active creators are the workers. For that reason, the Papal Encyclical recommends that "there should be a modification of the wage system so as to give the worker a share in the profits, management and ownership in the industry wherein he works."

Much of the tension that exists in the economic order today is between the stockholders who do not work and the laborer who does. There is no doubt as to who has the clearer title to profits; certainly the man who clips the coupons and sends in his postcard for a vote by proxy to the corporation is less entitled to the profits of the industry than those who helped create the wealth and the profits. The man who keeps his stock in a safety vault has less claim to the fruits of industry than the worker who wipes sweat from his brow at the end of a day.

One means suggested for helping ownership and labor to coalesce is worker-ownership of stock in industry. Labor leaders are not always favorable to this idea because they lose their power over workers once the workers become satisfied, but this short-sighted policy would be of short duration once the workers see the logic of the situation. Undoubtedly, labor today is striving for some property rights in industry, though it is going about it very clumsily. Labor's claims will be stronger and its demands more just, when it sees that since finance capitalism has separated ownership and responsibility, it is wrong for capitalism to claim all the profits, as it is wrong for the Communists to claim that the state should have all the profits. Neither capital nor labor must be excluded from sharing in the profits. By the same token, workers in industry should refuse to accept labor leaders whose only work is the management of labor unions.

Labor would be within its rights in making such demands, because hired labor has a double aspect: individual
and social. It has an individual character because John
Smith labors and John Smith is tired at the end of a day.
But labor has a social side, because John Smith has helped
to create social wealth in conjunction with other workers.
He is part of a combination of finance, labor and management. For his individual contribution, he should receive a
living wage sufficient to support a family, and for his social
contribution, his constantly increasing contribution to the
common good, he ought to receive a share in the wealth he
helps to create. Wages compensate him for his contribution
by the clock; but he receives no recompense either for his
co-operation with capital and management in the production of new wealth, or for his contribution to the common
good. This could be remedied by giving the workers some
share in the profits, management or ownership of the industry. Profit sharing should not be in the shape of a bonus
given at Christmas, which is paternalistic; but an agreement
by which employees will become participating shareholders
should be a normal and legitimate feature of the contract of
employment so as to make the worker more a partner than
a servant. This dignifying of the worker has been inhibited
generally in two ways: by the slowness of capitalists to perceive its merit before the government began taking excess
profits to pour through bureaucracies in which neither capital nor labor shares. Also, by a lack of statesmanship on
the part of labor leaders who constantly demand more and
more and more, which may kill the goose that laid the capitalistic egg, instead of seeking the more flexible, realistic and
sounder principle of participation in earnings.

The advantages of this system are many. It would make
class struggle which communism tries to incite irrelevant.

A man is willing to sit down on someone else's tools, but he is not willing to sit down on his own. Labor will be interested in capital when individual workers have capital to defend. Secondly, there would be a greater abundance of the fruits of the earth. Men work harder and more readily when they labor on that which is their own. Thirdly, it would make men less susceptible to foreign ideologies and the wild promises of revolutionaries, for no man would exchange his country for a foreign land if his own land afforded him the means of living a tolerable and happy life. Fourth, it is the intelligent answer to Communists who want to break *up* capitalism: this solution is in favor of breaking it *down*. Instead of concentrating wealth in the hands of a state administered by a few bureaucrats, the humane way is to distribute that wealth to those who create it. Communism advocates giving all productive property to a dictator; Christians advocate sharing it with the workers. The capitalist solution is to allow one man to own most of the hens and in turn to distribute eggs to workers who prepare the nests for him. The Communist solution is putting all the eggs into the hands of a dictator cook, who makes an omelet which is bound to be unsatisfying because not all the people like omelets, and some do not like the way the dictator cook prepares them anyway. The Christian solution is to distribute the hens so that every man can cook his eggs the way he likes them, and even eat them raw if that is his definition of freedom. By distributing a wide mass of property owners throughout a country with their scattered powers, privileges and responsibilities, one creates the greatest resistance in the world to tyranny either political or economic, for just as a man is free on the inside because he can call his soul his own, so he begins to be free on the outside, because he can call things his own. Then property becomes what it was always intended to be—the economic guarantee of human liberty. Deprive a man of his right to fashion things according to his own will, and you deprive him of the social basis of his freedom.

The Church is asking only that men begin to think of property as they might of love, in the sense that to possess means also to be possessed. One is not possible without the other. The beatific vision consists in being oneself and at the same time being God's. The economic vision of happiness likewise consists in possessing a garden, but also being possessed by it, in the sense that you work for it. Rights arise from possession; duties arise from being possessed, and each is inseparable from the other. The joy of a man being half possessed by the pipe he smokes, the woman he loves, the field he digs, finds its counterpart in the economic structure in possessing and being possessed by the industry. Thus is he elevated to the dignity of a producer-owner, a copartner and a sharer; for if a man surrenders all power of self-determination in regard to the profits, management or ownership of the place where he works, he not only loses that special prerogative which marks him off from a cow in a pasture, but what is worse, he loses all capacity for determining any work. This is the beginning of a slavery which sometimes goes by the name of security. When capital and labor realize that they are both workers because both are persons, and that capital cannot exist without labor, and labor cannot exist without capital, a vision will come to both of them, a vision of a God who as the Lord of the Universe, descends to this trivial earth of ours, in order to labor for over two decades as a carpenter in the little village of Nazareth.

Christ stands in a unique relation to mankind as the only volunteer worker in the world. Labor was imposed on man as a result of primeval sin. Since He was without sin He was dispensed from its penalties. Furthermore, the Lord of the Universe had no need of toiling with His universe. And yet He freely chose as the Son of God incarnate to join the ranks of labor. Because it was voluntary, it was unique. He was not just a laborer in the sense that He was opposed to a capitalist who is living virtuously. This is the mistake many are apt to make. He was not just a poor man; He was a rich Person who became a poor man, for being rich He became poor for our sakes, that through His poverty we might be rich. The very profession He chose, that of a carpenter, was a proof that He owned that on which He worked, and He worked on that which He owned. He was not an employee working for a corporation; He was not an employer using capital to hire others to make it useful. He worked on the universe He owned as an artist works on the canvas he owns. Hence neither the employer nor the employee alone can invoke Him as his patron; neither can say, "He belonged to our class." He was outside all classes because He was the worker, and the worker is not the employee hating the capitalist; nor is the worker the capitalist enslaving the employee. The worker is he who by his work establishes bonds with God by submission to the penance of work; with neighbor by the creation of common needs; and with nature by giving it the imprint of a mind made to the image and likeness of God. It was the forgetfulness of these ends that made carpenters nail the Carpenter to the Cross; when that happens capital and labor both lose.

Moral: Another way to meet communism would be by the appointment of chaplains from each of the three faiths in all types and sizes of industry. The function of such a chaplain would be something like that which a chaplain exercised in the army. He was not the "privates'" chaplain, nor the commissioned officers' chaplain; he was rather the mediator between the two, always operating in the interests of the whole service, its order and its decency. In our large cities the police, fire, post office, sanitation and even some insurance groups have their chaplains. The chaplain's function in the group is different from that which he would exercise among the same individuals apart from the group. Since the largest and most important group in our national life is industrial, there is no reason why religion should abandon its claim, so confidently asserted in earlier centuries, to give moral directions in business matters. There is no escaping from the fact that once the individual enters into a new human relationship, and one at which he spends most of his waking days, almost his entire week, there is a specific need of ministering to him *in that relationship*, and not apart from it. This need is increased when it is realized that the basic causes of disputes are antisocial behavior, or the selfish concern of a particular group defying all co-operation. No class is always and universally right simply because it is a class. This situation can be remedied not by any balancing of opposing forces, but only by a representative of a moral order appealing to a conscience beyond the cruel and cold forces of the economic.

In order that the chaplain might better operate within an industrial group, he should build a church or synagogue very near the factory, wherein labor and management, capital and labor could worship, and learn that all who eat one bread are one body. If men would get down on their knees together, there would be less need of using fists against one another. But his functions would go beyond the factory church. As the army camps assign a chaplain an office within the army camp, so, too, the industry should assign quarters for a chaplain in which he may be freely consulted at all times by both labor and management, for there is no reason why the iron gates of a factory should prevent the modern worker from enjoying what the village blacksmith used to enjoy—accessibility to his priest, his minister or his rabbi. The industrial chaplain should receive no salary, no expense account from stockholders, management or labor, but only from his church in order that he be free from obligation to any side.

In due time the chaplain could establish factory reading rooms, discussion clubs and even organize factory worship where the minor hates of the working hours could be dissolved in the reminder that all men are brothers, because God is their Father. The supreme advantage of these and other functions of the chaplain, would be that men would be organized on a basis different from the competitive one. Communism thrives only by intensifying hatred, opposition, tension and struggle between a group which buys labor and one which sells it. The value of chaplains in industry would be the organization of men on a noncompetitive or spiritual basis. When the time came to elect labor leaders from the industry, the Communists who thrive in vociferous minorities at late hours would find themselves stalemated and checked by those who came out in great numbers, not to pass a resolution favoring Russia's confiscation of Lithuania or Poland, but to insist on the preservation of basic human rights derived from a sovereign God and recognized by a government of the people, by the people and for the people.

Education: Since Communists infiltrate their philosophy through lies and myths, it is imperative that people in a democracy be properly informed concerning not only the errors of its ideology, but also the great truths of human nature, history and religion. Schools are in operation only about six hours a day, most of them closing at three in the afternoon. It would seem in the present crisis advisable to use the later afternoon and evening hours for adult education. Courses could be given to adults by clergy, lawyers and doctors and other professional men. Among many subjects taught there would be courses in religion, the training of labor leaders, marriage and property and also the philosophy of peace. Such adult education would treat religion not in a private way which would result in the preempting of the social order by antireligious forces, but as the leaven of society. Our people would learn that the alternative between Right and Left is not the same as right and wrong; that social conscience need not make cowards of us all, and that we do not have to go Left to impress our social contemporaries; that it is well not to get behind social movements, but in front of them; that the issue before the world is not between the religious and secular, but the spiritual and the demonic, and that the tendency of the state to take over the functions which were once the province of solitary social units, such as the family, is bringing on national ruin; that labor leaders and capitalists have no rights without duties; that politics must cease to be a mobilization of masses for the achievement of power and begin to be an organization of freemen for the responsible fulfillment of a common purpose. But above all else there will be the teaching of Divine Wisdom where people will not only give an orthodox assent to the creed, but will have their heads, hands, heart and soul so suffused with Divine Grace that the world will become better because their lives are better.[6]

Spiritual: Communism has an appeal principally to two classes: the naïve and the frustrated who believe that communism is interested in the poor and the workers. This appeal does not last long when they come to know either the philosophy of communism or its actual practice, which results in the diffusion of chaos created by a dictatorship over the proletariat. They then reject it as opposed to right, reason and decency. That is why the Communist Party has such a rapid turnover, reaching as high as 40 percent within a few years. At one time, those who liked the Nazis joined the party because the Soviets made a treaty with the Nazis. Later when the Soviets broke with the Nazis, the Nazi-loving group left and other groups joined. As knowledge grows among men of good will, communism becomes less satisfying. The Papal Encyclical on communism mentions the alluring promises of communism as one of the reasons for its success. "How is it possible that such a system, long since rejected scientifically and now proved erroneous by experience, how is it, We ask, that such a system could spread so rapidly in all parts of the world? The explanation lies in the fact that too few have been able to grasp the nature of communism. The majority instead succumb to its deception, skillfully concealed by the most extravagant promises. By pretending to desire only the betterment of the condition of the working classes, by urging the removal of the very real abuses chargeable to the liberalistic economic order, and by demanding a more equitable distribution of this world's goods (objectives entirely and undoubtedly legitimate), the Communist takes advantage of the present worldwide economic crisis to draw into the sphere of his influence even those sections of the populace which on principle reject all forms of materialism and terrorism. And as every error contains its element of truth, the partial truths to which We have referred are astutely presented according to the needs of time and place, to conceal, when convenient, the repulsive crudity and inhumanity of Communistic principles and tactics. Thus the

Communist ideal wins over many of the better-minded members of the community. These in turn become the apostles of the movement among the younger intelligentsia who are still too immature to recognize the intrinsic errors of the system. The preachers of Communism are also proficient in exploiting racial antagonisms and political divisions and oppositions. They take advantage of the lack of orientation characteristic of modern agnostic science in order to burrow into the universities, where they bolster up the principles of their doctrine with pseudoscientific arguments."[7]

Toward the deluded people who believe the lies of communism there must be on our part a recognition of their good instincts and their passion for social justice. Deluded though they are, they are nevertheless unconscious and involuntary instruments of the Holy Spirit. Our task must be to educate the naïve, for as their attachment to communism grows in ignorance, so will it decrease with education. They must be shown that their basic craving for community and social amelioration are better served within the framework of democracy and the fellowship of a redeemed society where reigns the spirit of Love sent to us by the Father and Son.

By far the greater appeal of communism is to the disillusioned and the frustrated. Many follow communism not because they are convinced that it is *right*, but because they have a hidden *hate* against something or somebody. Those who feel individually impotent to vent their hate upon a person or a class or an institution feel that if they joined communism they could find a corporate expression for their pent-up animosities and their dammed-up hate. Something of this psychology is present in those who love gangster pictures or any movies where there are killing and violence. Through them they find an outlet for their own subconscious hatred; they find some satisfaction in seeing it exercised vicariously.

The appeal of communism to this group is not in its theory, but in its hates. That is why communism always has to have a devil. The first argument every Communist uses is to incite contempt of his devil or his neighbor's devil, whether it be Fascism, which is never defined, or capitalism or democracy or religion or morality. A man who is the husband of one wife and who is refused permission by the Church to marry a second or a fifth time is always a potential member of the Communist Party, because through it he can "get even" with religion which irritated his conscience. The more he subconsciously feels the wrong he has done, the more violent will be his opposition to religion. That is why the greatest persecutors of religion are those who have been baptized. "The corruption of the best is the worst." Hitler, Mussolini, Stalin and Marx were all baptized and fell away. When Communists reach a stage where their parents are no longer Christian, but followers of dialectical materialism, their hatred of religion will decrease. Never having lost as much as the older generation, they will be less angry at themselves for having surrendered the treasure.

In the same connection, those who started out with a great lust for wealth and never achieved it, or who became frustrated capitalists, will join the Communist Party to get even with the capitalists whose wealth they envy, and which they now want to possess by expropriation. Those who have more money than they know what to do with, or who have made it too easily, will seek to compensate for their ill-gained wealth by espousing antisocial causes to justify their uneasy consciences. At bottom their love of communism is due to an extreme form of pocket-consciousness. Those who have felt the sting of uncharitable fellow men who made fun of their race or color and refused to give them the hand of fellowship are also likely material for communism, not because communism can give them recognition, which it does not in practice, but only because they get a chance to get even with those who were unkind. Those, too, who have never been able to think clearly, and who have by much reading and little thinking taken more than they can digest, flock to communism where they will have to do no thinking whatever, but where their very obedience to a dictator will give them the illusion of power. Because they became disillusioned with their freedom, which produced chaos in their souls, they look for a Communist dictatorship outside themselves to organize their chaos. Because they lost the power of self-regulation from within, they seek a Communist-imposed regulation from without; because they lost the goal of existence and the purpose of life, they invite a Communist tyranny to impose a goal and dictate a purpose; because they have been isolated from their fellow man, they seek a restoration into a community not on the basis of spirit and love, but of matter and force.

The supreme advantage of all these hates is that they enable the frustrated and the disillusioned to combine the strongest social affirmations with the most contemptuous disregard for personal betterment. They could not become Christians—which in their hearts they want—because Christianity would demand personal righteousness, but in communism they can have a seeming sense of righteousness and justice by hating the wrongs of others without any obligation to better their own individual lives. If those who know communism want to combat it effectively, they must start with the assumption that these frustrated and

disillusioned individuals are not perhaps so far from the
Kingdom of God as it would seem. In fact they are probably much closer than the indifferent who have neither hates
nor loves. The charges these frustrated souls bring against
society are very often justified, but in their zeal to cure the
baby of whooping cough they accept the solution of cut-
ting off its head. Once they come to see that what they
hate is sin, and not a method of production, and what they
are seeking is God and not their own miserable atheism in
which each one makes himself a god and the other man an
"atheist," they are at the very door of that peace that only
Christ can open to them.

A distinction must be made between the ideology and
the person, between communism and Communists. Communism is to be hated as a doctor hates pneumonia in his
sick child; but the Communists are potential children of
God and must be loved as the sick child is loved. A Christian who starts with the assumption that they ought to be
annihilated or sent to concentration camps—which indeed
they would do to us—is not worthy of the name of Christ.
We are to seek not their extinction but their transfiguration. Does God hate us because we are sinners? Then shall
we hate them for being a particular kind of sinner? Was not
Paul in the early Church a greater persecutor of religion
than Tito or Stalin or Hitler? There must have been thousands of Christians who in their thoughts hoped that God
would send a coronary thrombosis to Paul, to take him
out of this life. Prayers were multiplied before God to send
someone to answer that fiery and zealous enemy. Would
that Heaven would send someone to answer Paul! Well,
God heard their prayers, and he sent Paul to answer Paul.
God's power is more manifested in the conversion than in
destruction, for He knows that the bitterest enemies make

the best saints, and not those weak-minded brothers and sisters who hate communism when the editorials condemn it, and love it when the newspapers glorify it. Rome was the greatest persecutor of religion until Russia in modern times, but Rome became the center of Christianity. May God so transfigure Russia that from it one day will radiate a light which will renew faith in Europe and give it to Asia!

CHAPTER SEVEN

The Attitude Toward
the Family in Russia
and America

Communism in its philosophy and its early practice was
so antimoral and antihuman that it was necessarily opposed to the family as the unit of society. But after trying
out so-called Communist morality and all the queer practices which the lower levels of democracy still believe, it
began to repudiate both its theory and practice. Without
even blinking a Communist eyelid, it completely reversed
its field. Communism did not say it was wrong. No government in the history of the world ever said it was wrong. It
just took up another attitude without any explanations.

In order to appreciate and understand the complete
turn-about-face of the Communist theory and practice,
consider first the early attitude toward the family, then its
present position. The philosophy of communism teaches
that all morality, art, literature and institutions repose on
methods of production. In keeping with this, the *Communist
Manifesto* states that the bourgeois family reposes on capital or individual gain, and that "the family will, therefore,

disappear with capital." Engels in his work on *The Origin of the Family* declared that the family was based principally on an economics which recognized private property, from which flowed the right of one generation to inherit property from another generation; and secondly, the domination of the husband over the wife, because he received the pay envelope from the employer. From this Engels concluded that if you do away with the right of inheritance which is founded on private property and give the women equal economic rights with men, then you dispense with the economic necessity of a family. If there were children from any unions, the state was to take charge of the education of the children. In that same work, Engels took love out of the will and put it into the glands, and then argued that "only a union based on love is moral; hence the union should last only as long as love lasts. When this love ceases to exist, or when it is succeeded by a new passion, divorce becomes a benefit."

When Russia became Communist and began to put this philosophy into practice, the Communist concept of morality was known as the "glass of water" theory. As Madam Kollontai, the Soviet Delegate to the League of Nations states: ". . . love is a glass of water one swallows to satisfy a thirst." You drink the water, and forget the glass, so you enjoy the pleasure, and forget the person. The Matrimonial Codes of 1918 and 1927 affirmed the law: "All children belong to the State." To this end, the family code of October 22, 1918, declared that all church marriages were invalid, and could be dissolved at the will of either party, simply by sending in a post card to the registration office, which in turn sent another post card dissolving the union. The Thirteenth Congress of the Communist Party even described the family as a "formidable stronghold of all the turpitudes of the old regime."

By a peculiar paradox, however, communism held the family collectively responsible for the anti-Sovietism of any of its members. "In the case of flight or the passing over the frontier by an adult soldier, the members of his family—if they have helped him in any way whatsoever, to prepare for and execute the treachery, or if they were merely aware of the fact but did not inform the authorities—are punished with the privation of their liberty for a period ranging from five to ten years, and with the sequestration of all their goods. The adult members of the traitor's family that remain, and who lived with him or who were maintained by him at the moment of the consummation of the crime, are deprived of electoral rights and are deported for five years to the most remote parts of Siberia."[1]

At the very beginning of the Communist Revolution in Russia a decree was passed declaring that all women between the ages of 17 and 32 became the "property of the State, and that the rights of husbands were abolished."[2] In keeping with the idea that liberation means working in a factory rather than in a home, we read in a Soviet book published in 1935: "Women's labor has become one of the main sources from which industry could draw fresh supplies of workers. During the earlier years of the first Five-Year Plan, there were about 6,000,000 housewives in the towns. All the local Communist organizations received orders to call up these reserves and attach them to production."[3] The women refused to accept what the Communists called "the emancipation for women from depressing domestic atmosphere," but they were ultimately forced into "emancipation" and began working in the mines and sewers, and in the manipulation of pneumatic drills. A few years ago 23 percent of the miners were women. The Soviet poets composed ballads for the women to sing as they were "released from socially unprofitable and exhausting domestic toil."[4]

> "Formerly women only knew how to cook soup
>   and porridge.
> Now they go to the foundry—
> At the foundry it is nicer."[5]

No reason was required for the separation of husband and wife, not even the permission of the other party. All distinction broke down between legitimate and illegitimate children. The young were encouraged to spy on their parents and report them to the Communist authorities at the least sign of Fascism and anti-communism. Inasmuch as the labor laws required that a person was obliged to accept any job given to him by the state, for under communism there is only one employer, it often happened that the husband was given a job in one city and the wife in another. The Labor Board settled this difficulty by decreeing that either spouse could find a partner in the new place of occupation. Abortion clinics were established by the state throughout the country, and every available means was used to weaken the family.

Soon Communist philosophy, which was already wrong in theory, because the family was not, as it alleged, founded on capitalism, now began to prove itself wrong in practice. Russia began counting heads, and those that should have been heads, and it was discovered that in Moscow alone only 57,000 children were born in 1934, while 154,000 abortions were performed. In the villages there were 242,979 births, but 324,194 abortions.[6]

This ratio of 3 to 1 in favor of death was accentuated by the divorces. *Izvestia* of July 4, 1935, stated: "In Moscow, in the first five months of 1935, there were 38 percent more divorces than registered marriages. In May, the number jumped to 44.3 percent. It is about time we declared that the frivolity in union is a crime, and that marital infidelity is an offense against the morals of a socialist regime. About 2.3 percent of divorced couples have children, and only 10 percent of such divorced parents can support them." Recorded divorces, of course, did not include the break-ups which never came to the attention of the authorities. Homeless children roamed the streets, stealing, assaulting and killing. The wife of Lenin estimated their number at 7,000,000. So great were crime and juvenile delinquency that a joint resolution of April 7, 1935, of the Central Executive Committee and the Council of People's Commissars of the U.S.S.R., one of them being Molotov, decreed a full measure of punishment for children over 12, while death in other cases was made mandatory.[7]

At this point the Communists began to repudiate communism. As Lenin once saw that collectivism was wrong, since it brought on starvation, and gave a measure of private property again to the people, so now the Soviets see that the disintegration of the family is the disintegration of the nation. Every single social practice it once propagated is now condemned: abortion, divorce, free love and even the death sentence. The State denies responsibility for children and affirms parental authority. Novels began appearing such as *The Third Front* of Shoubine, showing the evil effects of divorce and abortion, and reaffirming the maternal instinct too long ignored and repudiated. The Government ordered conferences to be held everywhere glorifying family life. The Communist press that ridiculed marriage 15 years before, now writes such editorials as: "One of the basic rules of Communist morals is the strengthening of the family. The right to divorce is not a right to sexual laxity.

A poor husband and father cannot be a good citizen. People who abuse the freedom of divorce should be punished." The official *Journal of the Commissariat of Justice* affirms the perpetuity of the marriage bond: "Marriage is of positive value only if the partners see in it a lifelong union. So-called free love is a bourgeois invention, and has nothing in common with the principles of conduct of a Soviet citizen. Moreover, marriage receives its full value for the State only if there is progeny, and the consorts experience the highest happiness of parenthood." The Soviet Government in 1936 began manufacturing wedding rings. Post-card divorces were abolished. Measures were taken to make divorce extremely difficult and rare. Fees for divorces were raised from 3 rubles to 2,000 rubles, in order that, as the Communist press stated: ". . . silly girls would think it over twice before marrying a man with 20 or 30 divorce records." The so-called "bourgeois" distinctions between legitimate and illegitimate children reappeared in Soviet Law.

"1. Prohibition of abortions. They are legal only when the life of the woman is endangered. The penalty is two years in prison for the physician and other responsible persons, and for the mother a public rebuke for the first offense and a fine of 300 rubles for the second.

"2. To combat gross irresponsibility in family relations, a divorce must be indicated in the passport. This is a Communist innovation.

"3. A noticeable increase in divorce fees. The first divorce costs 50 rubles, the second, 150, and the third, 300.

"4. Support. The father who deserts his children must pay one fourth of his earnings for one child, one third for two children, and 50 percent for three or more children: the penalty for the nonpayment of support is imprisonment up to two years.

"5. Upward revision of maternity benefits. Expectant mothers again receive eight weeks' leave before confinement and eight weeks after. They also receive an increase in financial aid. The contribution from the social insurance budget for the feeding of the child is raised from five rubles to 10. This increase is highly deceptive. In 1928 five rubles could buy 25 bottles of milk, but in 1937, 10 rubles could purchase only 10 to 12 bottles.

"6. As an effort toward the improvement of the material condition of the mother the social insurance fund will contribute a sum for the necessities of the new born. The indicated allowance is 45 rubles. Prior to the Five Year Plans the average allowance for this purpose was 20 rubles. Later it was increased to 32 rubles. From 1929 to 1937 the prices for all the needs of an infant, and particularly underwear, increased not less than five times. Therefore the 45 rubles were scarcely a guarantee of a 'happy motherhood.' In addition, the country which was overtaking and outstripping capitalism was lacking in the most essential of infant requirements. 'It is difficult to find a rubber nipple, adhesive plaster, a baby's bath or a tub for the infant's laundry.'"[8]

Abortion clinics were abolished as abortion became legally identified with homicide; anyone counseling abortion was sentenced to two years' imprisonment. Articles appeared in newspapers telling of its harmful effects. Children, who under the earlier Communist regime were told to spy on their parents, are now told: "One must respect and love his parents, even if they are old-fashioned and do not like the Young Communist League." Subsidies are paid to mothers with large families.

In August 1944 the Soviet press boasted that since the law against divorce went into effect there was not a single petition for divorce filed in the entire country. Taxes were imposed on spinsters, bachelors and families with less than three children.[9] *Pravda*, forgetting history and even present constitutions of Portugal and Ireland, boasted: "With us for the *first time in the history* of peoples and countries, motherhood became a matter of solicitude on the part of the State." Stalin began to have his pictures taken with children, and one day appeared in one of Moscow's gardens with his own children, the majority of Soviet citizens up to that time not knowing that he had any children.

The Communist publication, *Trud*, April 23, 1936, quoted Stolz, the President of the Commission of Jurists and Sociologists, who laid down the following reforms: "(a) Marriage is a social affair—until now divorce was always very easy. It is now time to make it more difficult, (b) The Soviet woman is the equal of man, but she is not dispensed from the great duty which nature has conferred upon her, namely, that of motherhood; her health is doubly precious, first as a human being, and then as a mother, (c) Abortion is inadmissible in a socialist country."

Izvestia of March 28, 1936, says some women immediately began adopting children and simulated pregnancy and went through the comedy of labor in order to fit better into the new party line. Thus Russia, after 20 years of communism in practice, rejects its entire Communist philosophy of the family, and without even intending to do so, proves that when we fail to obey God's laws, expressed in rational nature, we defeat ourselves, just as the man who uses a pencil to open a can, not only does not open the can but even destroys the pencil. There are two ways of knowing how true and good God is. One is by never leaving Him; the other is by abandoning Him, for in our ruin we rediscover that we dehumanize our hearts as we de-divinize our lives. When we pour religion out of the cup of life, every other draught put into the cup tastes bitter as wormwood. The women whom Lenin bade leave the hearth and the home for the mines and the monkey wrench are now told to return to their homes and be women. Those who glorified free love are told that free love is neither free nor love, but glandular egotism. But more important than this complete repudiation of its ideology is the generally ignored fact that by reaffirming the family as the unit of society, Communists rejected also the idea that the class is the foundation of society. As the Soviet Constitution quotes Sacred Scripture, and more explicitly St. Paul's Epistle to the Thessalonians, without knowing it, so now communism in its greatest defeat proclaims the victory of the family over the class, the person over the proletariat, the fireside and the child over the hammer and the sickle.

This changed attitude of Russia toward the family merits comparison with the materialism of the Western world. There is no doubt that the philosophy of America today regarding family life is just the same as Russia's between 1917 and 1935, namely, belief in divorce, free love and a queer system which in a compound word rejects both birth and control. Russia stopped decay of family in a single year, because it was a dictatorship and could enforce its decree with bullets, death sentences for twelve-year-old delinquents, concentration camps and secret police. America is a democracy; hence the only way—and the right way—we can arrest our dry rot is not by a Presidential decree, not by a uniform divorce law, not by handling the problem of juvenile delinquency in each new age without ever stopping it at its source—the home—but only by a conscience enlightened by religion and morality.

The disturbance of family life in America is more desperate than at any other period in our history. The family is the barometer of the nation. What the average home is, that is America. If the average home is living on credit, spending money lavishly, running into debt, then America will be a nation which will pile national debt on national debt, until the day of the Great Collapse. If the average husband and wife are not faithful to their marriage vows, then America will not insist on fidelity to the Atlantic Charter and the Four Freedoms. If there is a deliberate frustration of the fruits of love, then the nation will develop economic policies of plowing under cotton, throwing coffee into the sea, and frustrating nature for the sake of an economic price. If the husband and wife live only for self, and not for each other, if they fail to see that their individual happiness is conditioned on mutuality, then we shall have a country where capital and labor fight like husband and wife, both making social life barren and economic peace impossible. If the husband or wife permits outside solicitations to woo one away from the other, then we shall become a nation where alien philosophies will infiltrate as communism sweeps away that basic loyalty which was known as patriotism. If husband and wife live as if there is no God, then America shall have bureaucrats pleading for atheism as a national policy, repudiating the Declaration of Independence, and denying that all our rights and liberties come to us from God. It is the home which decides the nation. What happens in the family will happen later in Congress, the White House and the Supreme Court. Every country gets the kind of government it deserves. As we live in the home, so shall the nation live.

When the divorce rate in 30 major cities in our country is one divorce for every two marriages, when a nation has over 600,000 divorces compared with 2,285,500 marriages in one year, these are unmistakable signs that America is rotting from within. Added to this is the high incidence of rejections in our army. Among the applicants for the WACs, one-third were rejected because of neuroses and psychoses. Over 1,500,000 men were rejected by the Army for the same reason. The rise in homicide from 3.4 per 100,000 in 1900 to 6 in 1941 proves a distinctly antisocial state of mind. Mental disease due to alcohol has increased 500 percent since 1920. It is now a definitely established fact that many of the neuroses and psychoses in modern woman are due to her fear of motherhood, her flight from the fulfillment of the high vocation to which God called her. The reason, too, for the instability of man is due to a flight from fatherhood. Divorce is an expression of unhappiness, and it is always preceded by a state of mental disequilibrium. Eighty-three percent of the divorces in the United States come from marriages in which there are no children. Education is not the cure, because women with a college education are failing to reproduce themselves by 45 percent and high school graduates by 21 percent.

Unless America reverses the attitude toward the family and ceases to try to make a success in the domain wherein Russia proved to be a failure, then, apart from all moral and religious considerations, three disastrous consequences will follow. First of all, America will be in danger of becoming a nation of traitors. If the nation reaches a condition where 50 percent of the married couples feel that they can throw overboard pledged loyalty in order to suit their own pleasure or convenience, then the hour has struck when citizens will no longer feel a need to keep their pledges to America as citizens. Once there is a citizenry that does not feel bound to the most natural and most democratic of all self-governing commonwealths, the home, it will not be long until it no longer feels bound to a nation. When a

Mrs. White is ever ready to call herself Mrs. Brown, then it will be only a minute before Americans will be calling themselves Soviets. The traitors to the home today are the traitors to the nation tomorrow. If a husband and wife feel justified in disrupting a marriage because there has been some mismanagement in a home, then why not repudiate the nation because there has been some mismanagement in its government? It used to be that people stayed married and worked to resolve difficulties, because loyalties were final. In those days citizens felt it necessary to stay in a country even when it was badly run, in order to make it better. A people who are not loyal to a home will not be loyal to a flag.

A second possible danger to a nation that does not arrest the decay of the family is the creation of a mentality that will refuse to make sacrifices, suffer trials and inconveniences for the sake of the protection of our country. In families, each one learns to renounce the "mine" in the "ours" of the community. The family is a training school in self-discipline, the crushing of egotism for the sake of the group, and the learning of the supreme lesson of living with others for the sake of others. Just as the monks felt that the annoyances of monastic existence were self-inflicted, so formerly did the husband or wife, because they had chosen them "for better or for worse." But if there is the slightest disagreement resulting from eating crackers in bed in the present order, the marriage is broken. If a condition is revealed where separation is permitted because the other party fails to give pleasure, or because greener pastures make the present grazing less appealing, or because every whim, appetite and fancy has a right to be satisfied even at the cost of another person, then what shall happen to the spirit of sacrifice so necessary in time of crisis and conflict?

The fewer sacrifices a man is required to make, the more loath he is to make those few. His luxuries become necessities, children a burden and the ego a god. Whence will come our heroes of a nation, if we no longer have heroes in a home? If a man will not put up with the trials of a home, will he put up with the trials of a national crisis?

We still respect a soldier not because he is going into battle to die, but because he is ready to endure a torture, if need be, rather than surrender his honor. That is the way it used to be in a family; a husband or wife would put up with the failings of the other for the sake of the salvation of both, or because of a devotion to a vow. If a man can get a divorce because his wife is incompatible—and what two people in the world are completely compatible—then why should not a soldier desert his army or his nation because he has to take his K rations out of a can? When we were Christian, heroism was overshadowed by holiness, but as Christianity ceased to cast the shadow of the cross on the family, luxury and self-will took the place of it. Granted this, how shall we meet a barbarian power that has demanded and exacted bitter sacrifice from people for years? Once sacrifice is separated from the home, sacrifice is uprooted from its nation.

Only a nation that recognizes that sweat, toil, hardship and sacrifice are normal aspects of life, can save itself—and this is first learned in the home. If our birth rate should again decrease as it did 15 years ago, and that decrease should continue, would we not become the prey of other nations? History does not reveal the survival of a single nation with a declining birth rate in a moment of trial and crisis. On the occasion of the fall of France in 1940, a French general gave the failure of the family to perpetuate itself as the basic reason for the nation's debacle. In

150 B.C. Polybius, in writing about the decline of Greece, said: "For the evil of depopulation grew upon us rapidly, and without attracting our attention, by our men becoming perverted to a passion for show and money, and the pleasure of an evil life, and accordingly either not marrying at all, or if they did marry, refusing to rear children that were borne, or at most one or two out of great numbers, for the sake of leaving their well-being assured, and bringing them up in extravagant luxury. The result, houses are left heirless, and like swarms of flies, little by little, the cities became sparsely inhabited and weak."

The decline of populations always begins at the economic top; those who could most afford to have children do not. The group less economically blessed produces more. Soon the infection against the family spreads from those in high economic brackets to those below, and a civilization goes into a decline. There is no doubt that the State will claim more power for itself as the family declines, but the state and society are not identical. As the vital energy of society goes into a decline, the mechanized bureaucratic machinery grows by leaps and bounds. As softness and effeminacy take possession of a nation, other peoples become more envious of it, and it becomes the prey for lustful eyes and ravishing hands. America is not in danger from the outside, but it is in grave danger from the inside. The internal danger can become the source of external danger. Invasion was a possibility from the time Roman morals began to decline; it became an actuality when they reached a universal law. There is no reason to believe that the laws of history should operate in a different way as regards America.

Thirdly, the decline in family life is intrinsically bound up with the decline in democracy. Here democracy is understood in its philosophical sense as a system of government which recognizes the sovereign worth of man. From this flows the notion of the equality of all men, and the repudiation of all inequalities based on race, color and class. But where in all the world is this dogma of the worth of man better preserved and practiced than in the family? Everywhere else man may be reverenced and respected for what he can *do*—for his wealth, his power, his influence, his charm, but in the family a person is valued because he *is*. Existence is valued in the home, not possessions or influence. That is why the cripple, the sick and those who are of no economic value to the family are given more affection than those who normally provide for its subsistence. The family is the training school and the novitiate for democracy. When a nation ceases to put the highest value on the home, it will not be long before it ceases to put a value on a person. Soon a man will begin to be valued because of what he can do for a *revolutionary class*, and then comes communism.

When men and women reach a point where they are no longer interested in watching a seed that they have planted grow, or caring for its flower; when they are more concerned about increasing dollars in their bank account than obeying the primitive impulse to increase and multiply— then know ye that a night has dawned when a *thing* is more important than a *person*, and *Hic jacet* must be inscribed on the tombstone of democracy. Beyond and behind all the schemes and blueprints of politics and economics, there is nothing more fundamental to the revival of true democracy than the restoration of the family. In that circle shall our citizens learn that there is other wealth than paper wealth, paper money, paper stocks, paper joys, namely, the tingling, vibrating wealth of children, the unbreakable bond between husband and wife, the pledge of democracy and the future heirs of the Kingdom of Heaven.

But though Russia has turned from the class as the unit of the nation to the family, though it has sought to restore that which it once sought to destroy, it must not be assumed that it has done so out of either Christian reasons or out of obedience to natural law. Circumstances have forced the Soviet Government to the view that the nation cannot endure without the family, but this is not because it places a value on the family, but only on the survival of the Soviet system. Its advocacy of separate education of boys and girls is principally for the purpose of preparing boys for war. Education is primed not to the communication of truth but to the glorification of communism and Stalin. In 1935 Kirov published verses in which Stalin was envisaged as being able "to see through a wall and illumine the world like the sun." The official newspaper of the Communist Party in Russia published this hymn to Stalin by Ayak Bergen:

> He commands the sun of the enemies to set.
> > He spoke, and the East for friends became
> > a great glow.
> Should he say that coal turn white,
> > It will be as Stalin wills. . . .
> The master of the entire world—remember—
> > is now Stalin.[10]

Though Russia is restoring the family, and though America, according to Sorokin in his *Crisis of Our Age*, is tending to increasing disorganization of familial and marital patterns until marriage will be only the shadow of real union for life, it must not be forgotten that, from another point of view, America has far the better record. Firstly, America provides a higher standard of living for the family, and America does not in a mad rush of imperialism disrupt family life in other nations of the world. The United States Labor Department recently released a comparison of economic life in the United States and Soviet Russia, based on an official study of Soviet prices and wages. The Russian head of the family can buy for his weekly wage 23 loaves of bread, but the American can buy 390. The Russian worker can buy 17 pounds of sugar with his week's wages, but the American can buy 500 pounds. The Russian would have to spend every cent of his weekly wages to buy 16 quarts of milk, but the American could buy 275 quarts and get some change. The Russian can buy 10 pounds of beef with his income, but the American can buy 82 pounds.

More important than the standard of living is the fact that America has no concentration camps, while according to conservative figures Russia has 15,000,000 of its own citizens in prison camps. Though Russia prides itself in its new attitude toward the family, it destroys the family by forcible separation of husbands and wives in assignments to such camps. When for example, the Soviet took over Lithuania, there immediately began a wholesale disruption of family life. In the Varkuta concentration camp, which lies at the confluence of the Pechora and Usa rivers in the subarctic Northern Urals, there are 60,000 Latvians, 50,000 Estonians and 100,000 Lithuanians who work in the mines seven days a week, and those who fall below the quota imposed by the Stakhanovite system must be content with only ¾ of a pound of black bread a day. At the concentration camp of Bykomys in the Komi "autonomous" republic bordering on the Arctic Ocean, are Poles and Lithuanians who are called *Spetzposlentsky* or "special settlers" who never had any formal charge drawn up against them. They arise at 3:30 A.M. and work until

6:00 P.M. under the guard of MVD police. At night they sleep on wooden floor boards. In the gold mines along the Kolyma River more than 1,000,000 prisoners toil under the whip. When General Sikorski, the late Prime Minister of Poland, intervened for the Poles, Stalin retorted: "Why do you protest that there are 1,500,000 Poles in Siberia? I have 12,000,000 Russians there."

On October 7, 1946, all the clerks, technicians and skilled workers of the Polish coal mine Rozwar in Bytom (Upper Silesia) were ordered by the Soviets to appear in the local school. The MVD surrounded 2,000 of them, including 100 women. All were loaded in freight cars and deported to Russia. At Riga, 72 attempted to escape and were shot. In addition to this, in order to destroy the national and religious culture of the satellite states there is a mass importation of Asiatics to "atone for" the mass deportation of the Christians and the Jews. In the Polish Western territory, near the rivers Oder and Neisse, 1,250,000 acres were allotted to importees. In Estonia 53,397 people were deported during the first Soviet occupation, and during the second there has been such a decrease that out of the 974 doctors in the country now only 320 remain. One historical incident describing the break-up of a Polish family gives some idea of the tragedy in Eastern Europe if multiplied by tens of thousands.

"Natalia C., recounting this parting from the loved and familiar scene, tells how she rose early one morning, still full of sleep, to see her husband off to the town where he had some business. After the cows had been milked, she decided to lie down and to sleep again while the bread rose. As she was pinning a sheet across the window to darken the room, she saw her husband returning in the company of four men. They entered the house, and her husband with a deathly pale face smiled at her and the children. The children were aged six and four, Tomus, a boy, and Wandeczka, a girl. After a pretended search of the premises, the family were ordered to leave. The children, seeing their mother begin her preparations, broke into violent grief, dragging at her arms and legs and urging her to stay. When they saw that this was no use and that she was already seated in the cart, they climbed determinedly onto the cart themselves—'crawling to me,' she says, 'like worms' over the bundles and baggage on which she was seated. When they reached the station, the father was separated from them and put into another wagon. The mother hoped much that the train would leave in the night, for the track went round a low hill just beside the homestead, and she hoped that the children need not see it, and feel all their sorrow freshly burst out again. Unfortunately, the train left during the day. As the homestead came in sight, they saw neighbours and other members of the family standing on the hill and the parish priest with a crucifix in his hand. As the train approached, he raised and held out the crucifix in the sight of the first cars. The wife thought with joy that his blessing was falling on her husband who was in this part of the train. The crucifix shone in the sun. As the chimneys, the orchard, and the trees came clearly into sight, Tomus cried out in a terrible voice, 'Mammy, Mammy, our orchard, our pond! Mammy, our Gierba (the cow) grazing! Mammy, why do we have to go away?'"[11]

Along with the physical disruption of the family is the poisoning of youth by false propaganda such as the new "10 Communist Commandments" published for Polish youths and first issued by the Soviet headquarters in Novosibirsk in Soviet Siberia:

1. Never forget that the clergy is a declared enemy of the State and of Communism.
2. Try to convert your friends to Communism. Do not forget that Stalin, who gave to the Russian people its new constitution, is the leader of the anti-Gods, not only in the Soviet Union but throughout the world.
3. Try to persuade, but do not force, your friends to stop going to Church.
4. Watch out for spies; denounce sabotage.
5. Spread atheistic literature among the people.
6. Every good Komosol is also a militant atheist. He must know how to shoot and be expert in military discipline.
7. Work eagerly to prevent any religious element you may notice from influencing your neighbors.
8. Every atheist must be a good Communist. Watching the security of the State is the duty of every anti-God.
9. Support the Atheist Movement by financial gifts that will especially aid the propaganda of foreign organizations, obliged through circumstances to work in secret.
10. If you are not a convinced atheist you will not be a good Communist and a faithful citizen of the Soviet State. Atheism is permanently linked with Communism and the two ideals are the basis of Soviet power in Communist Russia.

CHAPTER EIGHT

Passion

The condition of receiving peace is the rebirth of passion. About the only time we ever hear the word "passion" is in a movie or a modern novel. But passion was once something real in the world. It was born on the fringes of the Roman Empire, on a hill called Calvary and on a Friday called Good. That passion was Love, Fire, Enthusiasm, its ecstatic peak appearing seven weeks later on Pentecost as tongues of fire, and then as martyrdom, mysticism, missionary activity and an apostolate that swept off the world the Greek ideal of moderation and the Roman indifference to truth. Men were so much devoured by this Passion of Love that they left homes to spread the Good News; young women became so absorbed that they set their hearts on divine espousals without the intermediary of the human. From generation to generation this torch of Passion was passed on, and millions have so loved their Lord that all the blandishments of earth could not make them turn from that possession which makes all other possessions vain.

This Passion made some want to give everything to the Divine Lover, and thus was born the vow of poverty. It also inspired the young to give the best that one has to God, and since the best is not in the body but in the soul, there was born the vow of chastity. It inspired others to dispossess their own wills so as to be identified with the will of the one loved, and thus was born the vow of obedience. This kind of fire is what Thompson calls the "passionless passion, a wild tranquillity," and the "love we fall just short of in all love."

Though this Passion still continues to dominate a few of the faithful, as far as the world is concerned Passion has now passed out of existence; our fires have gone out. The Western world became secular, if not atheistic, in a vague sort of way. Even though the Western bourgeois or liberal no longer went to Church, it seemed not quite cricket to him to change his cathedrals into godless museums; even though he refused to have religion taught in schools he still wanted his statesmen to talk about freedom of religion; even though he denied sin he still felt that selfishness could be overcome by education and labor-management relationship; though he never adored God, he felt that if a man wanted to adore Him, that was his privilege, just as it was his right to vote Republican or Democrat.

There is no more Passion, Zeal, Fire, but rather broad-mindedness, which is now considered the greatest of all virtues, as the man who cannot be made to make up his mind about anything is called broad, and he who has discovered a few principles to guide his life is condemned as narrow. Tolerance has degenerated into indifference to truth, as right and wrong, good and evil are given an equal footing. Once the world, like Pilate, gives Christ and Barabbas, virtue and vice, good and evil an equal hearing, and allows a vote to determine which will be chosen, there is no need to count the ballots. Goodness will invariably be led to a Cross. One wonders if the Crucifixion of Our Lord was not interpreted more kindly by Him than modern indifference to Truth. G. Studdert Kennedy compares Christ of Golgotha and Christ in the modern, broad-minded city of Birmingham.

> When Jesus came to Golgotha, they hanged
>   Him on a tree,
> They drove great nails through hands and feet, and
>   made a Calvary;
> They crowned Him with a crown of thorns,
>   red were His wounds and deep,
> For those were crude and cruel days, and human
>   flesh was cheap.
>
> When Jesus came to Birmingham they simply passed
>   Him by,
> They never hurt a hair of Him, they only let Him die;
> For men had grown more tender, and they would
>   not give Him pain,
> They only just passed down the street, and left Him
>   in the rain.
>
> Still Jesus cried, "Forgive them, for they know not
>   what they do,"
> And still it rained the winter rain that drenched Him
>   through and through;
> The crowds went home and left the streets
>   without a soul to see
> And Jesus crouched against a wall, and cried
>   for Calvary.[1]

The Crucifixion was more bearable than the broad-mindedness which was neither hot nor cold, and therefore that which God said He would vomit from His mouth. But the world could not long live without fire and passion. Why did Europe at the close of the First World War adopt the totalitarian systems of Nazism, Fascism and communism? Brown, black and red Fascisms never could have engulfed Germany, Italy and Russia if they had not had some basic appeal and did not satisfy a long pent-up yearning. The Western man might go on with indifference to religion, but it was never a stable condition. Tolerance always gives way to cynicism, and cynicism to persecution. No civilization can long remain indifferent to religion. Eventually men will either love it or hate it; the Nazis, the Fascists and the Communists made the decisive steps. They were not faint-hearted. If the Western world would believe in individual atheism they would be bold enough to make it corporate and official and put it into practice. Communism, Nazism and Fascism were revolts against half-hearted materialism in the name of total materialism; protests against individu-alism in the name of collectivity, the only difference among the three forms of totalitarianism being that Nazism ab-sorbed the person in the race, Fascism in the state, and communism in the class. All three systems represented re-volts against the disintegration of the world.

Never will we be able to understand our times if we naïvely think of these systems as the work of a few gangsters or the creation of a pack of criminals. The appeal of Na-zism, Fascism and communism was principally negative; they were protests against a milk-and-water liberalism, a spineless indifference to causes, a failure to recognize that nothing was evil enough to hate, and nothing was good enough to die for. The people of Europe wanted something

they had lost in giving up the Church; without ever knowing it, they wanted a faith, a religion, a belief in an absolute;
they wanted dogmas, infallibility, discipline, authority,
obedience and sacrifice; they wanted to relieve the boredom that comes from a false sense of freedom or license,
so they flocked to a dictator; they wanted a compulsory organization for the chaos resulting from a liberalism which
judged progress by the number of responsibilities and
self-restraints it had; they wanted pilgrimages, and since
they wrecked the Churches of the Virgin, they would replace them with tractor factories; they wanted to believe
there was something evil in the world; for some it was the
Jew, for others the capitalists, for others the Christians, for
others parliament, and for others democracy, but at least
it made them feel that life had a purpose, that a woman's
desire to give life could be sublimated by taking life as a military Amazon, and that sacrifice could be made for the sake
of the party, the class or the nations by receiving a bullet in
the back. Passion returned, fires burned again—though it
was a passion for a vague collectivity, which, Molochlike,
canceled out personal dignity, disqualified all moral values
and denied all celestial loyalties.

Totalitarianism gave the European man a religion; a
counter-church to supplant a Church, a faith to fight the
Faith; the inspired gospel of Marx for the abandoned Gospel of Mark; a god of earth for a God of Heaven, a new
mystical body with its visible head not in Rome but in
Moscow, infallible when he speaks ex cathedra on the subject of politics and economics; and also an invisible head
too terrible to be named. Germany, Italy and Russia were
right in wanting a change; they were wrong in their solutions. The prodigal son was right in being hungry; he was
wrong in living on husks.

That terrible void which Europe filled with totalitarian systems at the close of World War I now exists in the victorious nations at the close of this war. Why is youth inclined to be revolutionary? Not for a bad reason but for a good one. Youth is beginning to distrust the so-called liberal world that is trying vainly to preserve individual freedom in a social environment which has abandoned all moral and religious codes. It wants an absolute to take the place of the relative; it sees the inconsistency between sitting in a classroom and hearing a professor say there is no distinction between good and evil, and then being inducted into the armed services to die because there is a distinction between good and evil. Our young people see the shallowness of the emotional anesthesia of the optimists that everything will come out right in the end through evolution and education; they see the vanity of trying to maintain a respect for religion without ever practicing it; and that life is vain if they have to go on through the night as sleepwalkers lighting matches while the rest of the world is lighting torches.[2]

Modern youth wants what Europe wanted at the close of the last war—Passion, Fire, Enthusiasm. It too wants to believe that there is evil in the world, and that a man ought to fight against it. But unfortunately, both the capitalists and the Communists have convinced them that the only evil is in the economic order. As a result the Communists believe it is possible to combine a passion for social justice with a complete unconcern for individual righteousness. They have a social conscience to right the wrong of others but no individual conscience to right their own; they organize to combat the alleged wickedness of others, but dispense themselves from all personal obligation to morality, conscience and God. As long as they fight for the underprivileged they feel privileged to do all the wrong.

Thus does youth feel a merciless aggression against wrong which fills up the void made by the loss of the Grand Passion of Love, but which only increases the world's disorder, for now their fires burn their neighbors' houses and not the dross of their own hearts.

Our civilization is in the state described by Our Blessed Lord in the parable of the empty house. We have driven out a devil from the house of Europe, but because Goodness, Justice, Truth, Responsibility and Love did not occupy that house, seven other devils worse than the first have come to dwell there. We of the Western democracies have no faith, no philosophy of life, no common purpose. We knew what we hated when we went to war, but we cannot agree on what we love now that the war is over. Our emptiness has made us preys to the Great Dietitian who offers us Red Fascism, as an alcoholic will give to another alcoholic an extra drink to put him on his feet. It fills up the void though it fills it as a vulture might fill the nest of a robin. This tyranny would never have had an appeal in any other age, when the atmosphere of the world was still Christian. If it appeals now it is because, though we have turned from the Divine Light, we have not lost the need of it, but like moths burn ourselves in the tiny flame of totalitarian candles and firebrands.

How shall this passion and fire and enthusiasm for the new religion of totalitarianism be met? Humanism alone cannot restore the needed passion, first of all because no man has an intrinsic value except as a creature of God. If he is only a descendant of the beast, then nothing better can be expected of him than to act like a beast; if he is one with nature, and psychology is nothing else than physiology, then like all natural things he may be used as a means or a tool or a steppingstone. If man is essentially one with nature and not transcendent to it because possessing an immortal soul, then it is hard to see how the so-called human values differ from physical values. Once man is reduced to the one-plane level, there is nothing left to do but to organize him, and organization on a one-plane level ends in the dehumanization of man.

Without the revival of religion, there will be an ever widening gulf between culture and the masses, for faith has been in Western culture the only common ground between the two. Deprived of religion, a culture becomes snobbish and the masses become standardized and then victimized by uncultured leadership. As Berdyaev observes: "The upper intellectual class has long been living a closed and isolated life, deprived of any broad social basis and apart from the common life of the people."[3]

A passion can be conquered only by a passion; it takes faith to conquer faith; a dogma to match a dogma; a philosophy of life to combat a philosophy of life. At the present time all that we of the Western world have to offer to this new passion is a change in editorial policy, a shift in national moods as revealed by the Gallup poll or an occasional change in a cabinet member. Why is it that our diplomats of the Western world have been helpless before the apostles of the new passion? Certainly not because they were wanting in a desire to preserve some form of decency and order and freedom in the world. But simply because their position has been illogical from the beginning. *The Western world has been attempting to preserve the fruits of Christianity after having surrendered the roots.* It is trying to preserve respect for the dignity of man, human freedom and the inviolability of human rights, after having surrendered a belief in God Who gives man a dignity because he is made to His Image and Likeness; after having surrendered the spirit which is the foundation of freedom, and after having denied the Creator Who is the Author of our inviolable rights. In vain will our Western world try to keep crosses on the tops of its church steeples after having knocked out the foundations of the edifices. The position of the enemy is much stronger. It says to us: "You deny the fruits of democracy and Christian humanism just as we do. . . . Why then do you illogically try to preserve these things which are already baseless?"

The situation resolves itself down to this. Modern Christians have truth but no zeal; materialists have zeal but no truth; they have the heat but no light; we have the light but no heat; they have the passion but no ideals; we have the ideals but no passion. Neither of us is perfect. They sin against the Light, we sin against Love. Which of the two is more pleasing to the eyes of God? Our Lord told the story: "A certain man had two sons; and coming to the first, He said: Son, go work today in my vineyard. And he answering said: I will not. But afterwards, being moved with repentance, he went. And coming to the other, he said in like manner. And he answering said: I go, Sir; and he went not. Which of the two did the father's will?" (Matthew 21:28–31) Our Blessed Lord implied that it was the son who was at first unwilling to go, and then afterward went, who merited praise from Him. In like manner, it is we who claim to believe in Christianity, and in the existence of God, and in the moral law, and who nevertheless act not out of these beliefs who are to be condemned. Our crime is our unfulfilled Christian duty, our sprinkling the fires of passion with the cold waters of indifference, our mediocrity which blinds us to the fact that the day of broad-mindedness is over and that all humanity is in search of a soul.

Hitler once said: "Something has come to an end," and what has come to an end is the nonreligious phase of modern history based on materialism and positivism. The post-Renaissance chapter is closed; the era that man is the measure of all things has ended in disillusionment. The world is discovering it cannot live without a religion, and without an absolute, and that the days of neutrality and indifference and broad-mindedness are over; humanity is looking for God, and its choice is between a true or an ersatz religion. There will be no side lines; either man will burn with hate toward those who would prevent the building of the city of man on the ruins of the city of God, or they will burn with love for the destroyers themselves, and pray even among their ruins: "Father, forgive them, for they know not what they do."

Whence, it may be asked, comes this passion of communism for evil and for destruction and for violence? Can it be that the Pentecostal fires have been stolen by the forces of anti-God as their missionaries equal in zeal the very missionaries of the Gospel itself? Whence comes this spirit of sacrifice of Red Fascism by which they put off immediate gain for future profits and powers? How explain the fact that an antifaith has such a passion for its faith? The answer is: these enormous sacrifices are possible only because of the Christian influence left in the world, and because the Shadow of the Cross still falls across their path. Their passion is real only because they have caricatured the Great Passion of Him Who said: "Greater love than this no man hath, that a man lay down his life for his friends." (John 15:13) If this antireligious passion of Red Fascism ever succeeded in blotting Christianity out of the world, which is impossible, then Red Fascism itself would become impossible, for it would no longer be able to interpret service in terms of higher purposes. No longer would it have a great passion to imitate, no longer a great love to pervert.

The antireligious fervor of totalitarians comes only from religion; their blind obedience is a parody on submission to Divine Truth; their atheism would be silly if there were no God, for they would all be like Don Quixotes dueling with imaginary windmills. It is only the reality of God that gives fire to their atheism. They would be crazy if God were a figment of the imagination, but they are not crazy because they are fighting against something just as real as a sword thrust or an embrace. The truth of this statement is borne out by the fact that just as Red Fascism succeeds in its antireligious campaign in any one country of the world, all of its members lose enthusiasm, and settle down as spineless capitalists into Czarist palaces fulminating against capitalism from their ivory towers. It is the reality of Christianity which makes sense of their anti-Christianity, for the Devil would not be so busy if there were no God.

As Berdyaev, who knows the Russian soul so well, expressed it: ". . . the attainment of Communism demands the religious energy of the spirit, postulates the capacity for self-sacrifice in the service of a super-personal purpose. Where shall this spiritual energy be obtained, this capacity for sacrifice, this ability to devote oneself to high causes? When the religious springs of life are finally dried up, when under the influence of anti-religious propaganda the religious energy of the spirit is quenched, the realisation of Communism will become impossible, for no one will care to make the terrible sacrifices necessary, or to serve a super-personal aim. Although it is so hostile to Christianity and to religion in general, Communism is utilising the results of the Christian training of the spirit, the Christian formation of the soul. All the movements in the world, even when they take anti-Christian forms, are utilising the results of centuries of Christian influence. If these results were to be finally eradicated from the spirit of man, it would put an end to all his capacities for any sort of unselfish social effort; it would mean reducing man to the level of the beasts. No matter how much European Communism denies Christianity, it is living unconsciously on Christian elements. The recognition of the worth of each individual, the value of each human soul, freedom of conscience—all these truths are drawn from the Christian revelation. Once complete Christianity is denied—the Christian doctrine of man— there can be no argument against a return to slavery, against man's exploitation of man; nothing can prevent the apotheosis of unbridled force, quite merciless in its attitude toward the weak. And inasmuch as Communism breaks completely with Christianity, it permits the enslavement of man in the Communist State; it leaves room only for the strong, and is merciless toward the weak. But even for the realisation of its own anti-Christian purposes it needs the enthusiasm and unselfishness aroused by super-personal ideals. Communism is concerned with man; it must be realised by men; it demands not much, but all of man's powers. But in setting its aims it forgets about the individual and considers him as simply an instrument, just as in the capitalist system."[4]

For unless we of the Western world love someone more than ourselves, on whose side shall we stand when passions meet and lovers quarrel? History has reached a point now where the Pilates of the world bring out only two candidates, Christ and Barabbas. The day is at hand when we must choose, not between good things, but between spiritual leaders and spiritual demigods. In this conflict between the two passions, no counsels of optimism will have any relation to reality. The struggle is not between political systems for material mastery, but between religious systems for the human soul. The world is too far gone for any tinker to fix it, and all the political and economic solutions are basically forms of tinkering. Nothing short of a passion for truth, fiery enough to make our enemies call us dreamers and fools and fanatics, will save the world.[5]

Communism is a futile attempt to compensate psychologically for loss of faith. Man cannot long live without a Great Love, and having turned his back on Infinite Love, he staggered for a century with a tawdry love of self. But individualism or egocentrism produced boredom. Here is where the passion for communism comes into play for those who are not willing to return to the Passion of Divine Love. It gave him relief from the ennui produced by a license that was too exhausting. Freedom is man's only to give away. He will give it to public opinion, to a dictator, or to God—but give it away he will. Without knowing it, the man who understands liberty as freedom *from* something, and not freedom *for* something, produces a chaotic society. Communism in its first stages furthers license to produce chaos and then takes advantage of the chaos to seize power and enslave man. Never before in history did man escape boredom at so great a cost.

Another reason for the appeal of the passion of totalitarianism is the denial of human guilt. The psychological conditions for a dictatorship become present when vast numbers of our populations surrender all personal responsibility and are educated to believe that man is determined not from the inside, but the outside, by insufficient playgrounds, Grade B milk, naughty ductless glands, bad environment or a Narcissus complex. Modern education from Darwinism to Freudianism is geared to the denial of the fact that man has any sins to confess. All irresponsibility brings in its train the desire to be possessed; either by music which excites him viscerally, or by alcohol, sleeping tablets and noise, all of which help him to escape the responsibility of conscience. Once men admit themselves determined by alien influences outside the moral law written in their hearts, they become raw material for a propaganda of repetition which submerges them in the divinized power of the anonymous. As responsibility implies religion, so irresponsibility implies anti-religion, as the new collectivism gives the depersonalized men an object of worship in place of God. Totalitarianism grows in direct ratio and proportion to the decline of responsibility in the individual.

This loss of personal morality is compensated for by an intense devotion to social morality. Social conscience takes the place of individual conscience. That is why the followers of the new demonic mysticism feel that by blaming others they relieve themselves of blame; by liquidating certain persons guilty of injustice, they dispense themselves from the guilt of their own personal injustices. That too is why in all totalitarianism there goes hand in hand a great passion for social reform with a complete disinterest in the need of individual reform. By lifting the beam out of their neighbor's eyes, they need not be concerned with the mote in their own. Politics then becomes the new theology. Acceptance of an ideology becomes the measure of the Good Life rather than loving relationship to Life and Truth and Love. Denial of morality necessarily widens the area of evil, and every increase of evil clamors for a repressive power on the part of a dictator. The more refined and sensitive the conscience, the less there is need of coercive power. Only those who recognize personal morality are free. The old-fashioned and despised insistence on

individual holiness as a condition of social apostolate produced a far better social order than the present one based
on idealistic ideologies and antimoral actors in ideologies.
Communism is destined to fail precisely at this point: it
tries to force Love and Righteousness into the framework
of compulsory regulation and therefore destroys them.
The third reason for the appeal of the passion of totalitarianism is the need of social unity. When a civilization
loses a unifying philosophy of life and a common purpose,
like a body without a soul, it begins to break up into a thousand discordant and warring elements. For a while—and
this is the present tactic—an attempt is made to balance
opposing forces and keep them in equilibrium. Men then
begin to recognize the need of unity and authority. Having
surrendered a spiritual bond of unity, like to that which the
soul gives to the body, or morality to the state, they seek to
compensate for the loss by a compulsory organization from
without in the form of a dictatorship. The unity now comes
not from within—but from without like a whip. Thus does
a society which lost its faith in the authority of a Church
sneak authority back into society through the door of the
counterchurch, as Kant who exiled God through *pure reason*
sneaked him back through *practical reason*. Inner authority
based on the Truth of God revealing gives way to external
authority based on the party line of the dictator dictating.
Once inner faith is lost, a dictatorship becomes imperative to
reestablish some kind of order by force. Everyone is looking
for a way out other than by making himself better. Communism does have the merit of an all-out Passion, though its
great demerit is that its fires destroy but do not enlighten.
But both communism and monopolistic capitalism suffer
from the basic fallacy of thinking that if you change the externals you change the internals, and that if you paint the

bus, saints and not sinners will ride in it. One of the characters in *Brothers Karamazov* summarizes well the basic fallacy
of the Communist Passion. "They mean to build justly, but
by denying Christ, they will end by spilling blood over the
earth." Our greatest sins perhaps have not been so much
sins of commission, as sins of omission—the sin of not loving—the sin of which no one ever accuses himself.

Up to this time we have only dreamed that we wanted
God, and now we have nothing else in our hands but a
newspaper, and nothing in our ears but the din of a radio.
When shall our fires come back? They shall come back
when we realize why we have lost them, and we have lost
them for the same reason that Peter did. On one occasion
while the apostles were out in the midst of the sea during
the fourth watch of the night, the Divine Saviour came
to them walking upon the waters. Peter cried out, saying:
"Lord, if it be Thou, bid me come to Thee upon the water
and He said: 'Come,' and Peter going down out of the boat
walked upon the water to come to Jesus." (Matthew 14:28,
29) Then it was that Peter began to sink beneath the waters. Why did he sink? Sacred Scripture gives us the reason:
"Seeing the wind was strong." In other words, he began to
take account of the opposition, to measure the velocity of
the wind and the strength of the tempest. We are sinking
because like Peter we have concentrated our whole attention upon the winds of public opinion, upon the currents
of indifference, upon the military, economic and political
opposition from this quarter or from that. We are sinking
for the same reason that Peter sank: *We have taken our eyes
off the Master.*

Perhaps when we have sunk a little more because of
our want of faith and love, there shall well up out of our
hearts the cry of Peter: "Lord, save me." Out over the

troubled waters of the dark night, he felt the Hands of His Master taking hold of him, and heard a voice saying: "Oh, thou of little faith, why didst thou doubt?" Not until we, who drown in a stormier sea than Galilee, utter from the depths of our seeming ruin the same cry and plea will the winds cease. Then we will be gathered into the boat with the other apostles, saying with them as they did when the storm was over, "Indeed, Thou art the Son of God." Then our passion, as His Passion, will conquer the world, and the enemies of our passion will be at peace with us, for our victory will be not power, but the Love of God.

CHAPTER NINE

Russia and the Faith

It is part of the general confusion of our time to assume that when a man speaks against communism he thereby is anti-Russian. It is this confusion which must be dissipated. An ideology is distinct from a people. The ideology of Nazism has passed, but the German people survive. In like manner, Russia existed long before communism came into being, and will continue to exist long after communism has been forgotten. Communism is so little a part of the Russian people that it has existed only about 30 years in the almost 1,000 years of the Christian history of Russia.

Russian historians claim that Christianity was first preached to Russia by Saint Andrew who came into that country by way of the River Dnieper to a place which later on became Kiev. In support of this tradition there is the testimony of the early Church historian Eusebius,[1] who tells us that Saint Andrew preached to the Scythian nations. The official date given for the conversion of Russia dates from the baptism of the Emperor Vladimir in 988, though

a great number of his people were baptized before him.[2] At
the time of the conversion of Russia, the Greek and Roman
Churches were one, though there was a temporary schism
under Photius (857). The missionaries from the Western
Church traveled freely in Russia to propagate the Christian
Faith and were invariably well received by Vladimir. No-
table among those who came was a monk from Ratisbon
by the name of Mauritius; later on there came Bruno, who
was famous for his miracles. He was martyred later while
preaching the Faith to the Russians, who later dedicated
a monastery to him. After Bruno came Boniface, who became known as the apostle of Russia.

The breach between the Eastern and Western Church
became final at the time of Cerularius (1053), but Russia
did not break off with the unity of the Church at this time.
This is evident from the following facts: the two Cardinals
and the Archbishop carrying the Bull of Excommunication
against Cerularius from Leo IX passed through Russia on
the way to Constantinople and returned to Rome through
that same country. Furthermore, 30 years after the rup-
ture between the Eastern and the Western Churches, Pope
Urban II intervened to save the body of the Russian Saint
Nicholas from desecration at the hands of the Moham-
medan invaders, and had it transferred to Bari in Italy on
the ninth of May, 1089. The Russian Church then introduced into its liturgy a feast commemorating the transfer
of the relics of that saint. That a feeling of cordiality still
existed between Russia and the Western Church is evident
from the fact that in 1097 a pilgrimage to the Holy Land
was organized under the Latin king of Jerusalem, Bald-
win I, and many Russians went on this pilgrimage under
Metropolitan Nicholas. In 1073 the Russians complained
to the Latin Church about the injustices of the Poles who

apparently had stolen some money from Russia. This appeal to their spiritual leader vindicated the Russians as Gregory VII in 1073, in a communication to King Boleslaw, asked: "in the name of God and according to justice" that the stolen money be restored.

Though Russia continued to have relations with the Holy See until well after the fall of Constantinople, there were a few historical events that acted as a kind of "iron curtain" between the East and the West. The most important of these events was the Tartar invasion which came at the very time that Western civilization was flourishing in the riches of Thomas Aquinas, Bonaventure, Dominic, Francis and the Gothic Cathedrals. This domination of Russia by the Tartars lasted about 240 years. The Holy See was greatly concerned with the threat to Russian civilization and Innocent IV called upon Poland to resist the Western advance of the pagan hordes. Inside of Russia at the same time there was a growing tendency on the part of the political rulers to take over the power of the Church and to discourage any interference on the part of the Patriarchs. Finally, Ivan IV (1533–1584) assumed the title of "Father of the Church and State." After the fall of Constantinople (1453) when the Patriarchs of Jerusalem and Antioch and Constantinople came into Russia, they formally acknowledged the Czar as the protector of Christianity. From this time on archbishops and bishops literally became enslaved to the Czar. At the ceremony of coronation the Czar himself placed the crown on his own head, and opened the Sanctuary door, took bread and wine from the altar and communicated with the bishops and priests. Reunion with the Western Church was now made impossible because of the opposition on the part of the Czars.

There were several attempts at reunion; one was the Council of Lyons in 1274. Russia, then under the domination of the Tartars, did not participate in this Council. On the way to Lyons to take part in the Council Saint Thomas Aquinas died. Another attempt was made at the Council of Florence in 1437. The political conditions were now ripe for reunion inasmuch as the Eastern Church was in danger of invasion by the Turks. The Greek Church was then most enthusiastic for the articles of reunion, and one of the leading Greeks in the Council was Isadore, who had become Metropolitan of Russia in 1431. Accompanied by 100 delegates, Isadore journeyed for 20 days less than a year and finally arrived at Florence. In 1439, before Isadore left Rome, he was created a Cardinal and was appointed by the Holy See as Papal Legate to Lithuania, Russia and Poland. On his return to Moscow on the nineteenth of March, 1441, prayers were offered for the Church and the State. The deacon pronounced the prayer for the Holy Father Eugene IV. The Czar then imprisoned Cardinal Isadore, though he finally was allowed to escape and seek asylum in Rome. In 1589 Moscow became the center of the Eastern Faith when its Metropolitan was raised to the rank of a Patriarch with the sanction of four Eastern Patriarchs.

During five centuries after the Tartar invasion Russia had very little contact with the Western world. Then in 1702, Peter the Great opened the windows of Russia upon the West. After a visit to Europe which lasted almost a year, he brought back the idea of the lay government of the Church, and in 1721 ordered the institution of the Holy Synod which continued until the time of the Bolshevik Revolution in 1917. In 1897, the religious census of Russia revealed that the Greek Orthodox constituted 71 percent of the population, the Roman Catholics 9 percent, the Mohammedans 9 percent, Protestants 5 percent, Jews 3 percent. The remainder was distributed between Old Believers and other minor sects.

In the first years of the Bolshevik Revolution the Communists officially published figures concerning religion in which they revealed that between 1918 and 1919, 30 bishops and 1,414 priests were executed. The unofficial figures given out by the Cheka stated that during that same period there were killed 2,691 priests, 1,962 monks, 3,447 nuns and clerics, and 8,100 Orthodox clergy.

At the time of Hitler's invasion of Russia after 24 years of the Soviet Regime, Russia had lost:

> 75 % of the bishops
> 90% of the priests, the number falling from
>   50,960 to 5,665
> 96% of the monasteries, falling from 11,926 to 37
> 90% of the Churches, falling from 40,474 to 4,225

The Catholic Church in 1936 stated that none of the eight bishops serving in 1917 was alive; only 10 of the 810 priests had survived; and only 11 out of 410 Churches were open.[3] After almost 30 years of religious persecution Yaroslavsky, the head of the Society of Militant Atheists, announced in 1937 that two-thirds of the village population and one-third of the city population still believed in God.

During and following the war there came a change in Russian policy toward religion, dictated partly by a desire to use the Russian Orthodox elements in Russia as a political instrument for pan-Slavism, and partly to win over by a pretended favoritism toward religion the dissident elements in the nations which it absorbed. On the thirty-first of January, 1945, the Commissars in charge of the administration of the Russian Orthodox Church conceded the following rights to the Church inside Russia:

To arrange prayer meetings
To administer property in the form of a loan from local Soviet authority
To conclude civil law agreements in connection with the administration of the cult and property
To take part in religious conferences
To appoint ministers of the cult for the performance of religious duties.

On the other hand, however, the legislation did not recognize the Church as a legal person, nor did it grant those rights essential for the conduct of freedom of religion: The Church has no right:

To own property
To administer public or private instructions to children under 18
To publish books on religious instructions
To discharge many other functions which are prescribed by Canon Law.

Simultaneously with the granting of these concessions to the Russian Orthodox Church there developed in a parallel fashion attacks upon the Catholic Church. This was due in part to an identification of Russian foreign policy with the activities of the Russian Orthodox Church. The Patriarch wrote to Stalin at this time stating: "In these days of tense struggle of peace-loving humanity against sanguinary Fascism, our Church gives itself *wholly* to the service of the dear mother land." Outside of Russia, the Orthodox Churches of the world are divided into two groups, the anti-Moscow group and the Moscow group.

The Soviet attitude toward religion is most clearly revealed in the persecution it visits upon all Catholics in its satellite states. This does not mean to say that others are not persecuted for other reasons, such as want of sympathy with the Soviet authorities. Cardinal Mindzsenthy, the Primate of Hungary, recently stated in a Pastoral: "So many souls are deprived of Faith, hope and charity that the light of Faith does not illuminate them, neither does belief in the Eternal Life thrill them, nor the warmth of charity comfort them. They sit in darkness and live in the shadow of death." Many of the Benedictine, Franciscan, Cistercian and Piarist schools in that country have been closed and the Catholic University Federation has been dissolved by the Communists. They have forbidden the publication of Catholic textbooks and are now preparing new Communist textbooks for schools. They are preparing a new method of automatic divorce when the couple have lived apart for two years. In order to convince the people of Hungary that they are not opposed to the practice of religion, the Communists have asked that all their members attend Mass on Sunday.

On July 12, 1920, the Soviet Government signed a peace treaty with Lithuania in which Russia stated: "Russia, without any prejudice, recognizes the self-rule and independence of the State of Lithuania with all its juridical consequences . . . and *for all time* denounces with good will all the sovereignty rights of Russia which it has had in regard to the Lithuanian nation or territory." Despite this treaty and the nonaggression pact of September 28, 1926, the Soviet Union occupied Lithuania on the fifteenth of June, 1945, and since has absorbed it into the Soviet Republic. During the first occupation extending from June 15, 1940, to June 22, 1941, the Soviets deported to Siberia

34,260 Lithuanians. In the town of Czerverne, 6,000 persons were shot by the NKVD during the short occupation. During the second occupation, the Soviets deported within the first few months 80,000 to Siberia. The *New York Herald Tribune* of December 1, 1946, reported that Russia had sent 115,000 to labor camps. One of the underground newspapers of Lithuania recently stated: "Every day we suffer the brutalities of the Bolsheviks by paying with the blood of our brethren and the cries of the innocent people who are being deported and murdered. We wonder whether the world knows about our sufferings, and our difficult and heroic struggle for the right and freedom of mankind to democratic ideals which the leaders of the Western democracies have proclaimed. Every drop of our blood spilled in the fight against the Bolshevik tyranny is a sacrifice not only for Lithuania's freedom, but also for the world." In Vilnius, according to the Lithuanian Legation in Washington, the Red Army detachment numbers 50,000 soldiers; in Kaunas there are 80,000; in the city of Siaulia there are 20,000. Scattered throughout the country there are 50,000 members of the dreaded MVD.

In the Soviet zone of Germany, clergy are spied on constantly. Nowhere in the territories under Soviet jurisdiction have any religious publications been licensed. This applies to both the Protestant and the Catholic Churches. The six Catholic parishes of Leipzig are not permitted to promote any kind of religious activity outside of the Church. Cardinal von Preysing protested against "unlawful deportations and arrests. . . . I raise my voice to ask for justice. I am thinking of the thousands and thousands of civil internees who in many cases have been deported without their families having been given any notice. I am thinking with sorrow that it has not been possible in my diocese to send priests into their camps, and I am in great distress about the lot of parents in Berlin whose children and young people have disappeared for over a year without any news and without reason." The Cardinal goes on to say that there is no record of a court holding trial for these children, and he puts it down to the same type of injustice which prohibits religious instructions in schools.

As a result of the Soviet annexation of the eastern part of Poland, the Church lost nine dioceses, 7,000,000 faithful, 5,000 priests, 4,300 churches and chapels. In the city of Lwów, the last Catholic church permitted to remain open by the Communists was closed.

In Yugoslavia under Tito there is also the typical Soviet suppression of religion. In 1939 Yugoslavia had 1,916 Catholic parishes; now it has only 394. In Macedonia not one Catholic parish remains. One hundred and sixty-eight priests have been arrested without any judicial formalities; 32 have been sentenced to long prison terms; 85 are under arrest waiting for trial; and 409 have been deported to concentration camps. Equally sad and tragic is the persecution of the Ruthenian Church which once thrived in the Western Ukraine. On the eleventh of April, 1944, the Soviets arrested all the Catholic Bishops and closed all schools and seminaries under the pretext that the Church needed administration. The Soviets set up a "Committee for Initiative" which was presided over by three apostate priests. These three apostate priests sounded out the 2,700 priests of Ruthenia, told them that they would not be deported on condition that they left the Church and allied themselves with the Soviet Church of Moscow. Only 42 of the 2,700 submitted and a few of these later on repented. Pope Pius XII on the twenty-third of December, 1945, addressed to the Ruthenian Catholics a Pastoral letter which was full of forebodings: "We are not unaware that most dangerous snares are being set for your Faith, and in truth there is reason to fear, it seems, that still greater trials will befall those who refuse to betray their sacrosanct religious heritage."

It would be beyond the scope of this book to enumerate the extent and the intensity of the persecution that is being visited upon the peoples of Eastern Europe who are guilty of only two "crimes": believing in God and believing in freedom. The world saw unspeakable horrors of persecution during the Nazi regime. It is now witnessing even greater horrors under the Soviet system. Some vague hint of the torture that is being inflicted upon helpless millions of people in the eastern part of Europe is to be found in the case histories of innumerable Poles which are recorded in *The Dark Side of the Moon*. For obvious reasons the author remains anonymous, but the preface of this documentary history has been written by the distinguished poet, T. S. Eliot. There is every reason to believe that there are more martyrs now for the Christian Faith in a single year than during any 25 years of the Roman persecutions of the first three centuries.

Now we turn to the other side of the picture, for there is another side, thanks to the distinction between an ideology and a people. This distinction made here between communism and Russia has its basis in the Christian distinction between the sin and the sinner: one can hate communism as an evil system, but still love the Communists as creatures made to the image and likeness of God. The Church has never once condemned communism without at the same time speaking of its affection for Russia. For example Pius XI, on February 2, 1930, wrote an Encyclical entitled *The Soviet Campaign Against God*, the major portion of which was concerned with prayers for Russia: "We approved and enriched with indulgences the ejaculatory prayer 'O Saviour of the world, Save Russia,' and again in the course of the last few months, two forms of prayer in which the people of Russia are commended to the protection of the sweet wonder worker of Lisieux, St. Theresa of the Infant Jesus." A later Encyclical directed against atheistic communism on the nineteenth of March, 1937, ends with these words: "We pray the Lord to enlighten the Russian people, that they may abandon the slippery path which will precipitate one and all to ruin and catastrophe, and that they recognize that Jesus Christ, Our Lord, is their only Saviour, for there is no other name under heaven given to man whereby we must be saved." All the prayers said at the end of every low Mass in Catholic churches daily throughout the entire world, are said for the intention of Russia. It was in 1930 that the Holy Father ordered that these prayers, which up to that point had been said for the settlement of the Lateran question, should now be said for the conversion of Russia. This means that now as ever in the past, the Church is willing to accept the erring into the treasury of her souls, but never the error into the treasury of her wisdom.

Two points are to be noted about the Russian people: first, their prophetic forebodings in the nineteenth century of twentieth-century godlessness, and secondly, their spiritual traits which are a basis of hope for world peace.

There has been a deep-seated tradition in Russia that it would one day become very wicked before it would ever become very good. Nineteenth-century Russia, which might be called the twilight of communism, foresaw the terrible upheaval. Unlike the Western writers who were babbling inevitable progress, the Russian writers were full of warning about bourgeois, materialistic civilization. Not shackled by standardized conventions, they saw more deeply the mystery of life and death. Leontiev believed the mission of the Russian people was to beget the anti-Christ. He foresaw the revolution as a tyrannical and bloody one, attracting the people of the East and then going on to annihilate the bourgeois world of the West, bringing not the end of the world, but the end of the epoch of materialism, nationalism and liberalism. Pecherin believed that Russia would bring "its own annihilation" for which one would hate his country for a time, but in the end it would inaugurate a new cycle of world history. Pushkin foresaw the possibility "of a Russian revolt senseless and merciless" but in the end freedom rising on "her light-shedding wings." Lermontov in his poem *Prediction* written in 1830 foretold the revolution given in Gorodetzsky's treatise:

> The day will come, for Russia that dark day
> When the Tsar's diadem will fall, and they,
> Rabble who loved him once, will love no more,
> And many will subsist on death and gore.
> Downtrodden law no shelter will provide
> For child or guiltless woman. Plague will ride
> From stinking corpses through the grief-struck land
> Where fluttering rags from cottages demand
> Help none can give. A famine's gnawing pangs
> Will grip the countryside with ruthless fangs.
> Dawn on the streams will shed a crimson light.
> And then will be revealed the Man of might
> Whom thou wilt know; and thou wilt understand
> Wherefore a shining blade is in his hand.
> Sorrow will be thy lot, grief melt thine eyes
> And he will laugh at all thy tears and sighs.

Tyutchev feared the dark, irrational elements in Russia would bring a catastrophe and foresaw Christianity as its saving power:

> A homeless orphan, man, bereft of power
> And naked, stands before the dread abyss,
> Stands face to face in this his direful hour
> With its dark emptiness: and all that quickens,
> Glad things and light seem now a dream long past;
> 'Tis unfamiliar things, unsolved, as darkness thickens
> Reveal his fated heritage at last.

Chaadaev foresaw the triumph of barbarism in Russia, saying: "It will triumph not because it is right, but because we are wrong." Dostoevsky, in *The Possessed*, studied all the phases of man's rebellion against his Creator, concluding that the denial of God meant the deification of man. Evil degenerates into arbitrary self-will and finally to the setting up of oneself as arbitrary law. "Boundless liberty leads to a boundless tyranny." Atheism brings man face to face with dark, irrational forces and finally suicide. Kirilov reaches this conclusion: "The whole of history is divided into two parts; the first from the gorilla to the destruction of God, the second from the destruction of God to the change of the earth and of man. Everyone who wants to attain complete freedom must be daring enough to kill himself. Who dares to kill himself becomes God."

The revolution that Dostoevsky saw coming was to him not a result of external forces, but an indication of a fracture of man's original relationship with God and His creatures. It would take on the form of socialism which is "concerned with atheism, a modern incarnation of godlessness, the tower of Babel built without God, not to raise earth to heaven, but to bring heaven to earth." Dostoevsky makes the Devil tell how socialism will organize everything: "We shall make them work, but in their spare time we shall organize their life like a children's game. . . . We shall allow them even sin, knowing they are so weak and helpless." Socialism was the escape from the burden of responsibility. Dostoevsky predicted that Russia would undergo the "temptation of bread and power" of a godless social teaching. It would almost seem that he was writing in the twentieth century as he describes how the godless regime would work: "Every member of society spies on the others, and it is his duty to inform against them . . . all are slaves, and equal in their slavery. Cicero will have his tongue cut out, Copernicus will have his eyes put out, Shakespeare will be stoned . . . slaves are bound to be equal. . . . A teacher who laughs with children at their God, and at their cradle is on our side; the lawyer who defends an educated murderer because he is more cultured than his victims and could not help murdering them to get money is one of us; the school boys who murder a peasant for the sake of sensation are ours; the juries who acquit every criminal are ours; the prosecutor who trembles in court because he fears he shall not be liberal enough is ours; among officials and literary men we have many adherents, and they don't know it themselves. . . . We will proclaim destruction, we will set fires going, we will set legends going, every scurvy group will be of use. Well there will be an upheaval; there's going to be such an upset as the world has never seen before. Russia will be overwhelmed with darkness, and the earth will weep for its gods." But he never saw communism as the final master of his country. *In the Journal of an Author,* published in 1881, he wrote: "Not in Communism, not in its mechanical forms is contained the Socialism of the Russian people. They believe that the final salvation and the all-illumining unity is in Christ and in Him alone. . . . The Russian people bear the image of Christ, and love Him alone."

Another Russian writer of the eighteenth century who saw both tragedy and hope ahead for Russia was Alexi Khomiakov. The triumph of individualism in the Western world meant for him not progress but degradation. "Modern society in its decay releases every individual to the freedom of his own impotence." Russia was taking too many lessons from the Western world which had forgotten its God, and was becoming "like a ship, on board of which only German words of command are heard." After a phase in which a godless fanaticism would possess Russia, he saw a dawn when Russia would give the Faith to Europe and be the medium of uniting Europe and Asia. He did not expect to see that day but believed it would come: "We must remember that not one of us will survive until the time of the harvest, but that our spiritual and ascetic labors of plowing, sowing and weeding are not for Russia's sake alone, but for the sake of the whole world. This thought alone can give permanence to our efforts. Russian life holds many treasures, not for her own people, but for many others, if not for all nations."

Soloviev, who died at the close of the last century, contended that the godless man had his origin in the rationalism and secularism of the Western world. Under its impact the Eastern people would degenerate into passive resignation to dictatorship. The Western people would become arrogant and proud. Despite the fact that he saw a vision of catastrophe ahead for the world because of its godlessness, he nevertheless believed that "Russia has a religious calling of world-wide significance. In the poverty and humiliation of her people are the signs of her special vocation."

Dostoevsky best expressed the evil and the goodness in Russia in the terms of a young man in the land of the Gerasenes. "All the sores, all the foul contagions, all the impurities, all the devils great and small, have multiplied in that great invalid our beloved Russia." But recalling that as the devil was cast out of the young man into the swine, which then plunged themselves into the sea, so the devils of Russia "will cast themselves down, possessed and raving, from the rocks into the sea, and we shall all be drowned— and a good thing too, for that is all we are fit for, but Russia will be healed and will sit at the feet of Jesus and will look upon Him with astonishment. . . . Sin is a stench, but stench will pass when the sun rises. Sin is transient; Christ is eternal; our people are subject to many sins, but they have only one idea, only one true love, and that is Christ."

There are three great qualities of the Russian soul[4] which warrant optimism as to the future brilliance of Russia: deep religious feeling, capacity for pain and suffering, and fellowship.

First, deep religious feeling. Atheism is not natural to the Russian people; rather it has been an importation from the Western world. The Russian people have never been concerned with the problem of atheism, but only the problem of God's dealing with men in a sinful world. Russian writers and philosophers have seen in their country's persecution of religion only its attempt to ignore the truth. What is it that gives substance to the violence of their atheism if it be not the reality of the object which is attacked? Could men espouse prohibition unless there was something to prohibit; could there be anti-Christians unless there were Christians? How could there be atheists unless there were something to "atheate"? All atheists would be fools fighting against imaginary windmills if God did not exist. They are capable of denouncing sacred ideals, of blaspheming and deriding the truth they have worshiped, only because fundamentally they believe in God. Men cannot be so violent against myths. Only the reality of the Christ Whom they hate saves them from being fools fighting a figment of the imagination. Whence comes their idea of the communion of all men in one body, which is so foreign to Western individualism, if it be not from the very religion they attack? Whence comes the idea of the brotherhood of men, of equal worth of all classes, so foreign to pagan Greece and liberal Europe, if it be not from Christianity whose fundamental doctrine they stole only to caricature? Dostoevsky tells the story of a Russian peasant who fires a shot at the Host in the Eucharist. This reveals not only how little Christ's followers could expect mercy at the hands of that kind of an enemy, but it also reveals the astonishing power of faith in the persecutors. They believe in God, but being unable to love Him, they want to attack Him and destroy all those who dare worship Him, like a man who cannot love a woman whom he knows to be good, so he begins to hate her.

The basic reason why communism appealed to Russia was religious. Deeply imbedded in the Russian soul were passionate religious convictions: the universal vocation of Russia to call all men to brotherhood, the need of sacrifice and pain to accomplish this mission, and the supreme need of resigning oneself to God's will. Communism in the face of a declining Church promised the people the realization of these three ideals, but without clearly telling them that they would be emptied of God. Brotherhood became a revolutionary proletariat; sacrifice became violence, and the Will of God became the will of the dictator. Communism is a religion, a surrender to an absolute. That is why it appeals to those who are without faith, and why *Soviet Russia is today regarded as the last hope of the Western man who lives without God*. As communism fills up the void in the Western world created by a loss of faith, so it filled up the void in Russia made by a secularized or state church. The Russian mind will not long remain satisfied with either atheism or a church that becomes the instrument of a Communist ideology. As Khomiakov said: "We Russians do not belong to this doomed world," and their failure to become atheistic after 30 years of persecution proves that they possess a power for spiritual resistance which makes them the natural allies of their suffering brethren in the eastern part of Europe. Did but the Western democracies think less of political categories and more about spiritual realities, they would see a great bond existing between themselves and the Russian people. Not in the realm of war, but of the spirit, the solution of the problem is to be found.

Russia's capacity for pain and suffering is insatiable. It is a paradox, but nevertheless true that the Russian soul is never completely happy unless its cup contains a few drops of the bitter draught of pain. While the Western Christian world emphasized the glory of the ascended Christ, Russia in its history has rather stressed the emptied Christ.[5] As Nekrasov put it:

> But only a Crown of Thorns
>   suited thy sullen beauty. . . .
> Thou lovest the sufferer, O Russian folk,
>   the sufferings made us one.

The Western world has stressed the Glorified Christ, but the Russian Church has stressed the Suffering Christ, or the Christ of the Transfiguration, Who in the midst of His anticipated glory spoke to Moses and Elias of His

Death. Many of the Russian churches in the north are dedicated to the Transfiguration, bearing witness to the need of sacrifice as the condition of betterment. Their word for ugliness, violence and disorder is "besobrazie," meaning "that which lost its image."

Even the very endurance, readiness for sacrifice, and power of faith that are revealed in the Russian Communists are a proof that they come from a dynamism of a soul far more intense than that of the dechristianized and disillusioned modern man of the Western world. Turgenev in the *Living Relic* tells of Lukera, the village beauty and best singer, who fell by accident from a staircase. Withered and paralyzed, left alone in a remote hut, hardly ever visited by anyone, she is all love and praise of God. Refusing to pray to be healed she asks: "Why should I worry the Lord God? What can I ask of Him? He knows better than I do what I need. He sent me a Cross which signifies that He loves me. We are commanded to understand it so." Asked if she wanted anything she answered: "I want nothing. I am content with everything, thank God, but you ought to persuade your mother to reduce the rent of the peasants."

It is no great mystery where the self-sacrifice of Russian communism has its font and origin. Although it is hostile to Christianity, communism is using the 1000-year-old Christian training of the Russian soul in the spirit of self-sacrifice and self-discipline. It is only because the shadow of Christ's Cross still falls across Russia that men are inspired to self-denial for a suprapersonal cause. Whether it knows it or not, communism is living on Calvary's heritage, still so deep in the souls of the peasants—the very word in Russian meaning "Christian." If the impossible ever came to pass, that Christianity should be blotted out of the world, even communism would lose its inspiration for sacrifice.

No transfiguration of the soul or society is possible without descent into the abyss, where sin is purged away, as the Cross becomes the prelude to the crown. Thus while communism attacks Christianity, it does so only by utilizing the very forces which Christianity has supplied. It was this that Soloviev had in mind when he said that the "poverty and humiliation are the signs of its special pre-election to a religious calling of world-wide significance." As the Christ by the example of His Love transformed the blasphemies of a suffering thief into a request for a heavenly kingdom, so too a day may dawn when another blasphemer with a capacity for pain will be lifted up by that same Christ, to hear the blessed words: "This day . . . Paradise."

There may then be verified the truth contained in the poem of Alexander Blok, who the very year after the Bolshevik revolution pictures the soldiers of the Red Army going through the country chanting: "Freedom, Freedom, hey, hey, Freedom without a Cross." They shoot a bourgeoise girl who happens to be unfaithful. A little noise disturbs them, and a half-vision moves in front of them; they can see nobody distinctly, and they receive no answer, so they fire in the dark. The poet continues:

> So they go with sovereign tread . . .
> Behind them a hungry cur,
> And at their head, with a bloodstained banner
> Invisible in the raging snow,
> Unwounded midst the bullets' flight,
> With gentle gait above the storm,
> Scattered o'er with pearls of snow,
> With a white aureole of roses,
> At their head goes Jesus Christ.

The third characteristic of the Russian people is a deep
sense of fellowship and solidarity with their fellow man. The
Western world is inclined to be individualistic in religion. A
society begins to decay when it "releases every individual to
the freedom of his own impotence." One of the most common words of the Russian language is "Sobornost," which
means the transcendence of all petty categories, races and
classes for the sake of humanity. It was natural for communism, with its emphasis on the collectivity to arise as an ersatz
and substitute for the Christian spirit of fraternity which
possessed the Russian soul for centuries. One finds something of this symphonic spirit in which all work together, in
the Russian writer Gogol. In his work *The Cloak* he tells of a
stupid clerk who, when teased in his office, used to ask: "Am
I not your brother?" One meets it also in Tolstoy's reflections
as he wandered about the poor quarters of Moscow: "I be-
held the misery, cold, hunger, humiliation of thousands of
my fellow men. . . . I feel, and can never cease to feel, myself
a partaker in a crime which is continually being committed,
so long as I have superfluous food while others have none,
so long as I have two coats while there exists one man without any. . . . I must seek in my heart at every moment, with
meekness and humility, some opportunity for doing the job
Christ wants done. Can I not be of some use to stop up a
hole? To wipe something with? Can I not be used as an example of meanness, of vice and sin?"

This deep sense of solidarity with one's brother is a perfect, natural medium on which Divine Grace can work, and
just as the Saviour once praised the Roman sergeant who
built a synagogue for the Jews out of a deep sense of the oneness of humanity, so too there may be reserved for a future
day praise for the Russians, who, though presently delayed
in the totalitarian drive of communism, are nevertheless on

the way to that Communionism where Christ is the brother
of all men and God their heavenly Father.

Though these writers of the nineteenth century knew
that the revolt against God was coming, and that Russia
would be at the head of it, enslaving men under the guise of
liberation, they nevertheless were convinced that the deep-
rooted faith of the Russian people would one day be a light
and beacon to the world. There are about 200,000,000
people in Russia, and it must be repeated that less than
6,000,000 of them are members of the Communist Party.
Hidden underneath the tatters of their crucifixion is the
promise of a resurrection. As one of their modern poets,
Andrai Bely, wrote of Russia's mystical expectation, in her
present agony of being nailed to the cross:

> "Russia—you are today the bride.
> Receive the message of spring."

The beginning of her world mission as a bearer of faith
to other nations may already have its dim beginnings in the
few concessions which the Communist Government has
granted to the Russian Orthodox Church. This Church,
though dissident and broken off from unity with the center of Christendom, is nevertheless a Divine Church, with
a Divine priesthood, Divine sacraments, and Bishops who
are successors to the Apostles. Though the meager tolerance granted it by the Communists has been purchased at
the cost of becoming a political lackey for totalitarian ideology; though this Moscow branch of the Church is sending
its "bishops" who are really MVD agents, to win the Russian Orthodox Churches throughout the rest of the world
to be foreign agents for Russia's foreign policy; though the
Church enjoys no genuine religious freedom because Soviet legislation does not recognize the Church as a legal

person, nor does it permit the Church to own property or give religious instructions to children under 18, it nevertheless remains true that every time a Mass is celebrated in Russia, Christ renews his Calvary in the midst of executioners; every time the waters of baptism are poured on a child, Christ takes residence therein as His temple; every tabernacle that houses the Eucharistic Lord is a furnace of love where the cold hands of hate may warm themselves; every time a priest takes the Lord on a sick call past the Kremlin, the shadow of the living Christ falls on its walls; every time a hand is lifted in absolution over a sinner in the hidden confessionals, there is a diminution of hate, a new cell of love; every monastery that is opened is a place where the "Yurodivys" or "born fools" allow evil to be visited upon themselves that, like Christ in Gethsemane, they might drink the chalice to its very dregs, so that none of it may ever be spilled on a land they revere and a soil that they love. Let not the political Commissars think that they have only a stooge in the Russian Orthodox Church—which indeed they might have if it were a Church only Christian in name—but rather let them know that the concessions that they have made to religion for base political motives in reality are the signing of their own death warrant. The greatest fifth column in the history of modern times is forming today in Communist Russia. Around those cells of Christians who refuse to take as final the destiny of man as revealed in the cadaver of Lenin, but look to the empty tomb where Christ's love is revealed as stronger than death, is the key to peace when Christian Russia shall illumine the world.

The reverse procedure is taking place here in America, where a new fifth column of Communist activity is permitted, like termites who eat away the foundations and fabric of national life. Thus while we are allowing an alien barbarism to destroy us from within, Russia is unwittingly preparing for a new birth through the zeal of those who were once called the addicts of an opiate. As the Holy Father, Pius XI, said of the peoples of the Russian Orthodox Church: "People do not realize how much faith, goodness and Christianity there is in those bodies now separated from the age-long Catholic truth. Pieces broken from gold-bearing rock themselves bear gold. The ancient Church bodies keep so venerable a holiness that they deserve not only respect but complete sympathy."

Not in the further spread of an ideology which denies the dignity of man and his vocation to a supernatural destiny, not in economic plans and political subterfuges does the hope of the peace reside, but rather in the conversion of Russia. When that day comes—and please God it is not too far off!—then the present defenders of Russia in all of its works and pomps will hate and despise the Church, and we who are presently called its enemies but are not, because we pray for Russia daily, will be its lovers still. It is not Christian to wish for the extinction of Communists, though it is most Christian to pray for the evaporation of communism. This phenomenon takes place daily in the soul of every convert, whose false ideas are dissipated by the Christ Who is abidingly loved. What is true of individuals is true of nations; it is their transfiguration, not their defeat, for which we must yearn. Magdalen the sinner was not crushed, but transformed so that the passion that once burned for the flesh now burned for the spirit. God did not raise up a saint to battle the Manicheanism of Augustine; Augustine the saint answers Augustine the rhetorician: "As I live, saith the Lord God, I desire not the death of the wicked, but that the wicked turn from his way and live." (Ezek. 33:11) Those who mock may one day pray; those who ignore may one day acknowledge; but those of the Western world who both know God and yet ignore, may be cast out. The patronizing indifference to religion of our Western bourgeois world never suited the passion of the Russian soul. One of two things had to happen: either radical denial with persecution, or integral acceptance. Russia is now in the first stage of persecution, but through our prayers and charities we can hasten the day when the Lord's words will be fulfilled: "Behold I do new things, and now they shall spring forth, verily you shall know them." (Isaiah 43:19) It would be wrong for those who remain in the Father's house to complain like the elder son against the return of the prodigal son, for he who would resent the return of a sinner, thereby makes himself unworthy of the Kingdom of God. Not in war, but in prayer must we trust that the land which once was known as Holy Russia may become again the wellspring whence a pure stream of Christianity may flow. Then shall we see fulfilled the words of the Russian poet Khomyakov who was conscious first of Russia's great sins:

> But now, alas, what sins lie heavy,
> Many and awful on thy soul!
> Thou art black with black injustice,
> And slavery's yoke has branded thee,
> And godless flattery and baneful lying
> And sloth that's shameful, life-denying,
> And every hateful thing in thee I see.

But then he saw in his land a vessel of election summoning souls to penance:

> For all that cries for consolation,
> For every law that we have spurned,
> For sins that stain our generation,

For evil deeds our Fathers learned,
For all our country's bitter passion,
Pray ye with tears the while we live.
O God of Might, of Thy compassion
May'st Thou forgive! May'st Thou forgive!

CHAPTER TEN

Our Lady of Fatima
and Russia

Our world has become so used to judging temporal events in terms of other events, that it is losing sight of another and greater standard of judgment, namely, the Eternal, which breaks into history to set to naught the petty and trivial values of space and time. Since those who live in a two-dimensional universe of only right and left could not be expected to know of these heavenly manifestations, it is worth recalling that the two most important of them came when the world needed them most and when it heeded them least. One such revelation took place in the year of the birthday of the ideas that made our de-Christianized world, the other the year when those ideas were translated into action.

If there is any particular year in which we might say the modern world began—and by the modern world we mean in contradistinction to the Christian world—it would be about the year 1858. In that particular year John Stuart Mill wrote his *Essay on Liberty*, in which liberty was

identified with license and absence from social responsibility; in that year Darwin had completed his *Origin of the
Species,* in which he took man's perspective away from eternal purpose, and made him look back to the animal past. In
the year 1858 Karl Marx, founder of communism, wrote
his introduction to the *Critique of Political Economy* in which
he enthroned economics as the basis of life and culture.
From these men have come the ideas which have domi-
nated the world for almost a century—namely, that man is
not divine but animal in his origin; his freedom is license
and escape from authority and law; devoid of spirit, he is
an integral part of the matter of the cosmos, and therefore
has no need of religion.

In that same important year of 1858, on the eleventh
day of February, at the base of the Pyrenees Mountains
in France, in the tiny village of Lourdes, the Blessed Virgin began the first of 18 appearances to a little peasant girl
whose family name was Soubirous. She is now known as
Saint Bernadette.[1] Four years after the Church had defined
the doctrine of the Immaculate Conception, the heavens
opened and the Lady, so beautiful, said Bernadette, that
she could not possibly be of earth, spoke to Bernadette saying: "I am the Immaculate Conception." The very moment
the world was denying original sin and, without knowing
it, saying that every person in the world was immaculately
conceived, Our Blessed Mother claimed the prerogative
solely as her own: "*I am* the Immaculate Conception." She
did not say, "I have been immaculately conceived." There
was somewhat an analogous identification between herself and the Immaculate Conception that God had made
from Mount Sinai when He said, "I am Who am." As it is
of the very nature of God to exist, so too it is analogously
the very nature of the Blessed Virgin to be the Immaculate

Conception. If she alone and uniquely was Immaculately conceived, then everyone else was born in the state of original sin; if there is no original sin, then everyone is immaculately conceived. Claiming the privilege as her own was a contradiction to every idea that the de-Christianized world was then beginning to spawn. To those who believe man belongs solely to earth, heaven protests as the Mother calls men to become as pilgrims to her shrine in testimony to the spirit; to those who reduce man to an animal, and the animal to nature, the Beautiful Lady summons men to rise above the animal to their supreme vocation in her Divine Son; to those who degenerate freedom into license, the eternal reaffirms that the Divine Truth alone makes us free with the glorious freedom of the children of God; those who say religion is the opium of the people, she comes to arouse from the opiate of the lie to the glorious possibility of man becoming an heir of heaven.

But the world heeded not the heavenly recall to the spirit. The pagan ideas of 1858, that man is an animal, that freedom is isolation from law, that religion is antihuman, soon crept out of the covers of a textbook and the four walls of a classroom and finally became the violence of World War I, 1914–1918. This was the flowering into action of the false ideas of 1858. The secular word became flesh as war. To concentrate on but one year of this World War, the year 1917 would seem to be the most significant because of events in three places of the world. On May 13 of that year Benedict XV imposed hands on Monsignor Eugenio Pacelli making him a successor of the Apostles. As the bells of Rome were ringing out the midday Angelus, a new Bishop had been given to the Church who would one day by the hidden designs of Providence ascend the throne of Peter and govern the Universal Church as our Holy Father, Pius XII.

In Russia on May 13, 1917, Maria Alexandrovna was teaching catechism in one of the churches of Moscow. She had 200 children before her in the pews. There was a loud noise at the front door; horsemen entered, charged down the middle aisle of the great church, vaulted the Communion rail, destroyed the altar, then rode down the side aisles destroying the statues and finally charged the children, killing some of them. Maria Alexandrovna ran out of the church screaming. It was the first of those sporadic outbursts that foretold the coming Communist Revolution. She went to one of the revolutionists who was later to become famous, and when she screamed at him, "The most terrible thing has just happened. I was teaching catechism in the church when men rode in on horses, destroyed the church, trampled the children and killed some of them," Lenin, the revolutionist, answered, "I know it, I sent them."

In Portugal, on May 13, 1917, three children from the parish of Fatima, Jacinta, Francis and Lucy were attending their flock when the Angelus bell rang from the steeple of the parish church.[2] The three little shepherds knelt down and as was their daily custom recited the Rosary together. When they finished it, they decided to build "a little house" which might shelter them on stormy days. But these little architects were suddenly interrupted by a blinding flash of lightning, and they looked anxiously at the sky. Not a single cloud veiled the brilliance of the midday sun. Frightened, they started to run when, just two paces ahead in the midst of the foliage of an evergreen oak, they saw a "beautiful lady," more resplendent than the sun. With a gesture of motherly kindness the lady said to them: "Fear not, I shall do you no harm." The lady was very beautiful; she seemed to be from 15 to 18 years of age. Her dress, white as snow and tied at the neck by a gold cord, reached down to her feet which were just visible, barely touching the branches of the tree. A white veil embroidered with gold covered her head and shoulders, falling to her feet like the dress. Her hands were joined at the height of her breast in an attitude of prayer; a rosary of brilliant pearls with a silver cross hung from her right hand. Her face of incomparable beauty shone in a halo as bright as the sun, but seemed to be veiled by a slight look of sorrow.

Lucy was the first to speak: "Where do you come from?"

"I come from Heaven," replied the lady.

"From Heaven! And why have you come here?" Lucy asked.

"I have come to ask you to be here on the thirteenth day of each month at this hour for six months in succession. In the month of October I shall tell you who I am and what I want."

Just at that very moment, when in the eastern end of Europe Antichrist was unloosed against the very idea of God and against society in one of the most terrible bloodlettings of history, there appeared in splendor at the western extremity of Europe, that great and eternal enemy of the infernal serpent.

Of the six appearances of the Blessed Mother to those children, the most important was the apparition of July 13, 1917. It must be recalled that this was the third year of World War I and speaking of it she said: "This war is going to end. If people do what I have told you many souls will be saved and will find peace."

"But," she added: "if people do not cease to offend God, not much time will elapse and precisely during the next Pontificate another and more terrible war will commence." As a matter of fact it was during the Pontificate

of Pius XI that the terrible Spanish War took place, which
was a prelude to World War II. During that time the Reds
in their hatred of religion massacred cruelly 13 prelates,
14,000 priests and religious, and destroyed 22,000 churches
and chapels.

The Blessed Mother then gave a sign as to when World
War II would actually begin. "When you see a night illumi-
nated by an unknown light, know that it is the signal which
God gives you that the chastisement of the world for its
many transgressions is at hand, through war, famine and
persecution of the Church and the Holy Father."

Later on, Lucy was asked when the sign actually appeared, and she said it was the very extraordinary aurora
borealis which lighted up a great part of Europe on the
night of January 25–26, 1938. Speaking of the war to come
Lucy said: "It will be horrible, horrible." All the chastise-
ments of God are conditional and they can be averted by
penance. The Blessed Mother, it is to be noted, said that
World War II could be avoided, for she added: "To avoid
this, I shall ask for the Consecration of the World to my
Immaculate Heart, and Communion in reparation of the
first Saturday of each month. If my requests are granted
Russia will be converted; there will be peace. Otherwise
Russia will spread its error throughout the world giving
rise to wars and persecutions against the Church. The
good will suffer martyrdom, and the Holy Father will have
to suffer much. Different nations will be destroyed."

The Bishop of Fatima has seen fit not to give us a part
of that message. What that particular message was we do
not know. It apparently is not good news, and it also would
seem to refer to our times. In any case, we are given the
conclusion of the message with hope and joy: "But in the
end my Immaculate Heart will triumph. The Holy Father

will consecrate Russia to the Immaculate Heart, and Russia will be converted and an era of peace will be given to the world."

The final revelation took place on the thirteenth day of October, 1917, when the Blessed Mother promised to work a miracle that all present might believe in Her apparitions. On the evening of October 12, all the roads to Fatima were packed with carriages, bicycles and pilgrims on their way to the apparition. The witnesses were a crowd of 60,000 which had gathered by the noon of the thirteenth, many of whom were unbelievers and scoffers.

We are not here concerned about proving the authenticity of these phenomena at Fatima, for those who believe in the realm of the spirit and the Mother of God are receptive, and those who reject the Spirit would not accept it anyway. What significance shall we attach to the apparent fall of the sun attested by the people at Fatima on that October day in 1917? We have no way of knowing for certain, but since its general effect was so frightening, we may speculate. Could it augur the day when men would steal some of the atomic energy from the sun and use it not to light a world, but as a bomb to thrust it down from the heavens on a helpless population? It used to be when famine was stalking the earth, when war was devastating the accumulated heritage of the centuries, when men were acting as wolves to men, and when great concentration camps like Moloch swallowed up millions, men could always look up to the skies for hope. If this earth were cruel, at least the heavens would be kind. Did this Apparition portend that now even the heavens for a time would turn against man and its fires would be released upon the helpless children of God? Whether or not it was a premonition of the atomic bomb we know not. One thing is certain, it was not the end of hope, for amid all of the clouds, there still is the vision in the heavens of the Lady, with the Moon beneath Her Feet, the stars a crown about Her Head, and the sun above Her. The Heavens are not against us, and will not destroy while she reigns as the Lady of the Skies.

It may be worth inquiring, however, why Almighty God in His providential dealings with the Universe should see fit in this day to give us a revelation of His Blessed Mother in order to bring us back to prayer and penance.

One reason immediately comes to mind. Since the world has lost Christ, it may be that through Mary it will recover Him. When Our Blessed Lord was lost at the age of 12, it was the Blessed Mother who found Him. Now that He has been lost again, it may be through Mary that the world will recover Christ their Saviour. Another reason is that Divine Providence has committed to a woman the power of overcoming evil. In that first dread day when evil was introduced into the world, God spoke to the serpent in the Garden of Eden and said: "I shall put enmity between thee and the woman; between thy seed and her seed, and thou shalt lie in wait for her heel." (Gen. 3:15) In other words, evil shall have a progeny and a seed. Goodness too shall have a progeny and a seed. It will be through the power of the woman that evil will be overcome. We live now in an evil hour, for though goodness has its day, evil does have its hour. Our Blessed Lord said that much the night that Judas came into the garden: "This is your hour, the power of darkness." (Luke 22:53) All evil can do in that hour is to put out the lights of the world; but it can do that. If then we live in an evil hour how shall we overcome the spirit of Satan except by the power of that Woman to whom Almighty God has given the mandate to crush the head of the serpent?

No longer does one hear the lie that the Catholic
Church adores Mary, or puts her on the same level with
God, or that she takes the place of God. Rather are men
beginning to recognize the truth of the Christian tradition
that as it was through Eve that sin came into the world, so
it will be through the new Eve, Mary, that Redemption
from sin comes into the world. Methodist Bishop G. Brom-
ley Oxnam, writing a commentary on the words of Our
Lord to John at the foot of the Cross, *Behold Thy Mother*,
says:* "Is moral purpose written into the nature of things?
Was the universe designed for madmen? Does doom await
the dictators who strut the stage for a little hour, refusing to
repeat the lines of the Eternal Playwright, disregarding the
instructions of the Divine Director? Is there to be a final
curtain, and are they to hear, 'Thou art weighed in the bal-
ances and found wanting'? In a word is there something in
what Jesus sought to reveal, this something that is revealed
in the life of a true mother? Is this something which we
have defined as the realization of self in the complete gift of
self for others, is this something the law that must rule? . . .
Does peace await fundamental revision of contemporary
concepts of sovereignty? Is the right to hold property to be
related to the use the owner makes of that property? These
are perplexing issues but they must be faced if we are to
have permanent peace. They cannot be faced unless they
be faced in the proper spirit. 'And there was with Him at
the foot of the Cross His Mother.' . . . Man needs a new
unifying enterprise, large enough to unite all men. Class,
race and nation are concepts too small. Is it to be found
in the Christian doctrine of the solidarity of the human

---

* From G. B. Oxnam, *Behold Thy Mother*. Copyrighted 1944 by The Macmillan
Company. By permission of The Macmillan Company, publishers.

family, in the ideal of brotherhood? And what of the spirit that must underlie it? 'And there was with Him at the foot of the Cross His Mother.' . . . The spirit that she had revealed in serving her son was none other than the spirit which He saw must be revealed if He would be the Saviour of all. And she went with Him. She carried a broken heart to Calvary, but revealed in that broken heart as He revealed in His broken body the spirit that must yet rule mankind. It takes a great act of faith to believe, as one believed long since, that Jesus Christ will become the Ruler of the kings of the earth. Before He rules men must behold the spirit incarnate in Him, revealed in large measure in the hearts of mothers everywhere. It is the spirit that must rule mankind. When men know that and practice it, when they realize the true significance of a mother standing at the foot of the cross, then He will become the Ruler of the kings of the earth.

"The self is realized in the complete gift of self for others, and all men become free in the spirit and practice of that law.

"'And there was with Him at the foot of the Cross His mother.'"

The revelation of Fatima is a reminder that we live in a moral universe, that evil is self-defeating, that good is self-preserving; that the basic troubles of the world are not in politics or economics but in our hearts and our souls, and that spiritual regeneration is the condition of social amelioration. Soviet Russia is not the sole danger to the Western world; rather is it the despiritualization of the Western world to which Russia gave political form and social substance. World War II came according to Our Lady of Fatima because there was no amendment in the hearts and souls of men. The danger of World War III is precisely in this point, not just in the Communist International. The Western world is scandalized at the Soviet system, but this is basically because it sees its own individual atheism socialized and put into practice on almost a cosmic scale. The great issue at stake is not individualism or collectivism, because neither of these is of primary importance; it is not between free enterprise and socialism in the economic order, for neither of these matters tremendously; rather the struggle is for the human soul. This is another way of saying that the crisis centers around freedom in the spiritual sense of the word. War will not settle the world atmosphere, but will result only in the atomization of man, a fact of which the atomic bomb is only a symbol. Since evil is not wholly external a war will not eliminate it. Any world war is really an objectification of evil in the lives of men. A micro-cosmic war is the reflection of microcosmic war inside of individual hearts. Because the Christian knows this better than anyone else, the responsibility for the world's condition is to a greater extent his. The world is the way it is because each of us is the way we are. It is the special responsibility of the Christian to discern in two world wars in 21 years the judgment of God on the way we live. As long as the Christian thinks that there are only two directions he can take, "Right" or "Left," not only will he make no contribution to the world, but he will make the world worse by failing to recognize that additional to the horizontal plane of life, there is also the vertical which leads to God and where there are the two more important directions of "inward" and "upward." Not by finding scapegoats, whether they be political parties or communism, will we escape the responsibility of bearing, as Christ did in Gethsemane, the burden of the world's guilt. The revelation of Fatima was a most poignant reminder to Christians that the so-called problem of Russia is the problem of Christians: that by prayer, penance and reparation, and not by war, abuse and attack will Russia join the society of freedom-loving nations.

There is no "iron curtain" for this vision of the world because prayers do not go through an iron curtain but over it, as radioactive particles released in the atmosphere are carried over mountains and continents. The conversion of Russia is the condition of world peace, but Russia's conversion is conditioned upon our own reconversion. It may very well be that the very hatred which Russia shows to Christianity today proves she is closer to it than is the "broad-minded" man of the Western world who never says his prayers. Russia has to think about Christ to hate Him, but the indifferent man does not think about Him at all.

There are only three possible attitudes which we can take toward life and history. First, that of fatuous optimism, which believes that life moves necessarily toward a prosperous goal, thanks to education, science and the laws of evolution. Secondly, the pessimism of totalitarianism, which believes that human nature is intrinsically wicked, and that the dictatorial power of the state is necessary to control the anarchic impulses of individuals, who are not to be trusted. Freedom in this scheme of things is to be taken away from persons and placed in the collectivity. This view of life has proved equally unsatisfactory inasmuch as it puts the hope in the distant future without any guarantee that it will ever be achieved. Thirdly, there is Christianity which comes to optimism through pessimism; to a resurrection through a passion, and to a crown of glory through a crown of thorns; to the glory of Easter Sunday through the ignominy of a Good Friday. It proclaims that unless the seed fall to the ground it remaineth alone, but if it dieth to itself, it springeth forth unto new life. This optimism of Christianity comes to pass not by a power that comes either from ourselves or from nature, but by and through the power of God; not through the taming of errant impulses by a state, nor by the shedding of another's blood, but by the law of sacrifice in which love is revealed.

To those who are momentarily disheartened by the persecution of the Church, it must be remembered that the Church is less a continuing thing than a life that dies and arises again. The Risen Lord said to the Magdalen: "Do not touch Me." (John 20:17) "Do not detain Me within the tomb, or think that I must always be as I was before my Resurrection." The Magdalen had forgotten that He was now in the garden and not in the grave, a living Source of Life, and not a dead body to be covered with spices. We too are apt to think that the Church is supposed to be the same in every age, forgetful that its God is One Who knew His way out of the grave. A charge that has often been alleged against the Church is that it does not suit the modern world. This is absolutely true. The Church has never suited the times in which it lived, for if it suited the times it would perish with them, and not survive them. There is something always the same about the Church, and yet something very different. What is the same is that "Jesus Christ is the same yesterday, today and forever." What is different is the fact that the Church is always converting every new age, not as an old religion, but as a new religion. The trees that are now budding in this springtime season are the same trees that were so firmly rooted in the ground last year, and there is something new about them, for if they did not die they would not be living again. The Church is not a survival. It has returned again and again in the Western world of rapid changes in order to reconvert the world. Time and time again, the old stone has been rejected by the builders, but within a century it was brought back from the rubbish heap and became the head of the corner of the temple of peace.

Here is the great difference between the Church and the secular civilizations: the Church has the power of self-renewal, civilizations have not. They become exhausted and perish but they never renew themselves. When a civilization such as Babylon, Sparta and Athens fulfills its appointed vocation and exhausts itself, it passes away from the face of the earth forever. There is not a single record of a civilization that ever perished which rose again. But with the Church it is different; it has the power of coming out of the grave, of apparently being defeated by an age, and then becoming suddenly victorious, "for the gates of Hell shall not prevail against it."

The Church has often been "killed," once with the Arian heresy, then with the Albigensian heresy, then with Voltaire, Darwin, and now with the three forms of totalitarianism, red, brown and black, but somehow or other, as each succeeding age tolled the bell for its execution, it was the Church that finally buried the age. At this particular moment, there are those who feel that because we live in days of persecution, and because the Church has gone down into the catacombs once again in Europe, they must shed pious and reverential tears over its sepulcher, never realizing that if they would look through their tears as the Magdalen did, they would see the Son of God walking once more victorious upon the hills of the morning. One would think that the world after 1900 years of experience would give up bringing the spices for its interment. It was supposed to have been killed during the first ten persecutions; it was supposed to have withered under the light of

the age of reason; it was supposed to have been swallowed
up by the earth in the age of revolution; it was supposed to
have been antiquated by the advance of science and evolution; and it is now supposed to be buried in the days of our
contemporary antireligious revolutions. But the fact is that
it is just being sepulchered in the bowels of the earth where
it is digging catacombs and whence one day it will emerge
to reconquer the earth. If at this moment we are going into
the catacombs, it is only as Christ went into the grave. The
world might just as well expect to see Him there permanently interred, as they might look for the freezing of a star,
for "heaven and earth shall pass away, but My Word shall
not pass away."

Francis Thompson at the beginning of the century described the coming persecution of the Church as *Lilium
Regis*, and then its ultimate victory.

> O Lily of the King! low lies thy silver wing,
>   And long has been the hour of thine unqueening;
> And thy scent of Paradise on the night-wind spills
> its sighs,
>   Nor any take the secrets of its meaning.
> O Lily of the King! I speak a heavy thing,
>   O patience, most sorrowful of daughters!
> Lo, the hour is at hand for the troubling of the land,
>   And red shall be the breaking of the waters.
>
> Sit fast upon thy stalk, when the blast shall with
> thee talk,
>   With the mercies of the King for thine awning;
> And the just understand that thine hour is at hand,
>   Thine hour at hand with power in the dawning.
> When the nations lie in blood, and their kings a
> broken brood,

Look up, O most sorrowful of daughters!
Lift up thy head and hark what sounds are in the dark,
   For His feet are coming to thee on the waters!

O Lily of the King! I shall not see, that sing,
   I shall not see the hour of thy queening!
But my Song shall see, and wake like a flower that dawn-
winds shake,
   And sigh with joy the odours of its meaning.
O Lily of the King, remember then the thing
   That this dead mouth sang; and thy daughters,
As they dance before His way, sing there on the Day
   What I sang when the Night was on the waters![3]

Catastrophe is the condition of greatness. The Church
is like a lamb that is shorn of its wool every springtime, but
it lives on. The particular season in which we live then is
the time of the shearing of Christ's lamb, when perhaps
even the shepherds shall have only iron staffs. It is always
the business of the Church to utilize defeat.

Toynbee tells us that there have been three philosophies concerning the relationship between Christianity
and civilization. The first is that Christianity is the enemy
of civilization. This view was developed in early Roman
days by Marcus Aurelius, by Julian the Apostate, in the last
century by Gibbon and in this century by Marx and his
followers. The second view is that of historical liberalism,
which believes that Christianity is the handmaid of civilization, a kind of transitional thing which bridges the gap
between one civilization and another. Religion has a useful
and subordinate talent of bringing a new secular civilization to birth after the death of its predecessor. The Church
is, therefore, a kind of morale builder, an ambulance, a steppingstone for a new order, a midwife to a more progressive

civilization. The third and correct view is that civilizations prosper and decay to facilitate the development of Christ's kingdom in this world. It is the breakdown of secular civilizations that constitutes the steppingstones to something higher. What Aeschylus of old affirmed, that it is through suffering that learning comes, was reaffirmed at Emmaus, that through trial and catastrophe glory comes. It may be that, as Toynbee said, "all the sufferings of civilizations are the stations of the Cross on the way to the Crucifixion, and religion is a chariot. It looks as if the wheels on which it mounts toward heaven may be the periodic downfalls of the civilizations of earth."[4]

Civilizations are cyclic, they are recurrent, they go through the same phenomena of birth and death and never come to life again. Religion, however, is a continuous upward linear movement, rising to new heights after the decay of each particular civilization. As a Christian civilization grew out of the decay of the Greco-Roman world, so a new Christian order will grow out of the decay of historical liberalism and communism. What we are witnessing in our day is not the decline of the Church, but rather the death of a civilization that has been egocentric and has been trying to make selfishness a success, and to balance opposing forces by tolerance understood as indifference to truth, or by having recourse to external organizations to compensate for the loss of personal vitality and virtue. Out of this tyranny when men walk in processions and think that they are original, out of its death in which the Church suffers, there will emerge a rebirth of faith in which a new generation will learn that the Church is not in the world to improve human nature, but to redeem it; not to make men better but to save them. What we are witnessing then is the death of an era of civilization, but not the death of Him Who is the Lord of the Universe.

As each civilization dies it persecutes, and in the midst of that persecution the Christ says to us as He did to the disciples of Emmaus: "Ought not the Son of Man to suffer in order to enter into His glory?" In the heart of apparent failure God's power is most clearly revealed. When the world's predicament is most desperate a new factor breaks in from the outside which completely changes the situation. When chaos and fear and the powers of darkness seem invincible, the purpose of God moves on as He makes His appearance at those moments of history when things are darkest. As there was a divine invasion in Bethlehem, so too there is now a divine invasion after Calvary. As the Jews of old were saved from bondage at the Red Sea by the hand of the Lord dividing the waters for them, and causing the same waters to swallow up their pursuers, so too now when men huddle together in fear, the power of God becomes manifest. The kingdom of God does not grow *out* of history, but manifests itself *through* history. The resurrection was the finding of meaning in history, for if the Crucifixion were the end, then the power behind Our Lord was not committed to the vindication of innocence.

In the midst of our fear today, when for our protection we have barricaded every door against the enemy, Christ appears in our midst and reminds us to be at peace. The worst thing that can happen to the Church is to be tolerated. Because the Church today is living in fear and is persecuted, it is psychologically placed in a more favorable position for preserving its true nature than ever before. If Christ were a worldly success, then He could only be imitated in worldliness. If He were a failure and never rose from the dead, then we would be vindictive and we who are His followers would hate the Jews and the Romans and the Greeks. If He were only a man, He would be forgotten as all men are. If He wrote a book, we would all be professors, but if He came into this world to bring us victory through defeat, then who shall ever be without hope? Though we in this generation have seen two world wars in 21 years, though the first war was fought to make the world safe for a democracy without God, and the second war was fought to make an imperialism without God, and the third war threatens us in which democracy without God may quarrel with imperialism without God, we shall still believe in the possibility that, though the doors are closed against Divinity, and though we shrink in fear, there will be another Divine Invasion of that extrahistorical power in this dark hour. We who have faith in the glory and certitude of His resurrection know that we have already won—only the news has not yet leaked out!

As Americans we cannot be unmindful of the relation of this country to the Woman to whom God gave the power of crushing the head of the serpent. The Council of Baltimore on December 8, 1846, consecrated the United States to the Immaculate Conception of Our Blessed Mother. It was only 8 years later that the Church defined Her Immaculate Conception. It was on December 8, 1941, the Feast of the Immaculate Conception, that the United States went to war with Japan. It was on May 13, 1945, Mother's Day, the day on which the entire Church celebrated Sodality Day of Our Lady, that the United States Government proclaimed a National Thanksgiving for V-E Day. It was on August 15, 1945, the Feast of the Assumption of Our Blessed Mother, that victory came to us in the war with Japan. It was the nineteenth of August, 1945, that the United States Government declared official V-J Day and this happened to be the anniversary of one of the appearances of Our Lady at Fatima. On September 1, 1945, the first Saturday of the month which Our Lady of Fatima asked should be consecrated to Her, General MacArthur accepted the surrender of Japan aboard the *Missouri*. It was on September 8, 1945, the Birthday of Our Lady, that the first American flag flew over Tokyo, and as it was unfurled General MacArthur said: "Let it wave in its full glory as a symbol of victory for the right."

Under the inspiration and suggestions of the Lady of Fatima, may it be America's destiny to see the great spiritual solidarity that exists between the 97 percent of the Russian people who are not members of the Communist Party and the idealism, love of peace, generosity and friendliness of the American people. Over the grave of Dostoevsky, Pushkin preached a eulogy that expressed the high destiny of the Russian people. "Our destiny is universality acquired not by the sword, but by the strength of brotherhood, and by our desire to see the restoration of concord among all men." This has always been the American ideal. When a minority would now disrupt those peaceful relations between the Russian and the American people, it is now the sweet burden not only of America, but of the conscience of the West, to restore our relations to God, to the Mother of Christ "up whose body as a tower of ivory, He climbed to kiss upon her lips a mystic rose."

> Thou art more kind to our dreams, Our Mother,
> Than the wise that wove us the dreams for shade.
> God is more good to the gods that mocked Him
> Than men are good to the gods they made. . . .
>
> What is the home of the heart set free,
> And where is the nesting of liberty,

And where from the world shall the world take shelter
And man be master, and not with Thee?
Wisdom is set in her throne of thunder,
The Mirror of Justice blinds the day—
Where are the towers that are not of the City,
Trophies and trumpetings, where are they?
Where over the maze of the world returning
The bye-ways bend to the King's highway.[5]

Prayer to Obtain a Favor Through the Intercession of Venerable Fulton J. Sheen

---

Eternal Father, You alone grant us
every blessing in Heaven and on earth,
through the redemptive mission of Your
Divine Son, Jesus Christ, and by the
working of the Holy Spirit.
If it be according to Your Will, glorify
Your servant, Archbishop Fulton J.
Sheen, by granting the favor I now request
through his prayerful intercession
(*mention your request*).
I make this prayer confidently through
Jesus Christ, our Lord. Amen.

Imprimatur +Most Rev. Daniel R. Jenky, C.S.C.,
Bishop of Peoria

For information on membership in the Archbishop Fulton J. Sheen Foundation, or to share any personal knowledge of the archbishop (letters, photos, life experiences), or to report any spiritual or physical favors in his name, please write:

The Archbishop Sheen Foundation
P.O. Box 728
Peoria, IL 61652-0728

ENDNOTES

CHAPTER ONE

1 Reinhold Niebuhr, *Reflections on the End of an Era* (New York: Charles Scribner's Sons, 1936), p. 3. Quoted by permission of the publisher.

2 History is not economically determined, but morally determined. Just as the violation of a law of health entails disease, so too the violation of moral laws entails certain consequences which are called judgments. The word "crisis" in Greek means judgment.

"War is the collapse of the Divine order which God is striving with man's co-operation to establish in the world. The collapse of this order is due to man's disobedience. The collapse itself is God's judgment." Charles Clayton Morrison, *The Christian and the War* (Chicago: Willett, Clark & Company, 1942), p. 43. Quoted by permission of the publisher.

"The judgment of God is executed not only at the end of history, it is executed periodically in history."

Reinhold Niebuhr, *Beyond Tragedy* (New York: Charles Scribner's Sons, 1938), p. 202. Quoted by permission of the publisher.

"The punishment that falls on the existing exploiting order comes from the inevitable results of its own activity. . . . God's justice is outraged by disobedience; disaster comes as the inevitable result of the working of God's moral law, not as irrational anger." Basil Mathews, *Supreme Encounter* (London: S. C. M. Press, 1940), p. 182.

"Europe will return to the Faith or she will perish." Hilaire Belloc, *Europe and the Faith* (New York: Paulist Press, 1939), p. 261. Quoted by permission of the publisher.

"The rejection of God's intention for man, sets man in opposition to himself, and leads to self-destruction; and this resistance itself bears witness to the truth and necessitates the victory of the truth." John Macmurray, *The Clue to History* (New York: Harper & Brothers, 1939), p. 117. Quoted by permission of the publisher.

"There is a Divine purpose underlying the ups and downs of history, and the original structure of humans is perverted to such an extent that only by Divine interference can history be rendered meaningful." Otto Piper, *God in History* (New York: The Macmillan Company, 1939), p. 42. Quoted by permission of the author.

"It belongs to the nature of ethical monotheism that history is grounded in the moral will of God and controlled by it, and that this moral will of God establishes a covenant relation with His worshippers." Eugene W. Lyman, *The Kingdom of God in History* (London: George Allen & Unwin, 1938), p. 88. Quoted by permission of the publisher.

3 Hilaire Belloc, *Restoration of Property* (London: Sheed and Ward, 1936).

4 Cf. Peter Drucker, *The End of Economic Man* (New York: The John Day Co., 1939).

"It is one thing to deny the profit motive entirely, with Communism, and another and different thing to restrain it with certain bounds for the good of society." John F. Cronin, *Economics and Society* (New York: American Book Company, 1939), p. 155. Quoted by permission of the publisher.

5 "Herein lies the dilemma of humanitarian modernism: that it condemns its own best impulses to continual thwarting and recurrent disaster. That is, for Christian faith a single variant of the central dilemma of mankind." Robert L. Calhoun, *The Christian Understanding of Man* (Chicago: Willett, Clark & Company, 1938), Part I. Quoted by permission of the publisher.

"All the slippery optimism which has so devitalized the democratic peoples has sprung not from accidental misjudgments about particular events; it has sprung from an essential defect, which is best seen in its intellectual nakedness, in the philosophy of pragmatic liberalism." Lewis Mumford, *Faith for Living* (New York: Harcourt, Brace & Company, Inc., 1940), p. 120. Quoted by permission of the publisher.

For a history of these ideas, cf. Christopher Dawson, *Progress and Religion* (London: Sheed and Ward, 1929); John V. Nef, *The United States and Civilization* (Chicago: University of Chicago Press, 1942); D. R. Davies, *The Two Humanities* (London: James Clark & Co., 1940); Norman Nicholson, *Man and Literature* (London: S. C. M. Press, 1944).

"It is clearly untrue that we are automatically progressing and that the Churches and religion ought to hasten to adjust themselves to all the novelties of the age." Karl Mannheim, *Diagnosis of Our Time* (New York: Oxford University Press, 1944), p. 132. Copyright 1944 by Oxford University Press.

6   Henry P. Van Dusen (ed.), *The Christian Answer* (New York: Charles Scribner's Sons, 1945), p. 5.

7   "First with Descartes, then with Rousseau and Kant, rationalism has set up a proud and splendid image of the *personality* of man, inviolable, jealous of his immanence and his autonomy, and finally good in essence. . . . Yet in a little more than a century, this proud anthropocentric personality has perished. . . ." Jacques Maritain, *True Humanism* (New York: Charles Scribner's Sons, 1938), p. 20. Quoted by permission of the publishers.

A very brief but excellent presentation of the idea that when "reason" becomes reasoning from social welfare, then rights lose their outside purchase, cf. William Ernest Hocking, *What Man Can Make of Man* (New York: Harper & Brothers, 1942), p. 42 *ff.*

8   Harold J. Laski, *The Rise of European Liberalism* (London: George Allen & Unwin; New York: Harper & Brothers, 1936), p. 36. Quoted by permission of the publishers.

9   R. H. Tawney, *Religion and the Rise of Capitalism* (London: John Murray; New York: Harcourt, Brace and Company, Inc., 1926), p. 253. Quoted by permission of the publishers.

10   Max Weber, *The Protestant Ethic and the Spirit of Capitalism* (London: George Allen & Unwin, 1930). Cf. John H. Hallowell, *The Decline of Liberalism as an Ideology* (London: Kegan Paul, 1947).

11 "In the 19th century Western Liberal votaries of Progress and the 20th century Russian Communist Marxians we see two predestinarian sects of an atheistic turn of mind whose ethos is manifestly akin to that of their theistic fellow votaries of the Idol of Necessity. . . . The historical link between 16th century Calvinism and 20th century Communism is 19th century Liberalism." Arnold J. Toynbee, *A Study of History* (London: Oxford University Press, 1939), Vol. 5, p. 616. Quoted by courtesy of the publishers and the Royal Institute of International Affairs.

For the relation of Catholicism to Liberalism, cf. Emmet John Hughes, *The Church and Liberal Society* (New Jersey: Princeton University Press, 1944).

Christopher Dawson does much to clear up the confusion surrounding the term "liberalism" by distinguishing between liberalism as a political party, liberalism as an ideology, and liberalism as a tradition. "Continental socialism, as represented above all by Karl Marx, is responsible not only for the discrediting of the liberal ideology, but also for the totalitarian change to liberty under the shadow of which we are living today." Christopher Dawson, *The Judgment of Nations* (New York: Sheed and Ward, 1942), p. 66. Quoted by permission of the publishers.

"Capitalism is unthinkable as a 'sacred' economy. It is the result of the secularization of economic life, and by it the hierarchical subordination of the material to the spiritual is inverted." Nicholas Berdyaev, *The End of Our Time* (London: Sheed and Ward, 1935). Quoted by permission of the publisher.

For the evil economic effects of historical liberalism as manifested in capitalism, cf. Herbert Agar, *The Land of the Free* (Boston: Houghton, Mifflin, 1935), pp. 90,

211; Amintore Fanfani, *Catholicism, Protestantism and Capitalism* (London: Sheed and Ward, 1937), p. 142 *ff.*

"The age of individualism and *laissez faire* in politics and of unrestricted competition in industry is gone. In the future we shall have a collectivist society; the only question is whether we shall have a collectivism of tyranny or a collectivism of freedom." Nathaniel Micklem, *The Theology of Politics* (London: Oxford University Press, 1941), p. 73. Quoted by permission of the publisher.

"As Liberalism did not create moral ideals, so, too, it cannot preserve them. It lives on the spiritual capital that it has inherited from Christian civilization, and as this is exhausted something else must take its place. Once society is launched on the path of secularization it cannot stop in the halfway house of Liberalism, it must go on to the bitter end, whether that end be Communism or some alternative type of totalitarian secularism." Christopher Dawson, *Religion and the Modern State* (New York: Sheed and Ward, 1935), p. 64. Quoted by permission of the publishers.

"Today the liberal individualism and the conservative traditionalism of the 19th century have alike disappeared, and the policy of *laissez faire* which has already been abandoned in economics, is rightly being abandoned in culture also." Christopher Dawson, *Beyond Politics* (New York: Sheed and Ward, 1939), p. 26. Quoted by permission of the publishers.

"The totalitarian revolt in its most intransigent form is a complete fulfillment of that dogma of becoming which had already formed the central assumption of the era of modern Liberalism." V. A. Demant, *The Religious Prospect* (London: Frederick Muller, 1939), p. 110.

"Historical dispute and distortion of certain Catholic Doctrines produced Capitalism and as a consequent indifference to those doctrines; but a complete denial of *all* Catholic doctrine and an intense atheism produced Materialist Communism." Hilaire Belloc, *The Crisis of Civilization* (Fordham University Press, 1937), p. 180.

12 Denis de Rougemont, *The Devil's Share* (New York: Pantheon Books, 1944), p. 46. Quoted by permission of the publishers.

13 Paul Tillich, *Interpretation of History* (New York: Charles Scribner's Sons, 1936), p. 87. Quoted by permission of the publishers.

14 Nicholas Berdyaev, *Meaning of History* (New York: Sheed and Ward, 1940). Quoted by permission of the publishers.

15 Nicholas Berdyaev, *Freedom and the Spirit* (New York: Charles Scribner's Sons; London: Goeffrey Bles Ltd., 1935), p. 168. Quoted by permission of the publishers.

16 Denis de Rougemont, *The Devil's Share* (New York: Pantheon Books, 1944), p. 23. Quoted by permission of the publishers.

17 "Here the Devil plays with our terror of recognizing ourselves responsible for our lives. Formerly he had recourse to the disguise of clothing. Today the costume no longer signifies anything. The phenomenon of disguise has turned inward and become a moral evasion. It is first of all before oneself, and as if in a dream, that one plays a role with impunity. The present day world is full of individuals who bear within themselves a borrowed costume. They hide before their own eyes. How could they know Satan, since they are unwilling to see their own true being, the one who makes their decisions, the only one to whom the Tempter might reveal himself?

"The fallen Angel says to us: I am your heaven, there is no other hope. The Prince of this world says to us: there is no other world. The Tempter says to us: there is no judge. The Accuser says to us: there is no forgiveness. The liar summarizes all by offering us a world without obligations or sanctions, closed on itself but ceaselessly recreated in the image of our self-indulgence: there is no reality. Finally Legion utters the last blasphemy: there is no One." Denis de Rougemont, *op. cit.*, p. 45.

18 C. S. Lewis, *Screwtape Letters* (New York: The Macmillan Company, 1943), p. 11.

19 Joseph Roth, *The Anti-Christ* (New York: Viking Press, 1935), pp. 4–6. Quoted by permission of the publishers. Cf. William Robinson, *The Devil and God* (London: Lutterworth Press, 1945); Karl Pfleger, *Wrestlers with Christ* (New York: Sheed and Ward, 1936); J. Huizinga, *In the Shadow of Tomorrow* (New York: W. W. Norton & Co., 1936).

20 Fyodor Dostoevsky, *Journal of an Author*, May-June, 1877.

21 *The Brothers Karamazov*, pp. 299–300. Cf. J. A. T. Lloyd, *Fyodor Dostoevsky* (New York: Charles Scribner's Sons, 1947); Nicholas Berdyaev, *Dostoievsky* (New York: Sheed and Ward, 1934); Edward Hallett Carr, *Dostoevsky* (Boston: Houghton, Mifflin, 1931).

22 Privately translated from the Russian.

23 *Decline of the West* (New York: Alfred A. Knopf, 1939).

24 *The Passing of the European Age* (Cambridge: Harvard University Press, 1943).

25 *The Crisis of Our Age.*

26 *Fate of Man in the Modern World* (London: S. C. M. Press, 1935).

27 Karl Marx, *Das Kapital.*

28 *Preface to Morals* (New York: The Macmillan Company, 1929).

29 *A Study of History* (London: Oxford University Press, 1939), 6 Vols.

30 Heinrich Heine, *Works of Heinrich Heine*, translated from German by Charles Godfrey Leland (London: William Heinemann, 1893), Vol. VIII, pp. 301–302, 303–305.

CHAPTER TWO

1 "Marxism and therefore Bolshevism does but voice the secret and unavowed philosophy of the bourgeois society when it regards society and economics as the absolute. It is faithful, likewise, to its morality when it seeks to order this absolute, the economic society, in such a way that justice, equality, freedom, the original war cries of the bourgeois advance, may be the lot of all. The rise of the bourgeoisie and the evolution of the bourgeois society has made economics the center of public life." Waldemar Gurian, *Bolshevism, Theory and Practice* (New York: The Macmillan Company, 1932), p. 237.

"The individualism of unlimited right of disposition over private property results in economic anarchy, but Communism results just as inevitably in totalitarian anarchy. . . ." Emil Brunner, *Justice and the Social Order* (New York: Harper & Brothers, 1946), p. 179. Quoted by permission of the publishers.

The grievances against bourgeois capitalism as expressed by Marxism are matched by the Papal Encyclicals. The fact that Christian morality should oppose both the economics of monopolistic capitalism and the economics of communism is a proof of their affinity. Pius XI in *Quadragesima Anno* wrote: "It is potent that in our days not wealth alone is accumulated, but immense power and despotic economic domination are concentrated in the hands of the few, who for the most part are not owners, but only the trustees and directors of invested funds, which they administer for their own good pleasure."

"Communism is on the one hand a product of this godless economy, and on the other a protest against it. Marx himself spoke of the influence Ricardo and the economics of his day had on his own economic doctrines. He derives most of his theory from the godless economy of the contemporary European society. Marx even believed himself that a godless economy guided exclusively by the interests of profit was the eternal basis of society and of culture. Just so is Capitalism godless, because at its centre is godless industrial development instead of man and his right to live a worthy life. The individualism of Capitalist society recognized, instead of the supreme value of human personality, the supreme value of the economic man, of an individual guided by personal interest and the profit motive in economic development." Nicholas Berdyaev, in *Christianity and the Crisis*, pp. 579, 580.

"We are most of us too phlegmatic to recognize the jest of the modern situation in its full implications. For it is the truth that Communism and Liberalistic Capitalism, so much vilified the one by the other, are similar beasts, provided with similar apparatus, seeking to devour the same prey." J. F. T. Prince, *Creative Revolution* (The Bruce Publishing Company, Milwaukee), p. 67.

2   "Far more powerful in its effects than philosophical immoralism is the relativisation of morals implied in

scientific systems like historical materialism and Freudian psychology. In the Marxist doctrine the domain of moral convictions and obligations can occupy no other place than one of the top shelves of the ideological superstructure which raises itself on the economic organisation of a particular period and which, conditioned as it is by the latter, is destined to change and to disintegrate with it. The ethical ideal here remains subject to the social ideal. It has only relative value, relative in the most literal sense of the word. . . . In spite of the fact that it does not absolutely preclude a certain independence of the spirit, Freudianism is essentially even more anti-Christian in its implications than the ethical theory of Marxism. For, in setting up the infantile appetites as the basis of all life of the soul and the spirit it ranges virtue—to speak in Christian terminology—under sin, it places the ultimate origins of the recognition of the highest values in the flesh." J. Huizinga, *In the Shadow of Tomorrow* (London: William Heinemann, Ltd., 1936), pp. 132, 134. Quoted by permission of the publishers.

"The modern world has no cement to bind together personal morals and the morals of political and economic life. It is the function of religion to furnish that unifying force. And it is the very nature of secularism, in the strict sense of the word, to prevent that function from being performed." F. Ernest Johnson, *Religion and the World Order* (New York: Harper & Brothers, 1944), p. 9. Quoted by permission of the publishers.

3   "Today the average university graduate understands far more of physical science than of Christian philosophy, and does not know that an intelligent Christian philosophy exists. He rejects the doctrines of religion because he is comparing his childish knowledge of religion

with his adult understanding of science, anthropology and politics; he contrasts the simple doctrines that he learned from his mother with the sophisticated polish of statistical mechanics or psycho-analysis, and firmly believes that he is 'thinking for himself.' And what the university graduate does on one level, the ordinary schoolboy does on another." Michael Roberts, *The Recovery of the West* (London: Faber and Faber, 1941), p. 100. Quoted by permission of the publishers.

"There is an enormous vacuum where until a few decades ago there was a substance of education. And with what is that vacuum filled: it is filled with the elective, eclectic, the specialised, the accidental and incidental improvisations and spontaneous curiosities of teachers and intellectual discipline. Yet the graduates of these modern schools are expected to form a civilized community. They are expected to govern themselves. They are expected to have a social conscience. They are expected to arrive by discussion at common purposes. When one realises that they have no common culture, is it astounding that they have no common purpose? That they worship false gods? That only in war do they unite? That in the fierce struggle for existence they are tearing Western society to pieces? . . . We have established a system of education in which we insist that while everyone must be educated, yet there is nothing in particular that an educated man should know." Walter Lippmann, Address to the American Association for the Advancement of Science, December 29, 1940.

4   "Marx himself tied up the proletarian completion of the world with a definitely bourgeois tradition. *There is nothing in the world more bourgeois* than rationalistic atheistic humanism. . . . When we see what have been

the fruits of anthropocentric humanism for bourgeois civilization, we may well ask what are the advantages the proletariat will gain by absorbing its philosophy, and if it implies any honor to make it the heir of the stupidest thing the world has ever known, *i.e.*, bourgeois free thought." Jacques Maritain, *True Humanism* (New York: Charles Scribner's Sons; London: Geoffrey Bles Ltd., 1938), p. 61. Quoted by permission of the publishers.

"A number of symptoms indicate that the democratic nations of the West are indeed about to inject into the blood stream of their political life some of the most dangerous germs of nihilism. Nihilism is other things beside the transposition of means to end and the ruthless application of the cynical old maxim that the end justifies any means. Nihilism is, above all, realism pursued to its logical conclusion. It is materialism, rational or biological materialism, which interprets man as a bundle of instincts, worthless in himself, but valuable as material. Material for governments, for social collectives. In a life robbed of all meaning and value, meaning and value are defined by the organ that possesses the power to validate its definitions by coercion. When that happens, all other values are denounced as sentimental moral philosophy, the occupation of idle 'perfectionists' who are in any case unfit for the real struggle of life." Hermann Rauschning, *Time of Delirium* (New York: D. Appleton-Century, 1936), p. 41. Quoted by permission of the publishers.

"Agnosticism and materialism of our era are not fundamental; they are the fruits of that spiritual heresy of Humanism by which man came to see himself as a whole, instead of as a spiritual-social-biological organism in living relation to the real world of spirit, of other men and things. This atomism on the spiritual plane gave birth to atomism on the social plane . . . then we have Collectivism both in the patchwork of decaying Capitalism and Russian Communism." V. A. Demant, *Christian Polity* (London: Faber and Faber, 1936), pp. 160, 161. Quoted by permission of the publishers.

5   "Without the philosophy of Hegel, scientific socialism would never have come into existence." Friedrich Engels, *The Peasant War in Germany*, p. 28.

6   "The current Socialist opposition of Communist and bourgeois society is in reality a false dilemma. . . . The Bolshevik philosophy is simply the *reductio ad absurdum* of the principles implicit in bourgeois culture." Christopher Dawson, *Enquiries* (New York: Sheed and Ward, 1933), p. 30. Quoted by permission of the publishers.

"There are reasons to believe that much of the philosophy of the era of Liberalism has been of the (Communist) spiritual atheistic type. An outlook made conscious in the philosophic developments that flower from Cartesian and Kantian dualism, had, while retaining the language of religion made the relation between the spiritual and the secular so abstract that for practical purposes the guiding thought of modern world has been atheistic. Communist Materialism has abolished the opposition between appearance and reality of Modern Humanism by giving up the appearance of religion." V. A. Demant, *op. cit.*, p. 162.

"Both the historical conceptions of bourgeois liberalism and of Marxist utopianism are involved in errors, similar to those which Christ castigated in his day. They assumed that history would culminate in either the triumph of the bourgeois classes over their aristocratic foes; or in the triumph of proletarian classes over their middle-class foes. . . . That is why the mystery of history can not be resolved except in the divine mercy. And that mercy can only be comprehended and apprehended by those who acknowledge that all classes and groups, all cultures and nations, are tainted with hypocrisy in their judgment of the contestants in and of the whole drama of history." Reinhold Niebuhr, *Discerning the Signs of the Times* (New York: Charles Scribner's Sons, 1946), pp. 19, 20. Quoted by permission of the publishers.

7   Emil Brunner, *op. cit.*, p. 7.

8   Lewis Mumford, *op. cit.*, Chapter I.
    "The Western World now finds herself at a pause, in a confluence of conflicting tides that raises questions in the best minds regarding the future, and also respecting much that we have considered necessary to the progress of civilization." Ralph Tyler Flewelling, *The Survival of Western Culture* (New York: Harper & Brothers, 1942), p. 3. Quoted by permission of the publishers.

9   William G. Peck, *The Salvation of Modern Man* (London: Centenary Press, 1938), p. 126. Quoted by permission of Goeffrey Bles Ltd.

CHAPTER THREE

1   Leopold Schwarzchild, *The Red Prussian, The Life and Legend of Karl Marx* (New York: Charles Scribner's Sons, 1947).
    Otto Ruhler, *Karl Marx* (London: George Allen & Unwin, 1929).
    Nicolaievsky and Maenchen-Helfen, *Karl Marx, Man and Fighter* (Philadelphia: J. B. Lippincott Co., 1936).

M. Beer, *The Life and Teaching of Karl Marx* (London: George Allen & Unwin, 1934).
Edwin H. Carr, *Life of Karl Marx.*

2   It should be immediately evident that the examples Hegel uses to prove his point are things that are not essentially contradictory but only affected with duality, relative to something else, perhaps their contrary. *Logik, Werke*, 8, p. 280.

In the preface to the 2nd edition of *Das Kapital* (1873) Marx looking back on 30 years of familiarity with Hegel and somewhat saddened by criticisms wrote: "I declare myself publicly a disciple of that great thinker" (p. XXVII). But he and Engels attributed errors in communism to ignorance of Hegelian dialectic: "That which is wanting to these gentlemen is dialectics . . . for them Hegel never existed." (Letter to Conrad Schmidt, Oct. 27, 1890). Lenin himself paid tribute to Hegel, though in Volume 8 of his Collected Works the word "contradiction" is spoken of as a "struggle."

Dühring wrote a criticism of Hegel in which he pointed out that Hegel failed to make a distinction between thought where contradiction could exist and things where there is only antagonism of forces. Engels answered Hegel in a work called "Anti-Dühring" in which he emphasized the contradictory nature of things, a point of view shared by Marx himself. "Hegel very often presents in the midst of speculative exposition a real exposition of things themselves." (*Heilige Familie, Gesamtausgabe*, 1, 3, p. 231). Dialectics for both now begins to be in things before it is in thought. This thought was finally crystallized in the second edition of *Das Kapital*. "My dialectical method not only differs from the Hegelian on the basis of method, but is the exact opposite. For Hegel the movement of thought, which he personifies under the name of Idea, is the demiurge of reality which is nothing else than the phenomenal form of the Idea. For me, on the contrary, the movement of thought is nothing but a reflexion of the movement of reality, transported and transposed in the brain of man." Marx is now prepared to stand Hegel on his head and to make the dialectic apply to reality rather than ideas. *Das Kapital*, 2nd Ed.

This takes place because of Marx's hatred of idealism. At Hegel's death his followers split into two groups: The Right and Left Wing. The Right Wing emphasized the *Idealism* of Hegel or the Primacy of the Spirit; the Left Wing emphasized the Dialectics. Marx never liked the Idealism of Hegel with its idea that spirit comes from matter.

3   As an example of the abstract way in which Marx arrived at his conclusions it is well to quote his rejections of the rude materialism of Feuerbach which was the negative side to his affirmation of Dialectical Materialism. In *Thesis I against Feuerbach*, Marx writes: "The chief defect of all previous materialism—including Feuerbach's—is that the object, reality, sensibility, is conceived only in the form of the object or as concept, but not as human, sensory activity, practice, not subjectively. That is why it happened that the *active* side in opposition to materialism, was developed by idealism—but only abstractly, for idealism, naturally, does not know real, sensory activity as such. Feuerbach wants to recognize sensory objects which are really differentiated from objects of thought, but he does not conceive human activity itself as an objective activity. Hence in the *Essense of Christianity* he regards only the theoretical attitude as the truly human one while practice is conceived as fixed only in its dirty Jewish form. Hence

he does not grasp the significance of 'revolutionary,' of practical critical activity."

4   F. Engels, *Ludwig Feuerbach*, printed in the U.S.S.R., 1934, p. 59.

5   "We may distinguish men from animals by consciousness, by religion, by anything you please. But they themselves begin to differentiate themselves from animals as soon as they begin to produce their own means of subsistence—a step necessitated by their own bodily organization." Karl Marx, *Gesamtausgabe*, Sec. 1, Vol. 5, p. 10.

6   Economic determinism is hereby tied up with his dialectical materialism. If spirit is dependent upon matter because matter is dialectical or revolutionary, it follows that the philosophy, art, literature and politics of any given period are due to the material or economic conditions underlying them. Translating this into more philosophical language: just as matter in motion produces spirit (dialectical materialism); just as the ideas of men are the reflections of their sensations in the external world (materialistic epistemology) so too the above principle translated into economic language means that technical transformations of economic life determine through the formation of social classes the ideologies of society, religion, law, etc. (economic determinism).

"The social history of men is never anything but the history of their individual development, whether they are conscious of it or not. Their material relations are the basis of all their relations. These material relations are only the necessary forms in which their material and individual activity is realized." Karl Marx, *Poverty and Philosophy*, p. 152.

7   Karl Marx, *Communist Manifesto*, 1848.

8   *Communist Manifesto*, Sec. II.

9   Marx's address to the League of the Communists in 1850.

10 F. Engels, *Anti-Dühring*.

11 From a speech given by Lenin to the 3rd All-Russia Congress of the Komsomol, October 2, 1920, quoted in V. I. Lenin, *Religion*, 1933, p. 47.

12 *Ibid.*, p. 48.

13 V. I. Lenin, *The Infantile Sickness of Leftism in Communism*.

14 Joseph Stalin, *Problems of Leninism*.

15 All of *Darkness at Noon* is a study of a sensitive man's refusal to accept this paradox.

16 Cf. A. Cornu, *Karl Marx, l'homme et l'oeuvre* (Paris: De L'hégelianisme au materialisme historique, 1934).

17 Ludwig Feuerbach, *Wesen des Christenthums, Werke VII*, pp. 55–62, 213–215.

18 *Ibid.*, pp. 362, 266.

19 *Ibid.*, pp. 62–63.

20 *Werke II*, p. 389.

21 *Ibid.*, p. 260.

22 *Ibid.*, p. 268.

23 *Ibid.*, p. 252.

24 Friedrich Engels, *Luther als Schiedsrichter Zwischen Strauss und Feuerbach*, in *Gesamtausgabe* I, a, p. 175.

25 Karl Marx, *Okonomisch–Philosophische Manuskript, Gesamtausgabe* I, 3, p. 164.

26 *Ibid.*

27 *Ibid.*

28 *Ibid.*

29 "Feuerbach resolves the religious essence into the human. But the essence of man is not an abstraction residing in each single individual. In its reality it is the whole of social relationships.

"Feuerbach, who does not enter upon the criticism of this real essence, is consequently compelled:

"(1) To abstract from the historical process and to fix-ate the religious feeling as something self-contained, and to presuppose an abstract—*isolated*—human individual.

"(2) To conceive the essence of man only as 'the species,' as an inner, inarticulate, *natural* tie, binding many individuals together.

"Feuerbach does not therefore see that the 're-ligious feeling' is itself a *social product*, and that the abstract individual whom he analyses belongs in real-ity to a specific form of society."

30 Karl Marx, *Judenfrage, Gesamtausgabe*.

31 Friedrich Engels, *Du Lage Englands, Gesamtausgabe* 1, 2, pp. 424–425.

32 Karl Marx, *Okonomisch–Philosophische Manuskript, Gesamtausgabe*.

33 *Ibid.*

34 *Ibid.*

35 *Ibid.* "Man is the source of his own life."

36 *Gesamtausgabe*.

37 *Heilige Familie*.

38 *Gesamtausgabe*.

39 N. Lenin, "Novaya Zhizn," No. 28 16/3; December 1905. Quoted in *Religion* by V. I. Lenin.

40 "Proletari," No. 45 26/13, May 1909. Quoted, *ibid*.

41 The best refutation in English of Marxism from the

philosophical point of view is Charles J. McFadden's *The Philosophy of Communism* (New York: Benziger Bros., 1939).

42 Though communism is a secularization of the Kingdom of God, it must be remembered that precisely because it is a secularization, both are not on the same this-worldly plane. It is important to remember some basic differences. As Alexander Miller has put it: "Not only is God free of historical necessity because He is history's living Lord, but the man who serves God may find himself, not in line with the historic process which is the Marxist's only sanity, but against it, even to the point of historically fruitless martyrdom. In other words, while on the Marxist view the only sane and valid action is action which accepts the logic of the historic process and conforms to it, the Christian who serves not the historic process but the living will of God, may be compelled to stand against the stream of history, even as a forlorn protesting voice." From Alexander Miller, *The Christian Significance of Karl Marx.* Copyright 1947 by The Macmillan Company, by permission of The Macmillan Company, publishers.

CHAPTER FOUR

1 A refutation of the lies circulated about the Church and Fascism by Communist-inspired propagandists is given in the scholarly study by D. A. Binchy, entitled *Church and State in Fascist Italy* (London: Oxford University Press, 1941), which was prepared for the Royal Institute of International Affairs.

2 Louis Budenz, *This Is My Story* (New York: Whittlesey House, McGraw-Hill Book Co., Inc., 1947), p. 234.

3 Harold J. Laski, *Communism* (New York, 1927), pp. 229,

230. Quoted by permission of the Oxford University Press.

4   Karl Marx, *Deutsch-Französiche Jahrbucher*, 1844. Marx-Engels Historical Critical Edition, Karl Marx Institute.

5   Quoted in *The Christian Understanding of Man* by Robert L. Calhoun (Chicago: Willett, Clark & Company, 1938), p. 104. Quoted by permission of the publishers.

6   "Democracy extends the sphere of individual freedom; socialism rejects it. Democracy attaches all possible value to each man; socialism makes each man a mere agent, a mere number." De Tocqueville, *Oeuvres completes*, IX, 5, p. 546.

7   "The irruption of the masses is the irruption of vast numbers of people in whom personality is not expressed, and with whom there is no qualitative definition but who possess great excitability and psychological readiness for slavery. This creates a crisis in civilization." Nicholas Berdyaev, *Slavery and Freedom* (New York: Charles Scribner's Sons; London: Geoffrey Bles Ltd., 1944), p. 121. Quoted by permission of the publishers.

8   Clare Boothe Luce, *Is Communism Compatible with Christianity?* (New York: Catholic Information Society, 1946). Quoted by permission of the publishers.

9   "Today our best plans miscarry because they are in the hands of people who have undergone no inner growth. Most of these people have shrunk from facing the world crisis and they have no notion of the manner in which they themselves have helped to bring it about. Into every new situation they carry only a fossilized self. Their hidden prejudices, their glib hopes, their archaic desires and automatisms—usually couched in the

language of assertive modernity—recall those of the Greeks in the fourth century B.C. or those of the Romans in the fourth century A.D. They are in a power dive and their controls have frozen. By closing their eyes they think they can avoid the crash. . . . The possibilities of progress will become real again once we lose our blind faith in the external improvements of the machine alone. But the first step is a personal one: a change in direction of interest towards the person. Without that change, no great betterment will take place in the social order. Once that change begins, everything is possible." Lewis Mumford, *The Condition of Man* (New York: Harcourt Brace & Company, 1944), p. 423. Quoted by permission of the publishers.

"A liberal and competitive economy and its society can function quite well with neutralized values as long as there is no threat from within or without which makes a basic consensus imperative. This is obviously the case when totalitarian states attack our societies. But not only this negative instance, the assault from outside, makes it a social necessity to have society integrated on those deep levels on which religion integrated pre-industrial societies; the need for planning within our own societies calls for a similar integrating bond. It is not a matter of chance that both Communism and Fascism try to develop and superimpose a pseudo-religious integration in order to create a psychological and sociological background for planning." Karl Mannheim, *Diagnosis of Our Time* (New York: Oxford University Press, 1944), p. 111. Copyright 1944 by Oxford University Press.

10 "There is a deadly danger for any philosophy or sociology or Theology which sets the end of history within history itself. It can do so only by neglecting the gigantic

overshadowing limiting fact of mortality and so throwing its whole perspective out, but it also involves the delusion that something *total* can be built in an order of things which of its nature is transitory, transitional and non-total, and that delusion breeds idolatrous and totalitarian claims." From Alexander Miller, *The Christian Significance of Karl Marx.* Copyright 1947 by The Macmillan Company. By permission of The Macmillan Company, publishers.

11 Nicholas Berdyaev in *Christianity and the Crisis*, edited by Percy Dearmer (London: Victor Gollancz, 1933), p. 175.

12 Repeated by Foster on page 5390, Hearings of the Committee on Un-American Activities, and on page 58 of hearings of the same committee in September and October 1945.

13 Such was the basis of the criticism of historical liberalism in the Encyclical *Libertas Praestantissimum*, of Leo XIII (New York: Benziger Bros., 1903).

14 William Ernest Hocking, *What Man Can Make of Man* (New York: Harper & Brothers, 1942), p. 15. Quoted by permission of the publishers.

15 Reinhold Niebuhr, *The Nature and Destiny of Man* (New York: Charles Scribner's Sons, 1943), Vol. I, p. 186. Quoted by permission of the publishers.

16 Nicholas Berdyaev, *Slavery and Freedom* (New York: Charles Scribner's Sons, 1941), p. 191. Quoted by permission of the publishers.

17 *Libertas Praestantissimum.*

18 "Man cannot live unless he is free—that is, unless he possesses this soul which is his own. Christ brought to men the full assurance of their personal being. He

taught them that in prizing their individual lives they were not mistaken, for God knew them and loved them separately, and saw something in each one of them which must not be allowed to perish." Ernest F. Scott, *Man and Society in the New Testament* (New York: Charles Scribner's Sons, 1946), p. 245. Quoted by permission of the publishers.

"Christianity teaches that the human soul is directly related to God. Such immediacy is the hallmark of the Divinity of the soul and the center of our freedom." Reprinted from *Freedom Forgotten and Remembered* by Helmut Kuhn by permission of The University of North Carolina Press. Copyright, 1943, by The University of North Carolina Press.

19 "If one inquires why and for what reason he was embalmed and exhibited in a kind of solemn shop-window, one soon arrives at the conclusion that the reasons are many and the purposes varied. It was desired to withhold from eternity at least a part of that which belongs to it. Since it is impossible to conquer death, they wanted at least to conquer the corpse, whose law is decay and not permanence. It is like an ostentatious, but of course at the same time childish, threat to Death, who is shown that his victim can none the less be preserved—like jewellery which is no longer to be worn. To afford visual proof of this was one of the most important aims. 'You have taken him from us,' the sweepers said to Death, 'but we shall show you that we can keep him. We shall exhibit him to the world as he looked in life.' If they had been able to hear the answer of Death, they would have heard something like the following: 'Your threat is childish and your pride is folly. It is my task to take from this earth not his countenance but that which was his life and which you love—namely his breath. He is extinguished,

like a lamp. I have taken wick and oil, and you may keep the vessel, with which I am not concerned. It was his flame which you loved, and his light! Why are you now flaunting the insignificant vessel in which they were contained? Many great lights have I already extinguished and monuments were erected to them.'" Joseph Roth, *The Anti-Christ* (New York: The Viking Press, Inc.), pp. 4–6. Quoted by permission of the publisher.

20 For further fallacies of communism in the philosophical order, cf.: Charles A. McFadden, *The Philosophy of Communism* (New York: Benziger Bros., 1939).

H. G. Wood, *Christianity and Communism* (New York: Round Table Press, 1933).

J. E. le Rossignol, *From Marx to Stalin* (New York: Thomas Y. Crowell, 1940).

Frank Sheed, *Communism and Man* (New York: Sheed and Ward, 1939).

E. Delaye, *What Is Communism?* (St. Louis: B. Herder Book Co., 1938).

Max Eastman, *Marxism Is It a Science?* and *The End of Socialism in Russia* (Boston: Little, Brown & Co., 1937).

Mauriac, Ducalleton, Marc, Berdyaev, de Rougemont and Rops, *Communism and Christianity* (London: The Paladin Press, 1938).

E. Stanley Jones, *Christ's Alternative to Communism* (New York: Abingdon Press, 1935).

Arnold Lunn, *The Science of World Revolution* (New York: Sheed and Ward, 1938).

Waldemar Gurian, *Bolshevism, Theory and Practice* (New York: Sheed and Ward, 1932).

Richard Coudenhove Kalergi, *The Totalitarian State Against Man* (Glarus, Switzerland: Paneuropa Editions Ltd., 1938).

Critiques from the more practical point of view are

to be found in: Arthur Koestler, *The Yogi and the Commissar* (New York: The Macmillan Company, 1945).

John Fischer, *Why They Behave Like Russians* (New York: Harper & Brothers, 1946).

George Moorad, *Behind the Iron Curtain* (Philadelphia: Fireside Press, 1946).

Louis Budenz, *This Is My Story* (New York: McGraw-Hill Book Co., Inc., 1947).

Alexander Barmine, *One Who Survived* (New York: G. P. Putnam, 1945).

William Bullitt, *The Great Globe Itself* (New York: Charles Scribner's Sons, 1946).

Hamilton Fish, *The Challenge of World Communism* (Milwaukee: The Bruce Publishing Company, 1946).

Victor Kravchenko, *I Chose Freedom* (New York: Charles Scribner's Sons, 1945).

Report of the Royal Commission, June 27, 1946, Ottawa, Canada.

W. L. White, *Report on the Russians* (New York: Harcourt, Brace & Company, 1945).

David Dallin, *The Real Soviet Russia, The Big Three, Soviet Russia's Foreign Policy* (New Haven: Yale University Press).

Rose Wilder Lane, *Give Me Liberty* (New York: Longmans-Green, 1936).

W. H. Chamberlain, *The Russian Revolution*, 2 Vols. (New York: The Macmillan Company, 1935).

F. A. Voigt, *Unto Caesar* (London: Constable & Co., 1938).

John K. Turner, *Challenge to Karl Marx* (New York: Reynal & Hitchcock, 1941).

Richard Hirsch, *The Soviet Spies* (New York: Duell, Sloan & Pearce, 1947).

Jan Ciechanowski, *Defeat in Victory* (New York: Double-day Doran, 1947).

Thomas G. Chase, *The Story of Lithuania* (New York: Stratford House, 1946).

Preface by T. S. Eliot, *The Dark Side of the Moon* (New York: Charles Scribner's Sons, 1947).

Edward H. Carr, *The Soviet Impact on the Western World* (New York: The Macmillan Company, 1947).

George Orwell, *Animal Farm* (New York: Harcourt, Brace & Company, 1946).

Arthur Koestler, *Darkness at Noon* (New York: The Macmillan Company, 1946).

James Oneal and G. A. Werner, *American Communism* (New York: E. P. Dutton, 1947).

Ann Su Cardwell, *Poland and Russia* (New York: Sheed and Ward, 1944).

David Martin, *Ally Betrayed* (New York: Prentice-Hall, 1936).

N. S. Timasheff, *Three Worlds* (Milwaukee: The Bruce Publishing Company, 1936).

Kurt Von Schuschnigg, *Austrian Requiem* (New York: G. P. Putnam, 1946).

N. S. Timasheff, *The Great Retreat* (New York: E. P. Dutton, 1946).

N. S. Timasheff, *Religion in Soviet Russia* (New York: Sheed and Ward, 1942).

Robert Ingrim, *After Hitler, Stalin* (Milwaukee: The Bruce Publishing Company, 1946).

Eugene Lyons, *The Red Decade* (New York: The Bobbs-Merrill Company, 1941).

Periodicals and magazines:

Plain Talk (240 Madison Avenue), New York, 16—monthly. Expert Diagnosis of Communism.

New Leader (7 East 15th Street), New York, 3. Competent Analysis and Criticism of Communism by Liberals and Socialists.

Todays World (St. Louis, P. O. Box 2566, Merchants Station) monthly. Factual Presentation of Catholic Position Against Communism.

Wage Earner (58 West Adams Street), Detroit, 26—weekly. Catholic Labor Paper.

CHAPTER FIVE

1 Dispatch to *New York Tribune*, March 22, 1853.

2 Dispatch to *New York Tribune*, June 14, 1853.

3 Dispatch *to New York Tribune*, April 12, 1853.

4 *New York Tribune*, April 15, 1853.

5 Cf. Christopher Hollis, *Lenin* (Milwaukee: The Bruce Publishing Company, 1938). William C. White, *Lenin* (New York: Harrison Smith & Robert Haas, 1936).

6 V. I. Lenin, *Collected Works*, Vol. XXIV, p. 122, Russian edition.

7 Boris Souvarine, *Stalin* (New York: Longmans-Green, 1939). Isaac Don Levine, *Stalin* (London: Nennes, 1931). Leon Trotsky, *Stalin* (New York: Harper & Brothers, 1941).

8 Joseph Stalin, *Leninism* I, p. 299.

9 Stalin's Letter to Ivanov, February 12, 1938.

10 Stalin's *Marxism and the National Question*, pp. 56–61.

11 From Stalin's Report to Twelfth Congress of the Communist Party, April 23, 1923. *Marxism and the National and Colonial Question*, p. 168.

12 Stalin's speech to the 18th Congress of the Communist Party, March 10, 1939.

13 Stalin's report to the 10th all-Russian Congress of Soviets, December 26, 1922. In *Marxism and the National Question*, pp. 121–124, 127–128.

14 Stalin to Ivanov, February 12, 1938.

15 Stalin's Report to Eighth Congress of Soviets, November 25, 1936.

16 Stalin's Political Report to the Central Committee of the Communist Party of the 15th Party Congress, December 1927. In *International Press Correspondence*, London, December 22, 1927, Vol. 7, No. 72, p. 1645.

17 Joseph Stalin, *Leninism*.

18 *Collected Works of Lenin*, Second Russian edition, Vol. XXV, p. 624. German edition, p. 737.

19 Words to Von Ribbentrop on the occasion of the signing of the Nazi-Soviet Treaty.

20 Molotov's speech before the Supreme Soviet, August 31, 1939.

21 Signed: "For the German Government, J. Ribbentrop; on behalf of the Government of the U.S.S.R., V. Molotov."

22 All extracts are from the 3rd edition, 1936, published by Workers Library Publishers, Inc. The full text was first issued as a U. S. government document and is now available along with the Constitution and Rules of the Communist International in *Blueprint for World Conquest* by William Henry Chamberlain (Washington, D. C.: Human Events, 1946).

CHAPTER SIX

1 Alessandro Manzoni, *Observations on Catholic Morals*, Chapter 7.

2 St. Thomas, *Summa Theologica*, 2–2, q. 34, art. 3.

3 "It may seem a paradox, but the most technically

perfect economic realization of capitalistic civilization is the Soviet system, in which all private and public efforts have only one end: the economic rationalization of the whole of life, to the point of abolishing private property and the family, and of attempting the destruction of all religious ideals that might threaten such materialistic rationalization. Russia has carried the rationalizing experiment of capitalism to its logical conclusion." Fanfani, *Catholicism, Protestantism and Capitalism* (London: Sheed and Ward, 1935), pp. 91, 92. Quoted by permission of the publishers.

Leo XIII in his Encyclical *Rerum Novarum* referred to the evil effects of Monopolistic Capitalism as producing "immense numbers of propertyless wage earners on the one hand, and superabundant riches of the fortunate few on the other." Pius XI in his *Quadragesimo Anno* mentioned a triple struggle resulting from the financialism of Monopolistic Capitalism:

"1. struggle for dictatorship in the economic sphere itself.

"2. struggle to acquire control of the State so that its resources and authority may be abused in the economic struggle.

"3. the clash between states themselves."

F. Ernest Johnson, *Religion and the World Order* (New York: Harper & Brothers), p. 9. Quoted by permission of the publishers.

4   "And if the Church, which is a Christian Society, is to exist, its mind and will must be set upon that type of conduct which is specifically Christian. Hence the acceptance by its members of a rule of life is involved in the very essence of the Church. They will normally fail, of course, to live up to it. But when it ceases altogether to attract them, when they think it, not the

truest wisdom, but impracticable folly, when they believe that the acceptance of Christianity is compatible
with any rule of life whatsoever, or with no rule of life
at all, they have ceased, in so far as their own choice
can affect the matter, to be members of the 'Church
militant here on earth.'" R. H. Tawney, *The Acquisitive
Society* (London: G. Bell and Sons Ltd., 1930), p. 236.
Quoted by permission of the publishers.

"We must abandon the notion that the Christian should be content with freedom of cultus, and
with suffering no worldly disabilities on account of his
faith. However bigoted the announcement may sound,
the Christian can be satisfied with nothing less than
a Christian organization of society—which is not the
same thing as a society consisting exclusively of devout
Christians. It would be a society in which the natural
end of man—virtue and well-being in community—is
acknowledged for all, and the supernatural end—beati-
tude—for those who have the eyes to see it." T. S. Eliot,
Idea of Christian Society (London: Faber and Faber; New
York: Harcourt, Brace and Company, Inc., 1939),
p. 33. Quoted by permission of the publishers.

"Nay, let us look at where we are. We find the secular
State, in the interests of a minimum humanity, impelled
to the almost impossible task of regulating industry and
business from without, because the community cannot
trust those activities to regulate themselves from within;
and a sort of trench warfare develops between the
community as sovereign and its own constituent organizations. In truth, it is futile for a non-Christian society to
rail at bureaucracy. Bureaucracy is its sole substitute for
virtue." William A. Orton, in *Affirmations*, edited by Ber-
nard Iddings Bell (New York: Sheed and Ward, 1938),
p. 29. Quoted by permission of the publishers.

5   "Two things are competent to man in respect to exterior things. One is the power to procure and dispense them, and in this regard it is lawful for man to possess property. Moreover this is necessary to human life for three reasons. First, because every man is more careful to procure what is for himself alone than that which is common to many or to all: since each one would shirk the labor and leave to another that which concerns the community, as happens where there are a great number of servants. Secondly, because human affairs are conducted in a more orderly fashion if each man is charged with taking care of some particular thing himself, whereas there would be confusion if everyone had to look after any one thing indeterminately. Thirdly, because a more peaceful state is ensured to man if each one is contented with his own. Hence it is to be observed that quarrels arise more frequently where there is no division of things possessed.

"The second thing that is competent to man with regard to external things is their use. In this respect man ought to possess external things, not as his own, but as common, so that to wit, he is ready to communicate them to others in their need." St. Thomas, *Summa Theologica*, IIa-IIae, q. 66, art. 1.

"The root cause of present injustices is not to be attributed to the division of goods, nor even to the inequality of the division, but rather to the fact that the mass of the people are practically bereft of ownership. Some means must be devised to admit the proletariat within the proprietory system. Widely distributed property makes for social stability. Any alternative offered lacks the moral discipline of responsible ownership. Perhaps the best summary argument for private property is the impossibility of finding any better general system to take its place." McDonald, *The Social Value of Property According to Saint*

Thomas Aquinas (Washington, D. C.: Catholic University of America Press, 1939), pp. 184–5, paragraphs 7 and 8. Quoted by permission of the publishers.

"In the past, the ownership of business enterprise, the only form of property with which we are here concerned, has always at least in theory, involved two attributes, first the risking of previously collected wealth in profit-seeking enterprise; and, second, the ultimate management of and responsibility for that enterprise. But in the modern corporation, these two attributes of ownership no longer attach to the same individual or group. The stockholder has surrendered control over his wealth. He has become a supplier of capital, a risk-taker pure and simple, while ultimate responsibility and authority are exercised by directors and 'control.' One traditional attribute of ownership is attached to stock ownership; the other attribute is attached to corporate control. Must we not, therefore, recognize that we are no longer dealing with property in the old sense?" From Berle and Means, *The Modern Corporation and Private Property*. Copyright 1937 by The Macmillan Company. By permission of The Macmillan Company, publishers.

6 "The Christian Churches need a fellowship of lay theologians or Christian scholars who would view it as part of their vocation as Christian intelligentsia to create a Christian world view." Arnold Nash, *The University and the Modern World* (New York: The Macmillan Company, 1943), p. 287.

"The times call for the establishment of a new college or for an evangelistic movement in some old ones which shall have for its object the conversion of individuals and finally of the teaching profession to a true conception of general education." Robert Maynard

Hutchins, *The Higher Learning in America* (New Haven: Yale University Press, 1936), p. 87.

7   Pope Pius XI, *Encyclical on Atheistic Communism*, pp. 11, 12.

CHAPTER SEVEN

1   Penal Code of U.S.S.R., Article 58 N.I.C.

2   "Novaya Zhizn," No. 54, 1918, p. 2.

3   Shaburova, *Woman Is a Great Power*, 1935 edition, p. 32.

4   Shaburova, *Ibid.*, p. 36.

5   *Ibid.*, p. 38.

6   *Izvestia,* July 12, 1936.

7   Cf. Nicholas A. Timasheff, *Three Worlds* (Milwaukee: The Bruce Publishing Company, 1946), pp. 88–90.
    Ibid., Religion in Soviet Russia (New York: Sheed and Ward, 1942).
    Ibid., The Great Retreat (New York: E. P. Dutton, 1946), pp. 197–203.
    P. Malevsky-Malevitch, *Russia, U.S.S.R.* (New York: William Farquar Payson, 1932), p. 236*f.*
    N. De Basily, *Russia Under Soviet Rule* (London: George Allen & Unwin, 1938), p. 296.
    Hélène Iswolsky, *Femmes Sovietiques* (Paris: Desclée de Brower, 1937).

8   Declaration of the Soviet of People's Commissars, June 27, 1936.

9   Decree of July 8, 1944, Articles 16, 17, 18.

10 *Pravda*, May 23, 1935.

11 *Dark Side of the Moon*, Anonymous, Preface by T. S. Eliot (London: Faber and Faber, 1946), p. 69. Quoted by courtesy of the proprietor.

CHAPTER EIGHT

1 Studdert Kennedy, *The Rhymes of G. A. Studdert Kennedy* (London: Hodder and Stoughton Ltd., 1940), p. 34. Quoted by permission of the publishers.

2 "The burden of the crisis has borne most heavily upon the youth of all nations. Not material cares—years of unemployment, inactivity and lack of economic prospects—these things are not the hardest to bear. Even more oppressive are the spiritual lacks: uncertainty, the absence of meaning and goals, the profound contradictions between what the world is supposed to be and what it is in reality. For youth sees it as deficient in standards and values, lacking guidance, pitching toward a frightful shipwreck. And they cannot understand the causes and interrelationships because all who attempt to explain offer only empty phrases, partisan schemes and scientific balderdash. What else can the young do but revert to primitivism, seek distractions and games?" Hermann Rauschning, *Time of Delirium* (New York and London: D. Appleton-Century Co., 1946), pp. 219–220. Quoted by permission of the publishers.

3 Nicholas Berdyaev, *The Fate of Man in the Modern World* (London: S. C. M. Press, 1935), p. 117.

4 Nicholas A. Berdyaev, *Christianity and the Crisis* (London: Victor Gollancz, Ltd., 1933), pp. 572–573.

5 "Communism is teaching Christianity, what it ought never to have forgotten, namely that real faith is asking for everything in the life of a man. There will be no 'private affairs' left." Dr. Hans Lilje, *The Christion Faith of Today* (London: S. C. M. Press), p. 53. Quoted by permission of the publishers.

CHAPTER NINE

1   *Church History*, Volume III, Chapter I.

2   Hélène Iswolsky, *The Soul of Russia* (New York: Sheed and Ward, 1943); Paul Miliukov, *Outline of Russian Culture*, Part I (Philadelphia: University of Pennsylvania Press, 1942).

3   An interesting story of the religious persecution at this time is to be found in the work of Francis McCullough, *The Bolshevik Persecution of Christianity* (New York: E. P. Dutton, 1924).

4   For a more remote background of the Russian soul, cf. George P. Fedotov, *The Russian Religious Mind* (Cambridge: Harvard University Press, 1946).

5   "The acceptance of humiliation is a national ideal." From Nadejda Gorodetzky, *The Humiliated Christ in Modern Russian Thought*. Copyright 1938 by The Macmillan Company. By permission of The Macmillan Company, publishers.

CHAPTER TEN

1   Margaret Mary Blanton, *Bernadette of Lourdes* (New York: Longmans-Green & Co., 1939).

2   Thomas Joseph Walsh, *Our Lady of Fatima* (New York: The Macmillan Company, 1947). Barthas-Fonseca, *Fatima* (Montreal: Fides, 1945). Finbar Ryan, *Our Lady of Fatima* (St. Louis: B. Herder & Co., 1939).

3   *The Poems of Francis Thompson* (London: Oxford University Press, 1937), p. 122. Quoted by permission of The Newman Bookshop and Burns, Oates & Washbourne Ltd.

4   Arnold Toynbee, *Burg Memorial Lecture*, p. 22*ff.*

5   G. K. Chesterton, *Queen of Seven Swords* (London: Sheed and Ward, 1926), p. 23. Quoted by permission of the publisher and of the author's executrix.